Faith-Style

The Christian's Mantra for Victorious Living

It's time for you to open up your spiritual ears and eyes, people of God; God has an abundance of prosperity available for every area of your life waiting for you to receive by Faith.

Sherrelle S. Davis

Faith-Style: The Christian's Mantra for Victorious Living

Copyright © 2018 by Sherrelle S. Davis

Printed in the United States of America

Library of Congress – Publication Division

ISBN: 9798594726048

Editorial & Publishing Assistance:
Jabez Books Writer's Agency
www.Jabezbooks.com

King James Version
Zondervan Publishing House, Grand Rapids Michigan 49506 USA – June 1978

The Message Bible
Notice of copyright must appear as follows on either the title page or the copyright page of the work in which The Message is quoted: "Scripture taken from The Message. Copyright © 1993, 1994, 1995, 1996, 2000, 2001, 2002. Used by permission of NavPress Publishing Group."

Weymouth New Testament
Scripture quotations marked WEY are from the Weymouth New Testament by Richard Francis Weymouth, 1912. Public domain in the United States.

New American Standard Bible
"Scripture taken from the NEW AMERICAN STANDARD BIBLE®, Copyright © 1960,1962,1963,1968,1971,1972,1973, 1975,1977,1995 by The Lockman Foundation. Used by permission."

Holman Christian Standard Bible
Holman Christian Standard Bible®
Copyright © 1999, 2000, 2002, 2003, 2009 by Holman Bible Publishers.
Used with permission by Holman Bible Publishers, Nashville, Tennessee. All rights reserved.

Merriam-Webster's Dictionary (2018). https://www.merriam-webster.com/

Strong, James. *Strong's Exhaustive Concordance of the Bible.* Abingdon Press,
    1890. Print.

Copeland, Kenneth. *"The Blessing of The Lord: Makes Rich and He Adds No
Sorrow with It."* Fort Worth. Kenneth Copeland Publications. 2011.

Acknowledgements

In honor and loving memory of my grandmother, Carrie L. Mixon (1936-2011). A woman of Faith, Courage and Strength. Where would I be without your prayers. Love and miss you always.

A special thank you to my husband and children, thank you so much for your love, patience, and encouragement every step of the way. I love you more than words can express. It has been quite a journey, but you have been my inspiration and motivation along the way. I am blessed and grateful to have you in my life. Love you always.

To my parents, thank you so much for encouraging my love for the Arts. From drill-team, dance, choir, and plays to music, you supported whatever I put my hands to. I thank you and love you very much.

Thank you to our pastor and spiritual mother for your prayers, encouragement, support, and counsel over the years. We are blessed and honored to have you in our lives.

It's time to open up your spiritual ears and eyes, people of God; God has an abundance of prosperity available for every area of your life waiting for you to receive by Faith.

Contents of Faith

(Dedicated to Increase the Use of Faith of Believers All Around the World)

INTRODUCTION

Faith-Style is a book written for believers around the world to impart one of the most precious gifts God has bestowed on His people. It is the gift of **Faith** which has been in operation since the beginning of time. **Faith** is the believers' answer for everything we could ever need in this world, and it is by **Faith** God expects us to live. You may be saying, how do you know this? I know this because there is a scripture verse in the Bible that declares, *"The Just Shall Live by Faith* **(Romans 1:17)!"** For the believer, living by **Faith** is a way of life that should eventually come natural to us all because living by **Faith** pleases God and it is clearly the life He planned for His children since creation took place. **Faith** in God is the distinguishing factor between the godly and the ungodly and between the seen and the unseen in this physical material world. As the children of the most high God, it is time for us to get our priorities in place. It is time for us to get back on track and live the life of **Faith** God intended for His children to live.

The Holy Bible is comprised of an abundance of promises God has made available to us through the *Death, Burial and Resurrection* of His Son Jesus Christ and it is only by **Faith** we gain access to these promises. In the times we are living in we see people trying to acquire everything they need in life by their own strength because this is the way the world is set up. What I mean by this is everything we need and achieve is predicated on what we can see, feel, taste and touch. I personally believe many have strayed away from the fundamentals of Bible **Faith** and its teachings. I truly believe many do not believe that the God of Abraham, Isaac, and Jacob exist in the manner of the miracles He performed thousands of years ago. I can recall a conversation my grandmother and I had a few years ago and she said to me, "People just do not have **Faith** like that anymore." I do not remember exactly what was said that led to her statement, but I know I have never forgotten her words. I believe it is because sometimes you can talk to people including believers and while you are professing your **Faith** and believing God for the miraculous, they are looking at you like you have missed it somewhere. It is like they are saying to you, "What tree did you fall from and how hard did you hit your head to come up with some mess like that!" This kind of reaction causes me to think, "Wait a minute, am I speaking to a believer or not?" It is like they want to shut you down instantly and bring you back to what they have deemed as reality. If you believe the Word of God and take His Word literally, you must have come across this same reaction. This is not good because do you know the affect this could have on a believer that is believing God to do the miraculous in their lives? Especially a babe in Christ? This kind of reaction could possibly shut them down. I know this because when I believed God and stepped out in **Faith** for many things the Lord was speaking to me, I was often rebuked for it. Now, if I were weak in **Faith** those rebukes would have made me feel foolish. They would have caused me to give up and shut up. But thank God, I knew how to hear God, talk to God, and read God's Word for myself. Now this is the attitude and ingenuity it takes to accomplish **Faith-Style** living!

People of God, any time you step out in **Faith** to see the miraculous performed in your life, you are going to have to do it by **Faith**. You are not going to see, hear, feel, taste, or smell your **Faith** but you must have total confidence and assurance that whatever you are believing for, your **Faith** in God is going to bring it to pass. Having **Faith** and stepping out in **Faith** is like seeing a big blank space of nothing, but knowing what you are believing, imagining and visualizing spiritually is there without a question or doubt, and then your **Faith** begins to go to work.

There are many examples of **Faith** in the Bible. One of the most illuminating examples of **Faith** in the Bible for me is found in the New Testament when Jesus spoke to the fig tree in Mark 11:13. Jesus came across a fig tree that did not have any fruit on it. Even though it was not the season for figs, Jesus was hungry, and He wanted to see some fruit on that tree. When Jesus saw that the fig tree had no fruit on it, Jesus spoke to the fig tree telling it no man will eat fruit from it ever again.

Mark 11: 13-14

[13] And seeing a fig tree afar off having leaves, he came, if haply he might find anything thereon: and when he came to it, he found nothing but leaves; for the time of figs was not yet.

[14] And Jesus answered and said unto it, No man eat fruit of thee hereafter forever. And his disciples heard it.

Jesus spoke to the fig tree and believed by **Faith** what He spoke would come to pass, so much so, He left and went on about His business. Jesus did not hang around the tree to see if what He said would come to pass. He didn't go back to the same tree and say, "Why haven't you withered away yet? I know I spoke to you yesterday; you should have withered away by now!" No, the Bible clearly states, Jesus spoke to the fig tree one time.

Jesus spoke His desired result for the tree, and this was for no man to eat from the fig tree ever again.

Later in verse 21 it says, "Peter called to remembrance the tree Jesus had spoken to had withered away." I can almost visualize Peter's reaction as he passed by the tree. I know he had to do a "double take" glance of the tree to make sure he was seeing correctly. When he realized the tree was dead, he suddenly called out to Jesus and brought the withering of the tree to the attention of the other disciples. This clearly illustrates the tree was indeed dead.

Mark 11:21

²¹**And Peter calling to remembrance saith unto him, Master, behold, the fig tree which thou cursedst is withered away.**

Can you imagine Peter's reaction when he noticed that the tree Jesus had spoken to did exactly what Jesus said for it to do! Can you imagine the thoughts that must have bombarded Peter's mind? I mean come on people we are talking about someone standing there talking to a tree, telling the tree no man will eat fruit of it ever again. When Peter and the other disciples heard Jesus speaking to the tree, they probably did not even take Jesus seriously. They probably thought Jesus was just messing around. For Peter to come back and see the actual tree that Jesus spoke to withered away, this must have shocked Peter to his core! What is really interesting in Peter's discovery of the withered tree is the Bible states, "And Peter calling to remembrance." This confirms to us readers what Jesus had spoken by **Faith** concerning the tree, He had the total confidence and assurance what He said would without a doubt come to pass. It also confirms to us, Jesus never looked at the tree again to see if what He had said happened or not, He knew it would! Outside of the disciples discovering the withered tree, Jesus was also teaching them a tremendous lesson about **Faith**. Jesus chose to use the fig tree to illustrate to the disciples how important **Faith** is and the massive results they could attain when they believed God and utilized their **Faith**. Let us take a look at what Jesus said to the disciples in the next two verses.

Mark 11:22, 23

²²And Jesus answering saith unto them, Have faith in God.

²³ For verily I say unto you, That whosoever shall say unto this mountain, Be thou removed, and be thou cast into the sea; and shall not doubt in his heart, but shall believe that those things which he saith shall come to pass; he shall have whatsoever he saith.

These scripture verses also tell me, Jesus was telling the disciples He wanted them to use their **Faith** to bring forth fruit in all seasons. He was showing them the use of their **Faith** was going to be essential to their lives and assignment in the earth. This is an incredible example of **Faith** in action. The next verse reveals one of the most important keys to using your **Faith** and this key is to believe.

Mark 11:24

²⁴ Therefore I say unto you, What things soever ye desire, when ye pray, believe that ye receive them, and ye shall have them.

As I previously mentioned Jesus spoke to the fig tree and spoke the desired result He wanted. Jesus believed He received what He prayed for and He walked away with confidence and assurance it would indeed come to pass. And it did! This story reminds me of when God spoke to Abraham about leaving his country and relatives.

Genesis 12:1

¹Now the LORD had said unto Abram, Get thee out of thy country, and from thy kindred, and from thy father's house, unto a land that I will show thee:

God spoke to Abraham and Abraham responded by doing what God said.

Genesis 12:4

⁴So Abram departed, as the LORD had spoken unto him; and Lot went with him: and Abram was seventy and five years old when he departed out of Haran.

Abraham did not know where he was going or how he would survive but he believed and trusted God.

Romans 4:3

³For what saith the scripture? Abraham believed God, and it was counted unto him for righteousness.

This action among many brought Abraham into a life of **Faith-Style** living. Abraham trusted God emphatically! From the time Abraham left his father's house and country, God was ushering Abraham into a life-long journey of **Faith** which would prove to bring victorious living to Abraham, and everyone connected to his life.

Abraham did not rely on his own ability to make the promises of God come to pass in his life, instead he trusted totally and wholly in God. God said it, Abraham believed it. Abraham did not trust in his physical five senses or human reasoning. He did not know how God would perform His promise, but he became fully persuaded God would make it happen.

Romans 4:20-21

²⁰ He staggered not at the promise of God through unbelief; but was strong in faith, giving glory to God;

²¹ And being fully persuaded that, what he had promised, he was able also to perform.

Now that's **Faith-Style** living!

The same life God provided for Abraham and many others in the Bible, is the same life God would like to provide for you and me today. One of the promises God made to Abraham those thousands of years ago, is through Abraham all the families of the earth would be blessed. And this was the blessing of multiplication and increase in every area of our lives. You may be asking, what do I need to do to receive this blessing? You need to do what Jesus and Abraham did: Walk by **Faith** and not by sight! Jesus spoke to the fig tree in **Faith** and never looked back and Abraham departed from his country in **Faith** without ever looking back. They did not look back because they trusted God to follow through on what they believed!

God has given to every believer a measure of **Faith** (Romans 12:3). Jesus said to His disciples, if you have **Faith** as the size of a mustard seed, you indeed have mountain moving **Faith** (Matthew 17:20)! When we look at the lives of Abraham and Jesus, it was their **Faith** in God that gave them the victory in every situation.

This book was written to demonstrate how essential **Faith** is to the believer and to increase the use of **Faith** in believers all around the world! This book was also written to give practical insight into what it takes to pursue and live a life of **Faith**.

Faith-Style: The Christian's Mantra for Victorious Living!

WHERE FAITH BEGAN

I believe there are two important factors to living a life of **Faith**. First, knowing where and how **Faith** originated. Secondly, knowing who we are and our rights and privileges as the children of God. God the Father demonstrates to us from the beginning of His Word in the book of Genesis how essential **Faith** was in the forming of creation. The Bible tells us in the beginning God created the heaven and the earth and it continues by describing to us the condition of the earth before creation.

Genesis 1:1-2:

[1]In the beginning God created the heaven and the earth.

[2]And the earth was without form, and void; and darkness was upon the face of the deep.

The scripture says the earth was without form and void and darkness was upon the face of the deep. Without form tells us that the earth needed some serious development. In other words, it was shapeless and chaotic, it needed structure. It goes on to say the earth was void, meaning it was a big empty space, it contained nothing. The earth was this vast space with no form or material substance. As I looked up the definition for void one word stuck out. It was the word lacking.

> **Revelation Point:**
>
> **This is how our lives can appear to be at times: chaotic, shapeless without form and substance - lacking everything.**

This tells me from the beginning God was never a fan of lack and He sure was not a fan of darkness. God looked on the condition of the earth and instantly knew this was not the kind of place He had in mind for His creation. He began to release His **Faith** into the atmosphere to create the environment He wanted, and it was far from what He was seeing in front of Him. God immediately went to work creating, shaping, and filling the earth, making it into the place He desired it to be.

As we read the scripture, do we read anywhere where God says, "Well, I hovered over the face of the waters and nothing happened?" No, when the Spirit of God hovered over the face of the deep this created an atmosphere for the miraculous to happen and God released His **Faith** by beginning to speak **Faith**-filled words to bring what He wanted to see into existence. Darkness was present in the earth, so God released His **Faith** and spoke light into existence, and light came. Then God immediately separated His creation, the "light" from the darkness that was already present.

> **Revelation Point:**
>
> **You can see a picture here of the difference of people in the earth, the children of light separated from the children of darkness; the believer and the unbeliever.**

> **Revelation Point:**
>
> **We are born into darkness. Why? Because, when we are born into this world we are born into sin; which constitutes darkness and dead things. But thank God we do not have to stay this way. Jesus, our Dayspring, enters our life and through His light we become the children of light; God's intended will for all creation!**

Genesis 1:3-4

³And God said, "Let there be light"; and there was light.

⁴And God saw the light, that it was good: and God divided the light from the darkness.

You are probably wondering so what does all this have to do with speaking **Faith**-filled words? Creation had everything to do with speaking **Faith**-filled words. God spoke and everything He spoke was created but these couple of scriptures should answer your question in more detail.

John 1:1-3

¹In the beginning was the Word, and the Word was with God, and the Word was God.

²The same was in the beginning with God.

³All things were made by Him; and without Him was not anything made that was made.

Okay, let us look at verses 1 and 2 in the Message translation to see if we can get a clear understanding of what is being said.

John 1:1-2 MSG

The Word was first, the Word present to God, God present to the Word.
The Word was God, in readiness for God from day one.

Do you hear the action in the last sentence when you read it out loud! The Word was God, in readiness for God from day one. This tells us God could and would use His Word by **Faith** to create everything He wanted to see in existence and the Word was present and ready to go to work!

Okay, we know there are three operating forces in the Godhead:

- God the Father
- God the Son
- God the Holy Spirit

Many have come to know as the Triune or Trinity; the three persons of the Godhead operating as one.

This is how I see it:

In Genesis, chapter 1, verse 1 is where we can see all functioning persons of the Godhead stated as being one.

Genesis 1:1

¹In the beginning God created the heaven and the earth.

In verse 2 is where we began to see the different functioning parts of the Godhead. The Spirit of God goes into action, by creating the atmosphere for God the Father, to release the spoken Word of God (the Son); which through **Faith** brought forth the physical manifestation of light into the earth.

Genesis 1:2-3

²And the spirit of God moved upon the face of the waters.

³And God said, Let there be light; and there was light.

Notice the light was spoken into existence first before God created anything else. The light had to come first, to bring life into the earth. This I believe was our first glorious picture of salvation!

John 1:3-5 MSG

Everything was created through him; nothing - not one thing! - came into being without him.

What came into existence was Life, and the Life was Light to live by.

The Life-Light blazed out of the darkness; the darkness couldn't put it out.

The first three verses of Genesis, illustrates to us **Faith** coming on the scene, first used by the Master Creator Himself. God Almighty gave us our first example of **Faith** by demonstrating how truly powerful **Faith** is. What I find interesting is during the creation process of the earth, God does not use the word **Faith,** but we can clearly see as Moses tells the story of creation it was indeed God's **Faith** in His Word that brought all these things into existence. What is also interesting is God later confirms this in **Hebrews 11:3, *"By Faith we understand that the worlds were framed by the Word of God, so that the things which are seen were not made of things which are visible."*** This scripture plainly tells us heaven and earth were created by the Word of God through **Faith**. Not by materials or anything we can physically see or touch but by the Word and **Faith** of Almighty God. This is truly amazing!

Hebrews 11:3 NET

³By Faith we understand that the worlds were set in order at God's command, so that the visible has its origin in the invisible.

It's time to open up your spiritual ears and eyes, people of God; God has an abundance of prosperity available for every area of your life waiting for you to receive by Faith.

God has graciously enveloped us with a wealth of promises in His Word that is all yours for the taking. It is time to grab hold of these promises and take them by **Faith,** so you too, can create the life you desire as God did in the book of Genesis.

YOUR IDENTITY

Now, please do me the honor of giving you the amazing details of your identity as a child of God. I truly believe, if we want to live a life of **Faith,** our identity is a vital component to our **Faith** walk as believers. This amazing truth is first revealed to us in the book of Genesis where God created the first male and female to ever walk the earth.

Genesis 1:26- 27

26 And God said, "Let us make man in our image, after our likeness..."

27 So God created man in His own image, in the image of God created he him; male and female created he them.

As we read about the creation of the first human beings, this is something we should be excited about! When you think about Adam and Eve what is the first thing that comes to mind? The first thought usually is Adam and Eve messed up in the Garden of Eden and caused mankind to fall and the ground to be cursed, which made everything from then on tough for mankind. Okay, we are going to dismiss these thoughts for a moment and just focus on who Adam and Eve were before this unfortunate incident took place.

The Bible says God made man in His image and after His likeness. What does this mean to you? I will tell you what it means to me. One day as I was meditating on some scriptures, I thought about what it meant to be a child of God. As I continued to ponder this, I thought, "This is a pretty big deal! But then why is it taken so lightly?" Okay, when you think of God what are some of the images or words that come to mind? When I think about God here are some words and images that comes to my mind. God is Creator, Father, Heavenly, Brilliant, Powerful, Just, Mighty, Loving, Faithful, Merciful, Majestic, Glorious, Imperial, Kingly, Royal, Splendid and Magnificent. Trying to find words to describe God can be difficult in a sense because in all reality, He is too big to cap with our mere words and definitions. But guess what? Everything we believe God to be, we were made in His image and after His likeness. Let us take a look at what this means for the believer. I looked up the words image and likeness in the Webster dictionary.

The meaning of image is - exact likeness; a person strikingly like another.

I can hear you saying that sounds good already!

The meaning of likeness is - the fact or quality of being alike; resemblance.

This is something to shout about people! To be made in God's image and after His likeness is a very big deal. This means we resemble and have the exact likeness of our Creator, the Heavenly Father. Do yourself a favor and rejoice in this truth. This is the reason why it was written. God wants you to know exactly who you are and what you mean to Him. God had to love us deeply to create mankind as a depiction of Himself. Look at His other creations, none was made in the image of God except mankind. If God wanted to be the only representation of Himself, He could have left mankind out and created something else. But God wanted someone in the earth who represented Him. Adam and Eve were what I like to call little gods. Think about it. When married couples have a child, the child will share some of the same features, attributes, and qualities of both parents. This is expected right? So, when their child is born and growing up looking more and more like his (her) parents; we would acknowledge this by saying, "You look just like your mom and dad." And what about when the child does something like their parents, we would say, "Your mom (dad) does that same thing." This is normal for us to recognize the assortment of qualities the child shares with his or her biological parents, right? It is the same way with God because we were created in His image and after His likeness. God wanted an earth filled with children that resembled Him and shared His character, qualities, and abilities.

God is sovereign, meaning Supreme Ruler. But when God created Adam and Eve, God gave them dominion over the earth. Dominion meaning, supreme authority and governs territory.

Genesis 1:26

²⁶And God said, Let us make man in our image, after our likeness: and let them have dominion over the fish of the sea, and over the fowl of the air, and over all the earth, and over every creeping thing that creepeth upon the earth.

There it is in the Word of God! This is our identity! God gave mankind dominion over the earth and everything in it! God gave us the power, the right and the privilege to govern this territory. God gave us the right to conduct and invoke His affairs in the earth. Praise God! Doesn't this make you feel good? Do this give you a new perspective about your role of influence in the earth? Not bad for a man made of dust, huh?

Adam and Eve were created by God to be royal, brilliant creative, and powerful beings in the earth. How did God ensure the man He formed out of the dust of the ground would have His traits and characteristics? We can find the answer to this question in the scripture verse below.

Genesis 2:7

⁷And the Lord formed this man of the dust of the ground, and breathed into his nostrils the breath of life; and the man became a living soul.

When God breathed the breath of life into man, God planted His very own nature and essence inside of man. Ecclesiastes 7:29 states, *"Lo, this only have I found, that God has made man upright (Righteous)."*

I am not writing something I thought up myself, I am merely repeating what is written in the Bible. It is my hope to give you practical insight and understanding into who we are as children of God. Hopefully, my writing is practical but the revelation of who we are is simply amazing!

You may be thinking, Adam and Eve lost all credibility to righteous living when they sinned and disobeyed God in the Garden of Eden. Yes, this is true. But when God's Son, Jesus, arrived on the scene, He gave man His identity back.

2 Corinthians 5:17

¹⁷Therefore if any man be in Christ, he is a new creature: old things are passed away; behold all things are become new.

You see, Jesus came to restore mankind to his original state but under better conditions. He came to restore every trait, right and privilege that was lost in the Garden of Eden but under better promises. You see our identity is no longer based upon who we are but is now based upon who Jesus is and what He did for us. Thankfully, we do not have to look back and focus on the fall of mankind in the Garden. But we are to rejoice in the "new" that is afforded to us through our Lord and Savior, Jesus Christ.

Ephesians 4:22-24

²²That ye put off concerning the former conversation the old man, which is corrupt according to the deceitful lusts;

²³And be renewed in the spirit of your mind;

²⁴And that you put on the new man, which after God is created in righteousness and true holiness.

Let us continue to explore righteousness a little more. This is Jesus speaking people!

Matthew 6:33

³³But seek ye first the kingdom of God, and His righteousness; and all these things shall be added unto you.

Let us take a look at the same scripture verse in the Amplified version.

But seek (aim at and strive after) first of all His kingdom and His righteousness (His way of doing and being right), and then all these things taken together will be given you besides.

Jesus is telling us in this passage of scripture, we are to seek out God's righteousness. This means to know who we are and our true identity in Him. Once we know this information, we can live accordingly to the guidelines He has set before us. We can live the life God designed for us to live from day one. But for us to do this we must receive what He says about us by **Faith**. The word righteousness in Hebrew means lofty. The word lofty means in short, noble. Noble means, illustrious and aristocratic. You are probably wondering what is with all the definitions? The meanings of these words are very important. I want you to get a clear picture of what I am trying to show you.

Through Jesus Christ and His Kingship, we have been divinely imparted the birthright of nobility and aristocracy. This means we are of royal bloodline. We are members of the ruling class. We are the cream of the crop, the crème de la crème. We are the best of our kind!

1 Peter 2:9

9But you are a chosen generation, a royal priesthood, an holy nation, a peculiar people; that you should show forth the praises of Him who has called you out of darkness into His marvelous light:

This is what God tried to convince the children of Israel of when they were released from bondage. He was trying to break them from their slave mentalities, so they could walk into their true identities as His chosen people. God even allowed the Israelites to leave Egypt looking like royalty and they still refused to step into their rightful places as the chosen people of God.

Exodus 12:35- 36

³⁵And the children of Israel did according to the word of Moses; and they borrowed of the Egyptians jewels of silver, and jewels of gold, and raiment.

³⁶And the Lord gave the people favour in the sight of the Egyptians, so that they lent unto them such things as they required. And they spoiled the Egyptians.

You see, God even helped the children of Israel by giving them a physical picture of royalty. They did not even leave Egypt looking like slaves, they left Egypt looking like royalty. They had beautiful and expensive clothes, what we would call designer clothing in this day and time. And they had the Egyptian's wealth!

Over the summer my husband and I were looking at some English films that dated back from the 1400s to around the early 1900s. What drew me to these types of films is how these people lived. Yes, some of the movies we watched were about royal families and some of them were not. Of course, when you think about royal families, you think about a family that has had every luxury afforded to them since the day they were born. It is what we would call, being born with a silver spoon in their mouths. If you are a child of royalty, you are going to have the best of the best right? You are going to have the best housing, foods, clothing, schooling and so on. You know what else grabbed my attention? It was the confidence these people had. These people were just like the description I described above. They were both noble and aristocratic. You could see these character traits in everything they did. The way they dressed, walked, ate, or even their depiction of royalty as they sat during conversations. These people knew who they were, they accepted and embraced their identities. Even the ones that were not born from royal bloodline but were rich, they still lived like royalty. They lived in their big huge homes, well castles really! They had acres of land and servants in abundance. There were even some movies where the families were neither royalty nor rich, they simply lived an amazingly rich life based on their family's name alone. Meaning they may have had a vast fortune and affluence at one point in time but now all they have is their family's name which keeps affording them the lifestyle they were accustomed to when they had their wealth.

I now say to you child of God, how much more for us being the true King's kids! The life described above just through mere flesh relation and affiliation is purely magnificent. You cannot tell me as children of God, we are not too, afforded an amazingly blessed life. This is our true identity! You know how I know this is true? This is the life God has given to many of His children in the Bible, such as, Adam and Eve, Abraham, Isaac, Jacob, Joseph, Ruth, Esther, Job, David, Solomon and many more!

Even though every person I named is from the Old Testament, remember, Jesus, came to restore us to our original state as the children of God. He restored us under better conditions and better promises. God sent His Son Jesus to recover our identity in the earth. Jesus came to redeem our Rights, Privileges and Authority that was stolen from us in the Garden of Eden. He came to restore humanity and to put us back in right standing with God through His finished works (*Death, Burial, and Resurrection*).

2 Corinthians 5:21

21For He hath made him to be sin for us, who knew no sin; that we might be made the righteousness of God in Him.

We are the RIGHTEOUSNESS of GOD in CHRIST JESUS! Know your true role in the earth! Our identity is securely locked up in Christ. We can now freely enjoy every benefit that has been made available to us as a child of the most high God. We can live by **Faith** with the full confidence of knowing who we are in the earth.

Appreciate your God-given identity: Know it, Love it, and Walk in it. It is Yours!

IT'S UP TO YOU!

2 Corinthians 8:9

For you know the grace of our Lord Jesus Christ, that, though he was rich, yet for your sakes he became poor, that ye through his poverty <u>might</u> be rich.

John 10:10

[10] The thief does not come except to steal, kill and destroy. I have come that they <u>may</u> have life, and that they <u>may</u> have it more abundantly.

You see, I have started this chapter with scriptures first. The reason being is because I want you to notice something, I believe is vitally important. Look at the words that are underlined. Let us start with the first scripture verse. The underlined word is **might.** I have read this scripture over and over until one day I took notice of the word **might** and *Selahed.*

I thought about the word might and said to myself, why would it say **might be rich** instead of saying **will be rich.** I then thought about the scripture verse, John 10:10 where Jesus says, "I have come that they **may have life, and that they may have it more abundantly."** You see the word **may** is used twice here. I continued to *Selah* on both scriptures and came to this conclusion.

The meaning of key words is vitally important when you are reading anything. Defining words can help you capture the true essence of what the author is interpreting in his or her work. When I am reading and come across a word, I may have a general idea of its meaning, I like to look up the word to fully understand the author's perspective. It does not matter how big or small the word is. It could be a word used in the definition I did not consider before that will give me a deeper understanding of what the author is implying. Like the words may and might, which are very simple words. We all know what these two words convey. Off the top of my head, I would say the words may and might would simply imply, a possibility. In the Webster dictionary the word **may** means, to have permission, be likely to and used to express desire, purpose, or contingency. The word **might** mean, used as a past tense of **may**, used to express permission or possibility or as a polite alternative to **may**. You see, the general meaning for these two words I came up with was one word, which was possibility. Which was not wrong, but the Webster dictionary gave me a broader understanding of both words. We can see here the definition of both words implies, to have permission. So, this tells me in both scriptures, the Lord is telling us, we have permission to receive what Jesus came to give us through His *Death, Burial and Resurrection*. Most importantly, we see here the words **permission** and **possibility,** simply implies: the choice is ours!

God gave mankind choices from day one! When God created Adam, He told Adam he had free access to everything in the garden, except for the tree of the knowledge of good and evil. When we think about it, God could have just put the cherubs and the flaming swords around the tree, to make sure Adam and his wife did not touch the tree, but He did not. This tells me, God gave Adam and Eve a choice as to whether they would honor His Word or not. Of course, we know Eve allowed Satan to beguile her. Both she and her husband disobeyed God and their choice caused them to be evicted from the garden of Eden.

God provided for Adam and Eve the life most would dream about today. God prepared the most beautiful provision-filled place for them to occupy freely without a glitch of stress or worry. All the beautiful couple had to do is what God had blessed them to do.

Genesis 1:28

28And God blessed them, and God said to them, Be fruitful and multiply, and replenish the earth, and subdue it: and have dominion over the fish of the sea, and over the fowl of the air, and over every living thing that moveth upon the earth.

God prepared for Adam and Eve the best life anyone could ever imagine. It was theirs for the taking. All they had to do was to believe God and walk in the blessing He pronounced over them and their lives. God gave Adam and Eve dominion over everything in the earth. Everything God gave them dominion over reproduced after itself which made their job a whole lot easier. All Adam and Eve had to do was to sow and reap, sow, and reap and enjoy every harvest, season and creation God put before them.

Genesis 8:22

22While the earth remaineth, seedtime and harvest, and cold and heat, and summer and winter, and day and night shall not cease.

It is evident the choice Adam and Eve made was not the brightest choice. Can you see going from a life of blessing and privilege to a life of misfortune all because of a choice you, yourself made? I know this had to be a horrible feeling. A feeling many of us can identify with, when we too, have found ourselves outside of the will of God.

In John 10:10, Jesus exposes the devil and his tireless mission against us. Jesus exposes the enemy's plot to steal, to kill and to destroy us. Satan is a thief and a liar. He wants us out of the will of God because by his choice this is where he found himself. This is exactly why he went after Adam and Eve. You know the saying, "misery loves company." I am sure we all may have run into this type of scenario at one point in our lives where we may have had an acquaintance in school, work or even at home with a sibling or friend. They do something they know is wrong by choice that will get them into hot water and they immediately look for someone to share the blame with them. This is the plan of Satan, but he operates out of absolute evil. He wants to plant wrong thoughts in the minds of people, to get them to make bad decisions that can potentially destroy them. He does not want them to live and see the glory of God and much less live in glory with the Father, Son and Holy Spirit. He was an angel, remember? He knows the glory and majesty of God and heaven all too well and he does not want us to have what he once himself was a part of.

Once you have been exposed to the glory and omnipotence of the Father how can you be satisfied with anything less than that? Jesus knew this also. Jesus knew what the will of the Father was for His life and He stayed true to the Father's mission. Jesus was not exempt from Satan's tactics. Satan tried the same tireless account of manipulation on Jesus as he did with Adam and Eve and later with us.

Matthew 4:1

[1]Then was Jesus led up of the Spirit into the wilderness to be tempted of the devil.

Thank God, He supplied us with an example, who in flesh and blood like us, stood strong and did not fold at the lie of the enemy. When I say like us this is what I mean, the scripture puts it perfectly.

Hebrews 4:14-15

[14]Seeing then that we have a great High Priest who has passed through the heavens, Jesus the Son of God, let us hold fast our confession.

[15]For we do not have a High Priest who cannot sympathize with our weaknesses, but was in all points tempted as we are, yet without sin.

I feel some cheering on at this point, don't you? These scriptures tell me if Jesus can overcome temptation so can I. Remember, this was a choice Jesus Himself made and He made it at a very early age. Jesus was twelve years old when He and His parents, Joseph, and Mary, went to Jerusalem to participate in an annual feast. After the feast concluded, Joseph and Mary departed Jerusalem without noticing Jesus was not with them. After they looked for Him for a while, they decided to return to Jerusalem to continue their search. Let us take a look at what transpired.

Luke 2:48-49

[48]So when they saw Him, they were amazed; and His mother said to Him, "Son why have you done this to us? Look, your father and I have sought you anxiously."

⁴⁹And He said to them, Why did you seek Me? Did you not know that I must be about my Father's business?

Jesus gives us a distinct picture of loyalty in the scripture verses above. Being loyal to His Father was a part of Him. His loyalty to His Father had come to the surface, bringing it to the attention of His earthly parents, Joseph, and Mary. But God was not about to break His own commandment. What kind of example would this set for His children? God does everything descent and in order. Jesus understood observing His Father's will included keeping His Father's commandments. The commandment to honor His father and mother which is the first commandment with promise.

Ephesians 6:1-2

¹Children, obey your parents in the Lord, for this is right.

²Honor your father and mother, which is the first commandment with promise:

Jesus made the solemn choice to return home with His earthly parents and was tremendously blessed as a result.

Luke 2:51-52

⁵¹Then He went down with them and came to Nazareth, and was subject to them, but His mother kept all these things in her heart.

⁵²And Jesus increased in wisdom and stature, and in favor with God and men.

Are we beginning to see how important the choices we make for our lives are? Choices are a very integral part of our lives and well-being in the earth. As you can see, we need to take the choices we are faced with daily seriously. Our choices can have a tremendous effect on our lives, as well as the people around us, especially if we have children. Jesus could have given Joseph and Mary a hard time. He could have said to them, "Do you know who I am, I am the Son of Almighty God and nobody tells me what to do." Or like so many kids who have stepparents in the home, "You are not my daddy. My Daddy is Almighty God. I do not have to listen to you." No, Jesus took on the character of His Father. Instead of exalting Himself, He lived in humility and waited for the promise of God to be made manifest in His life. Jesus made the right choice and because of His choice, He increased in wisdom and in stature and in favor with God and man (Luke 2:52). Once Jesus completed the Father's will in the earth, He ascended to heaven and sat at the right hand of the Father. Oh, but wait, that is not all. Even though sitting at the right hand of the Father would be enough. Everything, and I mean everything was put under Jesus' feet and He was given to be head over all things. Now this is a supreme example of promotion and elevation. Glory to God!

Ephesians 1:19-23

[19]And what is the exceeding greatness of His power to usward who believe, according to the working of His mighty power.

[20]Which He wrought in Christ, when He raised Him from the dead, and set Him at His own right hand in the heavenly place.

[21]Far above all principality, and power, and might, and dominion, and every name that is named, not only in the world, but also in that which is to come:

22And has put all things under His feet, and gave Him to be the head over all things to the church.

23Which is His body, the fullness of Him that filleth all in all.

What a glorious testimony! This is the last will and testament of Jesus Christ my friends. Jesus' example here on earth, shows the believer if we make the right choices, we, too, can have a wonderful testimony!

Child of God, the enemy is going to try to talk you out of all that Jesus has died to give you. Do not let him. Make the right choice today as you are reading this book and say with me with all power and authority: **Satan, Jesus has exposed you for the liar you are. My Heavenly Father adores me, and I am the apple of His eye. My Father has chosen and highly favored me to receive the grace, the undeserved and unmerited favor of His Son, Jesus Christ. The grace of Jesus Christ is working mightily in every area of my life. Every promise I need for my life, My Father has given to me; it is my inheritance as His child and citizen of His kingdom. I have access to receive and possess them all by Faith, Now! In Jesus Name, Amen!**

Okay back to the two scriptures that headed this chapter. Let us read them again.

2 Corinthians 8:9

9For you know the grace of our Lord Jesus Christ, that, though he was rich, yet for your sakes he became poor, that ye through his poverty <u>might</u> be rich.

John 10:10

10The thief does not come except to steal, kill and destroy. I have come that they <u>may</u> have life, and that they <u>may</u> have it more abundantly.

Do not let these promises be a <u>might</u> or <u>may</u> for you anymore. When I read these promises now, this is what I say.

2 Corinthians 8:9

9For you know the grace of our Lord Jesus Christ, that, though he was rich, yet for my sake he became poor, that I, through his poverty I <u>am</u> rich.

John 10:10

10The thief does not come except to steal, kill and destroy. I have come that Sherrelle and her family <u>will</u> have life, and that we <u>will</u> have it more abundantly.

Amen! Do you feel like those scriptures were written just for you? When you personalize the Word of God it does amazing wonders for your confidence and **Faith**!

These scriptures amongst many others are what we need to grab hold of by **Faith**. We need to possess them by decreeing and declaring we have the abundantly supplied life Jesus came to give us. Do not let the enemy deceive you another day. Possess the abundant life Jesus came to give you today! Jesus has supplied you with everything you need to live a victorious life!

Began pleasing the Father today by utilizing your **Faith** and by basking in the triumphant life of **Faith-Style** living!

YOU'RE QUALIFIED

Have you ever been surprised with a gift and wondered, "Wow, what did I do to deserve this!" It is one of the best feelings in the world, especially for a woman to receive an unexpected gift from someone she loves when it is not given on a birthday, holiday, or anniversary. It pleases you that someone took the time out to think of you and to give you a gift and say, "I just wanted to do something nice for you." This type of gesture makes you feel so special because you would view this specific gift as an unexpected and undeserved gift.

Well, we have received the most wonderful and valuable gift we could ever imagine from our Heavenly Father. This is the gift of salvation that came through His Son, Jesus Christ. It says in **John 3:16, *"For God so loved the world, that He gave His only begotten Son, that whosoever believeth in Him should not perish, but have everlasting life.***

This scripture tells us how we qualify to receive God's gift of salvation in our lives, and yes, it is just that simple! To qualify for salvation all we must do is to repent of our sins, acknowledge Jesus Christ as the Son of God, and receive Him as our Lord and Savior. When we do this, we enter a new life in Christ as a born-again Christian.

2 Corinthians 5:17

¹⁷Therefore if any man be in Christ, he is a new creature: old things are passed away; and behold, all things are become new.

When we receive salvation (the forgiveness of our sins), we are entering into this New Covenant of "grace." You may be asking, what is grace? Grace is the undeserved and unmerited favor of God through Jesus Christ on which lies the basis of our salvation.

John 1:17

¹⁷Grace and truth came by Jesus Christ.

John 1:14

¹⁴And the Word was made flesh, and dwelt among us, (and we beheld his glory, the glory as of the only begotten of the Father,) full of grace and truth.

You see, grace and truth came exclusively through Jesus Christ. It was not anything we did or could do to redeem ourselves. Jesus paid the full price for our redemption at Calvary.

Ephesians 1:7

⁷In whom we have redemption through His blood, the forgiveness of sins, according to the riches of His grace;

He took our place on the Cross and became our deliverer and escape from the powers of darkness.

Colossians 1:13

¹³ Who has delivered us from the power of darkness, and hath translated us in to the kingdom of His dear Son:

So, it is only right we come into the full knowledge of what Jesus has done for us and not take any credit for it ourselves. Our only part in this, is to believe and receive our salvation by **Faith.**

Ephesians 2:8

8For by grace are ye saved through faith; and that not of yourselves: it is the gift of God:

So, let us give thanks and praise to Almighty God, thanking Him for His extended mercy. Giving thanks and praise by acknowledging that it is only through His Son we are qualified to receive His free gift of salvation and every benefit that comes along with it. Now let us take a look at a scripture that really sums up everything I have said thus far.

2 Corinthians 8:9

9For ye know the grace of our Lord Jesus Christ, that, though He was rich, yet for your sakes He became poor, that ye through His poverty might be rich.

This scripture states Jesus became poor for our sakes. One of the definitions of poor, is of a low or inferior standard or quality. So, this means we can be poor in many areas of our lives. We could be poor in spirit, joy, peace, physical and mental health, and our finances. But the "Good News" is we do not have to be poor anymore! Jesus took on our poverty, so in Him we would be rich. Rich meaning abundantly supplied!

This is something to shout about people! Do you see what Jesus did for you? Jesus came to restore mankind's position in the earth. He came to give us the blessed and privileged life that was stolen from us thousands of years ago.

We already know the story of the fall of mankind. It has been discussed a couple of times in the book already. Satan, the thief and deceiver, cheated Adam, and Eve out of the wonderful, provision-filled life God prepared for them in the Garden of

Eden. Adam and Eve did not do anything to deserve this precious gift God spent five days in the earth creating for them. God created Adam and Eve on the sixth day, so they could spend the seventh day, enjoying all the beauty that surrounded them.

In reading the book of Genesis chapters 1 and 2, we can see the Garden of Eden was an undeserved gift placed in the hands of Adam and Eve. It was an amazing gift they received from God. Adam and Eve did not work for or earn any rights to the Garden God created. God knew He was going to create man, so He took the time out to create a beautiful heavenly place filled with every provision they would need, want, or desire. We can view God's creation of the Garden of Eden as another glorious picture of salvation. Let us take a look and see!

Genesis 2:7-8

⁷And the Lord God formed man of the dust of the ground, and breathed into his nostrils the breath of life; and man became a living soul.

⁸ And the Lord God planted a garden eastward in Eden; and there He put the man whom He had formed.

We can see what I was explaining in the scripture verse above. You see, Adam was not even formed from the dust in the Garden of Eden. God formed Adam from the dust outside of the Garden. Once God formed Adam, He took Adam and placed him in the Garden of Eden. I believe the picture God is giving to me concerning Adam's arrival in the earth is this. When I think about the Garden of Eden, I think of all its beauty, splendor, and richness. So, I would think the soil or dust in the garden would be a depiction of all those things. But again, God did not use this dust to form man. He used the dust from outside of the Garden. Sadly, after Adam and Eve disobeyed God they were removed from the Garden of Eden. The verses below affirm Adam was sent back to till the dust he was made from. Let us take a look at what God said to Adam.

Genesis 3:17-19 and 23

¹⁷And unto Adam he said, Because thou hast hearkened unto the voice of thy wife, and hast eaten of the tree, of which I commanded thee, saying, though shalt not eat of it: cursed is the ground for thy sake; in sorrow shalt thou eat of it all the days of thy life;

¹⁸Thorns also and thistles shall bring it forth to thee; and thou shalt eat the herb of the field;

¹⁹In the sweat of thy face shalt thou eat bread, till thou return unto the ground; for out of it wast thou taken: for dust thou art, and unto dust shalt thou return.

²³Therefore the Lord God sent him forth from the Garden of Eden, to till the ground from whence He was taken.

When God created Adam, God bestowed upon Adam the precious undeserved gift of the Garden of Eden, which was created to be a depiction of heaven on earth. It was not like Adam did anything to deserve this gift but God making Adam in His image and after His likeness desired for Adam to live on earth as God lived in heaven. Although Adam was not formed from the dust from the Garden of Eden, God still welcomed Adam into His family and into the Garden. It did not matter where Adam originally came from, Adam was still a part of God. Adam was God's offspring.

When I read this story, it reminded me of what Jesus did for us. Before we were born again, we were sinners, like outsiders. But because of God's grace and the finished works of Jesus Christ, we were adopted into the family of God. It did not matter where we originally derived from (who are earthly parents were) or the life we previously lived, we became God's offspring and the inheritors of His estate.

Galatians 4:4-5

⁴But when the fullness of time was come, God sent forth his Son, made of a woman, made under the law,

⁵To redeem them that were under the law, that we might receive the adoption of sons.

Romans 8:17

And if children, then heirs; heirs of God, and joint-heirs with Christ;

When we became born again, we were redeemed from the curse of the Law. But remember it was not by anything we did to earn salvation. Just like it was not anything Adam and Eve did to earn the right to be placed in the Garden of Eden. It was all by and through the grace of God, who always wanted the best for His children.

When you think about God the Father, think of Him in this manner when it comes to His children. With Adam and Eve, God was like an earthly father and mother eagerly preparing for the birth of their newborn baby. Parents will spend months ecstatically preparing to welcome their newborn baby home. They will go shopping to purchase every provision the baby will need, even for months down the road. You see, the baby is not even born yet, but they want to make sure the baby will have everything it needs as soon as it makes its entrance into the world. This is how God views His children and He is the same way with us. It does not matter whether we think we deserve it or not. God's Son paid the price and penalty for us to have it.

Child of God do not let Satan steal from you another day. Know that Jesus "qualified" you to receive every spiritual and earthly blessing God has made available for you before the foundation of the world.

Again, the choice is yours! Jesus stated in **John 10:10,** *"The thief cometh not but for to steal, and to kill, and to destroy: I am come that they might have life, and that they might have it more abundantly."* As I have discussed in the chapter "It's Up to You" we have a choice to make. Are we going to live a life of defeat or are we going to live a victorious life by **Faith?**

We need to boldly declare today, **"I know Jesus came, suffered and died for me to have an abundant life and this is the life I will receive and walk out by Faith! Not only did He justify me, He also qualified me!"**

This is what **Faith-Style** living is all about. It is about us standing as a believer and taking hold of every promise God has made available to us in His Word. Whether it be for love, joy, peace, health or wealth, it is all available to us now by **Faith**!

THE REVELATION OF FAITH-STYLE LIVING

This morning is the day after I completed an accomplishment I am really excited about. I devoted this past month to reading the New Testament four times consecutively. I was so exhausted last night after reading, I thought for sure I was going to sleep in a while, but I woke up feeling really good and energized. I believe the reason for all the energy I was experiencing is because, after reading all that Word, it had become like fire shut up in my bones (Jeremiah 20:9). Many times, I have found while reading the Word of God all kind of thoughts and questions tend to pop up in my mind. One day, I wrote down some of my thoughts and questions because as many may have experienced, you must reread and study the scriptures to get a clear understanding of what you have read. Many times, I have noticed, if I do struggle to understand what I have read, God will give me the understanding through a more seasoned man or woman of God. This also tells me I am on the right track and that God is indeed speaking to me, as well as, revealing some things to me. One thing I know for sure, there is nothing like getting into the Word of God and studying His Word for yourself. Being a student of the Holy Ghost is the best learning this world has to offer! I remember reading the Bible a few years back and I was reading the book of James. As I was reading the chapters, I was astounded by some of the principles and life applications that were in there. Amazed by what I was reading, I said to my husband, "Wow, I did not know these kinds of things were in the Bible." My husband laughed, but I was so serious. That day, I realized the Bible was a book about life and it was a book God had prepared for His creation. The Bible is an instruction manual for the life God has created for us to live. It reveals to the people of God, His will, knowledge, wisdom, desires, guidelines, and His plans and purposes for our lives. When any Bible reader discovers this truth, they can truly understand what is written in Hosea 4:6, ***"My people are destroyed for a lack of knowledge."***

When reading the Bible and I come across a promise I have never read before, I think to myself, "How would I know this promise ever existed if I never read it?" Or how about sharing the gospel of Jesus Christ? How can I share the gospel of Jesus Christ, if I do not know anything about Jesus Christ? How will I know the benefits of salvation and living the Christian life, if I do not read God's Word to know what He says about it? How will I know the solution to many of life's issues, if I do not read God's Word to find out? How will I live by **Faith** and fight the good fight of **Faith,** if I do not know anything about **Faith**?

If we are not reading the Word of God and living by **Faith,** are we really living a Christian life? A life without **Faith** is a defeated life and as Christians we are born again in Christ to live the abundant and victorious life, Jesus came to give us.

Hebrews 10:23

23Let us hold fast the profession of our faith without wavering; (for he is faithful that promised;)

Let us remember; Christianity is a **Faith** based upon **Faith** living. We receive Jesus by **Faith** and by receiving Jesus, we are receiving God's Word that was released and brought into full manifestation. Because Jesus is the Word made flesh.

John 1:14

14And the Word was made flesh, and dwelt among us, (and we beheld his glory, the glory as of the only begotten of the Father,) full of grace and truth.

God announced the coming of His Son in the book of Genesis to be a solution to the problem that occurred between Adam, Eve and the serpent in the Garden of Eden. Because of the part the serpent played in deceiving Adam and Eve, the serpent was cursed. Let us take a look at what God said to the serpent.

Genesis 3:14-15

14And the Lord God said unto the serpent, Because thou hast done this, thou art cursed above all cattle, and above every beast of the field; upon thy belly shalt thou go, and dust shalt thou eat all the days of thy life:

15And I will put enmity between thee and the woman, and between thy seed and her seed; it shall bruise thy head, and thou shalt bruise his heel.

It is amazing to see that Jesus was given to be a solution to a problem that occurred millenniums prior to His arrival in the earth. A solution that was not manifested right away but was spoken by God into the atmosphere and prophesied about from then on after. It took **Faith** from all that believed of the Messiah to come, to usher in His actual arrival.

Even though these prophets did not see, touch, or feel the promise of the Messiah, their **Faith** in God's Word assured them the Messiah was indeed coming. What is this **Faith** these prophets had? We can find the answer to this question in Hebrews 11:1.

¹Now Faith is the substance of things hoped for, the evidence of things not seen.

The Amplified Bible version gives us a more in-depth definition of **Faith**.

Now Faith is the assurance (the confirmation, the title deed) of the things [we] hope for, being the proof of things [we] do not see and the conviction of their reality [faith perceiving as real fact what is not revealed to the senses].

The Amplified translation is amazing, but the Message translation really ignites your trust in God!

The fundamental fact of existence is that this trust in God, this Faith, is the firm foundation under everything that makes life worth living. It is our handle on what we can't see.

As we can see, **Faith** is an important aspect of Christianity. Christianity without **Faith** equals Worldliness.

Christianity – **Faith** = Worldliness

The Bible states, *"Whosoever therefore will be a friend of the world is the enemy of God* (James 4:4)*."* It also states, *"Now the just shall live by Faith; but if any man draws back, my soul shall have no pleasure in him* (Hebrews 10:38)*."* God makes it very clear in these two scripture verses, the righteous must live by

Faith. And if we are not in **Faith**, our hope and confidence is not in God.

My dear brothers and sisters in Christ, **Faith** is the livelihood of Christianity. Therefore, as of today we need to be careful with how we use the word lifestyle. The word lifestyle can be perceived as a worldly term that attributes to the traditions of living by what we can see and what we can do for ourselves. This is not a life of **Faith;** it is the life of the world. My husband and I were having a conversation a while back and I said to him, "I'll believe it when I see it." But before I could finish the statement I thought, "All this time I have been using this statement so loosely, I didn't realize the implications and the impact this statement held, until this day." I have used this statement many times without thinking about it. Then I said to myself, "Wait a minute, this is not a statement of **Faith,** this is a total contradiction of **Faith.**" From that day forward, I have been on guard to not use this statement ever again. This is when the Holy Spirit began to give me the revelation of **Faith-Style** living. Again, my husband and I were driving and talking. I do not quite remember exactly what we were talking about, but we must have been discussing **Faith** and I just blurted out the word **Faith-Style.** I thought about the implications of the word after I said it. I said to my husband, "Wow, that must have come from the Holy Ghost," and my husband agreed. I believe something incredible was being birthed in that moment. From that moment on I continued pondering the revelation of **Faith-Style** living.

You may not agree with me, but when I think about the word lifestyle, I think about an image I try to attain on my own. When I think about the word life, it reminds me of a phrase we may have heard many times and probably have used many times ourselves. "It's my life and I will do whatever I want with it!" I am sure this sounds familiar to many of us because it is a stage many of us have been through in our own lives. We have used this phrase with our parents when they try to get us to do something we do not want to do, or we may have heard it from our own children. The point I am making is, this phrase implies, "I am taking on full responsibility for my own life!" We feel our lives belong to us and nobody has the right to tell us what we can or cannot do with it. Then this attitude initiates the behavior of trying to prove we have full control over our lives and work ourselves to death to attain a certain lifestyle. We work to have a prominent career, beautiful homes, luxury cars, and expensive clothes. We take on the role of providing all these material things for ourselves. When I think about it, it is not our fault we think this way. Is this not what the world teaches us? This is traditional thinking. It is the world's way and especially the American way. As we grow up most of us are taught to go to school, get a good education, then a good job, so you can buy your home, car, invest money into a pension fund (IRA), save money for your retirement and look forward to Social Security. These are the things the world wants us to put our trust and confidence in. But in recent years, due to the economic downfall, these have all proven to be fallible systems. Systems which have provided many with a weak sense of comfort. So pretty much this is what the word lifestyle means to me, "Take control of your life and live it to your best ability, without God."

Many cannot wrap their mind around the thought of not being provision minded. For instance, like this saying we may have heard many times, "If I don't take care of myself who's going to do it for me?" What did Jesus mean when He told Paul on the road to Damascus, it is hard to kick against the goads (Acts

26:14)? Jesus was saying to Paul why do you keeping fighting the truth (paraphrasing)? He was telling Paul, why do you keep pursuing spiritual blindness that will only bring you harm (paraphrasing)? In today's terms, Jesus' statement says to me, why do we as believers continue to refute the truth of God's Word? People are kicking against the goads today by refusing to believe God wants to provide for His children. God voices and demonstrates this so many times in His Word. We as human beings, think it is so hard to get our needs met because we can only see them being met and supplied our way. We can read a provision scripture many times and still walk away thinking, "How many hours of overtime do I have to work or how many jobs do I need, to acquire the money I need to buy a house?" I can say this because I have done it repeatedly myself. So, we must ask ourselves this question, if we believe God and have total **Faith** in Him, why do we think every day provision is so hard for Him? I am really contemplating this myself as I write this. We quote all these names for God such as, El Shaddai and Jehovah Jireh but we think it is so hard for Him to provide for His own creation? Why can't we wrap our minds around God having a plan for our provision? Could it be because we do not have the patience to wait on God? I believe it could be for many reasons, but I believe God has put it on my heart to express how much He wants to provide for His children. God do not want His children missing time with Him working all day, every day to purchase material things. He wants His children to put Him first and to spend time communing with Him. God do not want us stuck in a job we hate, just to pay bills. Being stuck in a place you do not want to be, does not do anybody any good. It will only make you unhappy, resentful, and despondent. You might be saying, how do you know this? I know this because of what the Bible says in **Matthew 6:31-33, *"Therefore take no thought, saying, what*** *shall we eat? Or, what shall we drink? Or, where-withal shall we be clothed? (For after all these things do the Gentiles seek:) for you heavenly Father knoweth that ye have need of all of these things? But seek ye first the kingdom of God, and his righteousness; and all these things shall be added unto you."*

Are you seeking the Kingdom of God and His righteousness (His way of doing and being right)? If you are not currently in the perfect will of God for your life are you seeking Him daily, inquiring of Him, His purpose and plan for your life? God has a God ordained purpose and plan for everyone in this earth. Proof of this truth is recorded in the book of Jeremiah!

Jeremiah 29:11 AMPC

11For I know the thoughts and plans that I have for you, says the Lord, thoughts and plans for welfare and peace and not for evil, to give you hope in your final outcome.

If God says His plans for you is peace, then why would He want you in a job, house, car, financial situation, or illness that disturbs your peace? He does not! I remember a few years back when I was working at this telemarketing firm. This was a job that really disturbed my peace. The owners of the company, the supervisors and coworkers were all nice people. I enjoyed the atmosphere of the office but what I did not enjoy was the nature of the business. It was pretty much a sales position where we were required to make outbound calls to residential homes to push the company's product. The pressure was on from the time you clocked in and sat down in your chair. The company wanted results in which was your ability to make these sales which also determined how long you will keep your position. I knew myself how irritating telemarketing calls could be from the ones I had received in my own home. I knew first-hand how the person felt on the other end of the phone when we would call their homes in the evening, phoning them at a time when they were just getting home from work or just sitting down to enjoy their dinner. Some were highly irritated by the phone calls, some were polite, and some were very vulgar. There were a variety of reactions you could be facing anytime the computer dialed a phone number.

The funny thing about this job was, it definitely was not for everybody. When I first went to apply for the job it was me and another young lady that went to apply together. She told me about the job and was sure we would get hired on the spot because someone she knew had worked there. She was right! We went to the office, filled out an application and we were hired instantly the same day. We had to do a couple of days of training which we did, and on the second day after training we went right to work. The day after, the young lady who was hired with me, quit. A few days after this, one of the girls we were in training with, one evening, jumped out of her chair crying profusely as she headed straight for the exit door. I must admit this job was grueling. I began to dread preparing to go to work. There were many times I wanted to give up and say, I am never going back to that place again.

One evening as I was sitting in the office chair staring at the computer, I felt like getting up and heading straight for the exit door just like the girl did a few days prior. I did not want to make another call to anyone else but something inside of me would not let me give up. The next number the computer dialed had reached an answering machine. On this answering machine was the voice of a woman reciting John 3:16.

John 3:16

¹⁶**For God so loved the world, that he gave His only begotten son, that whosoever believeth in Him should not perish, but have everlasting life.**

When I heard the woman's calm and soothing voice reciting scripture on the answering service, I felt a sense of relief come over me. I knew this was the Lord bringing peace into my situation. I then looked up and vowed to God that I would not leave this position until He opened

Revelation Point:

As I was thinking about this, while writing this segment, I thought what did my situation have to do with John 3:16? It came to me, must have been from the Holy Ghost, at that moment I was presenting my body as a living sacrifice: meaning, by me not getting out of that chair and leaving the job then, I was trusting God to bring me out when He was ready. I was no longer there on my own accord but for the will of the Lord to be done in that place and in my life.

another door for me. Hear me child of God, right there in that moment, I was releasing my **Faith** for what I believed. I had to believe God was going to rescue me from this position. The loving God I knew would not allow His child to suffer in a job like this for much longer.

Romans 12:1

¹**I beseech you therefore, brethren, by the mercies of God, that ye present your bodies a living sacrifice, holy, acceptable unto God, which is your reasonable service.**

It might have been the next day or a couple of days later, God indeed opened another door, or what was disguised as the open door I was hoping for. Before being hired for the telemarketing position, I had applied for a cashier position at this new retail store opening in a neighboring city. I had applied with them a while back, so when I did not hear from them, in the timeframe they said, I just assumed I did not get the position. They called me and said they would like to offer me the position and I needed to come into the store and fill out the employment paperwork. That is if I was still interested in the position. I was so happy because this was the opportunity, I needed to leave the telemarketing position. But my only concern was, it was quite a distance away from my home and the car I had at the time needed some repairs. But I did not let these issues discourage me. I was just happy about the new open door of opportunity God had provided for me.

I drove out to the new store and completed the required paperwork to start my new venture in retail. The next day I found myself scouring the help wanted ads looking to see what other opportunities they had closer to my home. As I was searching, I came across an ad that looked somewhat familiar. It was an ad for a nonprofit organization, I had seen in the paper a few months prior. The first time I saw the ad, they were hiring for a manager. I looked at the ad and thought, this would be a job I would love to do but did not have the qualifications for, so I dismissed the thought. But this time the same organization was hiring for a shelter assistant position. I thought, why not apply and see what happens. You know when applying for this position, there was a feeling on the inside of me, from the moment I laid my eyes on the ad, this position belonged to me. Think about it. I already had another job so all I needed to do was to give my notice to the telemarketing company. But thank God, He did not stop there. He revealed the real blessing when it was time for me to see it. I stepped out in **Faith,** believing the job was already mine. I sent my resume out, received the interview and was hired for the position. Glory to God! All due to me believing and having **Faith**, God had something better for me.

Do you see the operation of **Faith** here? Do you see how the Lord had a plan for my welfare and peace here? Yes, I had to endure the hardship for a bit, but that is okay. The hardship only taught me who God was in my life and the results I would receive, when my trust and confidence is in Him.

God has given to us all things that pertains to life and godliness (2 Peter 1:3). And He has thoroughly equipped us to deal with every trial that would come our way. It is during these challenging times we must remember the greatness of our God. We must know God is with us, even on our most dark and dreary days. Knowing that our **Faith** in Him, will be the sun shining in, throughout our adversities.

We can see by the testimony I just shared; God our Heavenly Father did not just put us here on this planet to figure things out for ourselves. No, not at all. God has a purpose and a plan for each of our lives. Everything God has for us, is available to us, in Him and His Word. Come on believer, this must be received by **Faith**!

The word **Faith-Style** has a totally different meaning to me than the word lifestyle. When we live by **Faith**, we are wholly and totally dependent on God and His Word (Jesus). For the believer, The Word of God (Jesus) is our life, and our lives are only viable in Him and through Him. You see, it is in the Word of God (Jesus) we will obtain everything we need to live on the earth. We can see proof of this in the scripture verses below.

Acts 17:28 KJV

²⁸**For in Him we live, and move, and have our being;**

John 1:3-4 NIV

³**Through Him all things were made; without Him nothing was made that has been made.**

⁴**In Him was life, and that life was the light of man.**

Faith in God and in His Word (Jesus) is the solution for everything we need in our lives!

Living by **Faith** is a life where everything is not on me, but on God my sole source and provider. It is a life where my Heavenly Father is leading me into a life of supernatural provision. It is a life that allows me to grab hold of every promise in the Word of God and see them physically manifested in my life.

Promises such as:

- **I will never leave thee, nor forsake thee (Hebrews 13:5).**

- **When my father and my mother forsake me, then the Lord will take me up (Psalm 27:10).**

- **But my God shall supply all my needs according to His riches in Glory by Christ Jesus (Philippians 4:19).**

- **I can do all things through Christ which strengthens me (Philippians 4:13).**

- **For I know the thoughts that I think toward you, saith the Lord, thoughts of peace, and not of evil, to give you an expected end (Jeremiah 29:11).**

- Yea, I have loved thee with an everlasting love; therefore, with loving kindness have I have drawn thee (Jeremiah 31:3).

- The blessing of the Lord, it maketh rich and He addeth no sorrow with it (Proverbs 10:22).

- Blessed shalt thou be in the city, and blessed shalt thou be in the field (Deuteronomy 28:3).

- The Lord shall make thee the head and not the tail; thou shalt be above only and not beneath (Deuteronomy 28:13).

- The Lord shall open unto thee His good treasure the heaven to give the rain unto thy land in His season, and to bless all the work of thine hand: and thou shalt lend to many nations and not borrow (Deuteronomy 28:12).

- The Lord shall command the blessing upon thee in thy storehouses, and in all that thou settest thine hand unto; and he shall bless thee in the land which the Lord thy God giveth thee (Deuteronomy 28:8).

- "Lo, I am with you always, even unto the end of the world (Matthew 28:20).

And there are so...many more!

You see, all these wonderful promises the Word of God offers to every believer can only be attained by **Faith.** It is not anything we can or want to achieve on our own, they were already prepared and made available for us before the foundation of the world! In every promise listed above we can see God is in them, showing us that everything we face in this world in our time on the earth, He is right there with us. These promises are God's gift to His children, we can freely receive through **Faith-Style** living.

I know some of you are probably reading this chapter thinking, "Well it sounds good, but you still have to work to get food on the table, pay bills, and meet other financial obligations." There is no doubt about it! We need money on this earth to live. I am pretty sure God knew this before He created Adam. We must remember God said everything was done before the foundation of the world. Do we not think God knew what was going to take place in the Garden with Adam, Eve and the serpent before it happened? Of course, He did. Did God know He would have to send His Son into earth to die a tragic death before that incident occurred in the Garden of Eden? Of course, He did. Our life may be a surprise to us as we live it out day by day, but it certainly is not a surprise to God. Remember God is the Alpha and the Omega, the First and the Last, the Beginning and the End. God is the Author and Finisher of our **Faith**! I believe everything has already occurred and taken place in the spirit; we are at this point just living it out.

As I was saying earlier, God knew we would need money to live in the earth. Or should I say, God knew in advance that paper money would serve as currency in the world system of buying and selling. He knew money would serve as the currency we would receive for wages earned from our labor. And we would in turn use this currency for paying rent and mortgages, purchasing food, paying utilities and for other daily amenities. Currency is how the world system works for buying and selling and this is fine. Even as children of God we are in this world and do use money to take care of and meet many of our needs. But we as children of God do not need to limit ourselves to the world system of operation looking to money as our only source of supply. We will discuss this more in the chapter "Testimony of **Faith-Style** Living." The Word of God says, "The Just shall live by **Faith**!" Remember our **Faith** should be in operation on a continuous basis and our **Faith** in God is not limited to or constricted to money alone.

It takes **Faith** to obtain a job, but after you have obtained the job, what are you then using your **Faith** for? You are at this point working and expecting to be paid for your labor. You know your pay schedule so when payday comes you know without a doubt you will receive your paycheck for services rendered. So, what will you believe God for now? How will you use your **Faith**?

Even though God uses all kind of avenues to bless His people, it does mostly come back to money because value and worth is the scale in which most things are measured by. Such as time, labor, and material things. I know some believe God is not concerned with His people having money, and this is not true. God does not mind His people having money; He just does not want money having His people. And He certainly does not want His people trusting in their money and not Him. God does not want His children being provision minded. Having your mind constantly on provision can cause you to have a desperate mindset. Desperate people with desperate minds will do anything for money. People will lie, cheat, steal and even kill for money. We see this all the time every day. Local news stories are plagued with murders, schemes, and robberies, with money as the motivation for these committed crimes. From corporate theft to street theft, people will take advantage of any situation to get money. This is where the difference between God's blessing and filthy lucre come into place. Jesus says in **Matthew 6:24,** *"No one can serve two masters: for* *either he will hate the one and love the other; or else he will hold to the one, and despise the other. Ye cannot serve God and mammon.*

I have discussed this scripture in detail in the chapter "Where is Your **Faith**?" So, I will not repeat what was said. However, I would like to approach this scripture from a slightly different angle in this chapter.

The word mammon in the Greek dictionary means, avarice. Avarice in the Webster dictionary means, extreme greed for wealth or material gain. This is where the words filthy lucre comes into play. Lucre in the Webster dictionary means, money; especially when regarded as sordid or distasteful or gained in a dishonorable way. This is where people get money and filthy lucre confused. Can you see why God desires for believers to walk by **Faith** and not by sight? Can you see why He does not want you making money your source of supply? God is the one who created you, so I am sure He knows what He is talking about? He knows the effect money can have on people if not acquired the right way. Pay careful attention child of God, please do not confuse having money with what the Bible refers to as filthy lucre. There is a tremendous difference between the two. Believers also get it confused when they say, God thinks money is evil, but this is far from the truth. It is the love of money that is the root of all evil.

1 Timothy 6:10

[10]For the love of money is the root of all evil: which while some coveted after, they have erred from the faith and pierced themselves through with many sorrows.

Do you see the difference? How can money be evil? Money is just a form of currency. It is a paper product made from a tree that is the holders guarantee for purchases made. It is not money itself that can be regarded as evil. It is the person's thought or intention toward money that will determine how he or she will be affected by it. It is stated in Proverbs 23:4-5, *"Don't wear yourself out trying to get rich; restrain yourself! Riches disappear in the blink of an eye; wealth sprouts wings and flies off into the wild blue yonder (MSG).* Now, let us take a look at the scripture verses below.

1 Timothy 6:6-7

⁶But godliness with great contentment is great gain.

⁷For we brought nothing into this world, and it is certain we can carry nothing out.

Being content means to be thankful for what you have. It is not telling you not to desire or want better for yourself. It is saying, be content so you will not be prompted to gain wealth and riches in an undesirable way. For this reason, it is imperative we walk by **Faith** and not by sight. Sight tells the story of the circumstances we see around us, but **Faith** says to our story, this situation is temporal and is subject to change! **Faith** initiates the miraculous. It achieves life changing results we cannot produce on our own.

As we visit the "The Hall of **Faith**" in Hebrews chapter 11, we can see all that was achieved by the **Faith** of our predecessors. There are many stories in this chapter but let us take a look at the life of Abraham, after all he is the father of **Faith**. Abraham is a tremendous example of walking by **Faith** and not by sight. At God's request, Abraham left his people and the country he was accustomed to for many years. So, what prompted this man who was 75 years old at the time to make such a huge transition during this time in his life.

As I was reading Hebrews chapter 11 in the Amplified Bible, something jumped out at me, I have never noticed before. While looking at verses 7, 8, 9, 21, 22, 23, 24, 27, 29, and 31; I noticed something interesting that is in the beginning of these verses. There were words in brackets which pretty much shared the same meaning. These words are urged, prompted, actuated, aroused and motivated [by **Faith**]. I then noticed every great man and woman of God that were discussed in these verses had a motivator for every action they took. This motivator was **Faith**. Since we are talking about Abraham, let us take a look at verses 8 and 9.

Hebrews 11:8-9 AMP

8 [Urged on] by Faith Abraham, when he was called, obeyed and went forth to a place which he was destined to receive as an inheritance; and he went, although he did not know or trouble his mind about where he was to go.

9 [Prompted] by Faith he dwelt as a temporary resident in the land which was designated in the promise [of God, though he was like a stranger] in a strange country, living in tents with Isaac and Jacob, fellow heirs with him of the same promise.

As we can see in these two verses, **Faith** was the motivator for Abraham in both cases. He was urged on by **Faith** to leave his country and he was prompted by **Faith** to dwell in a foreign land. Hopefully, this sheds some light as to why **Faith** is needed in the life of the believer. Walking by **Faith** prepares you to receive everything God has made available for you. It also opens the door for the miraculous to take place in your life. For by **Faith** our elders obtained a good report (Hebrews 11:2).

Abraham's **Faith** in God brought him, and everyone connected to his life riches beyond measure. It does not say anywhere in the Bible, Abraham's job or occupation made him rich nor does it say Abraham pursued riches. Abraham never had to result to dishonorable ways to earn money. Abraham never had to lie, cheat, or steal from anyone to amass his fortune. Every place where we read Abraham was blessed in abundance, Proverbs 10:22 was the catalyst for his amazingly blessed life!

Proverbs 10:22 AMPC

22 The blessing of the Lord–it makes [truly] rich, and He adds no sorrow with it [neither does toiling increase it].

Before Abraham left his country, God shared with Abraham the rewards he would receive for his obedience. Let us read what God said to Abraham.

Genesis 12:1-3

1Now the Lord had said unto Abram, Get thee out of thy country, and from thy kindred, and from thy father's house, unto a land that I will show thee:

2And I will make of thee a great nation, and I will bless thee, and make thy name great; and thou shalt be a blessing:

3And I will bless them that bless thee and curse him that curseth thee: and in thee shall all the families of the earth be blessed.

Abraham knew God would perform His promises, but he did not know how God would do it. Although he did not have all the answers, Abraham believed God and took a step of **Faith**.

Abraham's continuous demonstrated **Faith** in God was a huge part of Abraham's God-given assignment. No matter how daunting the thought of him leaving his country might have been, Abraham courageously accepted his assignment. Because of Abraham's obedience and **Faith** in God, he has been acknowledged as the "Father of **Faith**" for many generations.

God wants you on your God-given assignment. He wants you to live a life motivated by **Faith,** so you too, can enjoy a full and beneficial life attributed to **Faith-Style** living!

DESIRE IGNITES FAITH

The Bible is a compilation of events that can be incomprehensible to our natural mind and senses. It is a book from beginning to end filled with stories that will make you think—is this for real? It is a book comprised of **Faith**-filled accounts that can many times "fall through the cracks" of our natural ways of thinking. Many do not want to hear about **Faith** in the manner God intended because **Faith** goes beyond our natural mind and senses. They want to stay locked into their man-made traditions, according to the belief systems they have cultivated over the years. They want to stay in the natural mindset of "just face reality" and "this is the way we normally do things." But what happens when you are in a situation that is going to require more than just the norm? What do you do when the doctor says, there is nothing more he can do for you? But you have a desire to keep on living. What do you do when you have lost everything? But you have a desire to keep going. What do you do when everything around you appear to be dead and hopeless? But you have a desire to see things better? What do you do when you are in a situation that looks impossible? But you have a desire to see it all worked out? What do you do when you have extracted all your natural resources and you are left with nothing? But you still desire a change?

Let me introduce you to some remarkable men and women of God that shared a strong desire to see their lives changed forever. These men and women of God were some world changers and history makers. They did not just settle for what life was handing over to them. They had a burning desire in them to see their circumstances changed and that desire ignited their **Faith**.

This first man we have spoken of quite frequently already, after all he is the father of **Faith**. Abraham left the country he was accustomed to for 75 years. As I thought about his story, I wondered what made God approach Abraham to leave his country after all those years. Abraham is what we would consider to be an elderly man at this point in his life. Although it is not stated in the Bible, I have often wondered, did Abraham have a desire to venture out into new surroundings? Did God approach Abraham because he already had a preview of Canaan and desired to dwell there permanently?

Genesis 11:31

³¹**And Terah took Abram his son, and Lot the son of Haran his son's son, and Sarai his daughter in law, his son Abram's wife; and they went forth with them from Ur of the Chaldees, to go into the land of Canaan; and they came unto Haran, and dwelt there.**

Whatever the case, the thought of leaving everything behind may have been terrifying for Abraham, but I believe Abraham's desire ignited his **Faith** in God. I believe the same was true for Abraham's wife Sarah. When God announced to Abraham and Sarah, they would have a child, the Bible states, Sarah laughed.

Genesis 18:12

¹²**Therefore Sarah laughed within herself, saying, After I am waxed old shall I have pleasure, my lord being old also?**

Although Sarah laughed at the possibility of becoming pregnant, can you imagine what she was thinking on the inside? In the natural this was a totally impossible situation. Sarah's womb was dead. Not only was she barren from her youth, she was now also past child-bearing age. But when someone, especially that someone being God tells you that something you have been dreaming about for years is going to happen. Initially, you may wonder how this would be possible. But something inside of you begins to ponder the thought of this miracle actually coming to pass in your life. The desire for what Sarah's heart had been yearning for all those years began to rise again. Sarah's **Faith** was released. She began to imagine her whole pregnancy from the time of conception until the delivery of the child. All Sarah could see from that point forward was the new life she and Abraham would share with the child they desired to have together for years.

There is another story in the Bible that resembles Sarah's story, it is the story of a woman named, Hannah. Hannah was also barren. But Hannah desired a child so badly that anything else did not matter. Hannah's husband, Elkanah tried his best to console her. He loved Hannah dearly and was not bothered by the fact she was unable to have children. Elkanah wanted to be everything Hannah needed.

1 Samuel 1:8

⁸Then he said Elkanah her husband, why weepest thou? And why eatest thou not? And why is thy heart grieved? Am not I better to thee than ten sons?

Hannah could not bear the thought of not having children a moment longer. A strong desire in her rose as she went to talk to the only person who could help her. Hannah was so grieved

SHERRELLE S. DAVIS

over this situation that while she was in the temple talking to the Lord; her lips moved intensely without a sound coming out of her mouth. Hannah had an intense desire to experience motherhood even if it meant giving the child over to the Lord. Hannah's desire ignited her **Faith**. Hannah made a vow to the Lord in her moment of distress. She promised the Lord if He would indeed bless her with a son; she would in turn dedicate the child's life to the Lord, to serve the Lord all the days of his life.

1 Samuel 1:10-11

[10]And she was in bitterness of soul, and prayed unto the Lord, and wept sore.

[11]And she vowed a vow, and said, O Lord of hosts, if thou wilt indeed look on the affliction of thine handmaid, and remember me, and not forget thine handmaid, but wilt give unto thine hand maid a man child, then I will give him unto the Lord all the days of his life, and there shall no razor come upon his head.

Hannah left the temple with the peace of the Lord; she knew from that moment everything was okay.

1 Samuel 1:18

[18]So the woman went her way, and did eat, and her countenance was no more sad.

God blessed Hannah to conceive. After Hannah had the baby, she and her husband named their son Samuel. Hannah kept her promise to the Lord. Once the child was old enough, Hannah took her son to the temple and dedicated his life to the Lord. Samuel grew up in the temple and eventually became one of the greatest prophets to ever live. God blessed Samuel with the significant role of anointing the first two kings of Israel, Saul and David.

The next person exemplified a strong desire for change. Ruth the Moabitess from the country of Moab. The situation with Ruth and her mother-in-law, Naomi, looked very bleak, death was all around them. Ruth's husband was dead, her father-in-law, Naomi's husband, was dead, and her brother-in-law was dead also. This situation did not look good at all. What is one to think after experiencing such sorrow? How does one recover from such tragic loss? Naomi had enough! She was ready to go and leave all the pain she suffered in Moab behind. Naomi did not want to see anything that remotely reminded her of her suffering in Moab. When Naomi told her two daughter's-in-law she was leaving, Naomi was saying goodbye to everything that bellowed Moab. She wanted that miserable experience behind her for good.

As Naomi was saying goodbye to her daughter's-in-law, Ruth and Orpah, they wept profusely at her departure. They did not want to see Naomi go, they begged to go with her.

Ruth 1:10-11

¹⁰And they said unto her, Surely we will return with thee unto thy people.

¹¹And Naomi said, Turn again, my daughters: why will ye go with me? Are there yet any more sons in my womb, that they may be your husbands?

Ruth had no intention of seeing Naomi walk away and leave her in Moab. The scripture says, *"Ruth clave unto Naomi* (Ruth

1:14)." Ruth had a strong desire to leave Moab. It was as if she knew there was something in the city of Bethlehem just for her. Ruth could not let this opportunity pass her by and she was not taking no for an answer.

Listen to Ruth's words of conviction as Naomi continued to ward her off. Ruth's words were so sweet and filled with such fervor that even Naomi in all her bitterness could not refuse her any longer.

Ruth 1:16-19

16And Ruth said, Entreat me not to leave thee, or to return from following after thee: for wither thou goest, I will go; and where thou lodgest, I will lodge: thy people shall be my people, and thy God my God.

17Where thou die, will I die, and there will I be buried: the Lord do so to me, and more also, if aught but death part thee and me.

18When she saw that she was stedfastly minded to go with her, then she left speaking unto her.

19So they two went until they came to Bethlehem. And it came to pass, when they were come to Bethlehem, that all the city was moved about them, and they said, Is this Naomi?

Ruth's quest for change ushered her into a life she could have never imagined for herself. Coming from a life full of hardship and sorrow, to now living a life of total victory, was nothing short of amazing. Ruth married Boaz, the man of her dreams. She gave birth to a beautiful baby boy named Obed and she was able to take care of her mother-in-law, Naomi. Most importantly of all, Ruth became the great-grand mother of kings, even the great-grandmother of the King of kings and the Lord of lords. How awesome is that!

This next Woman had about all she could take of her situation. The Woman with the issue of blood had gone from doctor to doctor spending all her money and could not get the help she needed. The Bible declares, her condition only grew worse. This woman grew tired of her situation. She knew there was help out there somewhere, if only she could get to it. This woman suffered from this condition for a whole twelve years. Can you imagine her physical condition at this point? She had to be suffering terribly. She probably was so weak and feeble she could barely stand. If she was physically damaged for all those years, can you imagine her mental state after suffering for so long? Whatever state or condition this woman was in, she said, enough is enough! She heard about a man named Jesus who was going around healing all manners of sickness and diseases. A strong desire began to rise in this woman as she said to herself (paraphrasing), "I have to get to this man." She said, *"If I could just touch His garment, I shall be made whole* (Matthew 9:21)." This woman's desire ignited her **Faith**. It put her **Faith** in action, and she got the results she wanted. She was totally healed of her condition! Glory to God!

This person I am about to discuss exhibited and fulfilled the greatest desire man could ever imagine. This desire was to fulfill the will of His Father and this person is none other than Jesus Christ. When Jesus was a young man of only twelve years of age, He discovered the strong desire He carried for doing His Father's will. When He and His parents, Joseph and Mary, went to Jerusalem for the Passover feast as they did every year, they noticed as they journeyed home their son was not with them.

Joseph and Mary went looking for Jesus and after three days of searching, they found Him sitting in a temple back in Jerusalem. When they saw Him there, Mary asked Jesus, *"Son, why have You done this to us* (Luke 2:48)?" Jesus responded, *"Why did you seek me? Did you know that I must be about my Father's business* (Luke 2:49)?" At the time, Joseph and Mary did not comprehend what Jesus was talking about, but the Bible says, Mary kept His words in her heart.

We can see Jesus' desire concerning His Father's will had come to the surface. Jesus harnessed such a deep desire to carry out the will of His Father that he at twelve years old stayed in the temple for days listening and asking questions about the holy scripture teachings. Jesus experience in the temple served both as an announcement and introduction for the greatest ministry ever about to hit the earth!

When Jesus is mentioned again at the age of thirty years old, we can see He did not waste any time getting started in ministry. From the time of His baptism in the Jordan River until His death on the Cross, Jesus spent His life and ministry on a mission emulating His Father.

John 5:19

19Then answered Jesus and said unto them, Verily, verily, I say unto you, The Son can do nothing of himself, but what he seeth the Father do: for what things soever he doeth, these also doeth the Son likewise.

Jesus did whatever was necessary to get the will of the Father done. He traveled from region to region being about His Father's business. The Bible states, Jesus went around doing good by establishing God's Kingdom in the earth. Jesus healed the sick, raised the dead and fed the hungry. Everything He did was in accordance to fulfilling His Father's will. You know what is interesting about the life of Jesus Christ? I do not recall reading anywhere Jesus spoke about fulfilling His own will or agenda. From the time His ministry began, He was dedicated to fulfilling His Father's will. Nothing more and nothing less.

John 5:30

³⁰I seek not mine own will, but the will of the Father which hath sent me.

While reading the books of the New Testament many of us have come to love every account that was given about the works of Jesus Christ in the earth. The life of Jesus Christ serves as the greatest example given and demonstrated of the operation of **Faith** in the earth. Jesus used His **Faith** daily to meet His needs, as well as the needs of others. He used His **Faith** to cast out demons, to heal the sick, raise the dead, and feed multitudes of people. I personally believe we can attribute all the wonderful works Jesus did here on the earth to Jesus' desire to please God. Jesus' desire ignited His **Faith** and gave Him every confidence and assurance His God-given assignment would indeed be fulfilled!

Desire is one of the keys to **Faith-Style** living. Desire is something that is engrafted deep on the inside of us. It is a thought we become more aware of as it grows and grows. I believe God put desires on the inside of us for a reason. The reason being is to show us how much He is in tuned with our innermost thoughts and aspirations. God can take hold of our desires and do exceedingly abundantly over and above what we can ask or think, as stated in Ephesians 3:20 AMP.

20 Now to Him Who, by (in consequence of) the [action of His] power that is at work within us, is able to [carry out His purpose and] do superabundantly, far over *and* above all that we [dare] ask or think [infinitely beyond our highest prayers, desires, thoughts, hopes, or dreams]—

Another scripture that shows us how in tuned God is with our desires is in the book of Psalms.

Psalms 37:4

4Delight yourself also in the Lord, and He will give you the desires *and* secret petitions of your heart.

So, you see our desires are important to God. This scripture here is saying when you delight in the Lord, you are showing Him you have the **Faith** in Him to bring the desires of your heart to pass.

Jesus, Abraham, Sarah, Hannah, Ruth, and the Woman with the issue of blood all had this desire. Their desire gave fuel to their **Faith,** setting their **Faith** in motion to accomplish the impossible in their lives.

This indeed is Faith-Style **living!**

NO IDLE WORDS IN THE EARTH

D id you know the words you speak daily would have an impact on your life? I know in times past I didn't, I just spoke whatever I wanted to say at the time. Before reading the Bible, I always assumed words were just words. Of course, I knew words had meaning, but I did not know my words were so significant they were actually creating and framing the world around me. In the book of Genesis, God demonstrated the importance of words. God's Word played an integral part in the creation process. God used His **Faith**-filled words to create the earth and everything in it. The book of Genesis also demonstrates, God never intended for our words to be just spoken words. But we were to use His Word to create and get the results we wanted to see manifested in our own lives. We can see the truth of this statement all throughout the Bible, but the scripture below provides more insight on the importance of speaking **Faith**-filled words. As it also presents evidence on how effective God's **Faith**-filled Words were to the creation process.

Hebrews 11:3

3Through faith we understand that the worlds were framed by the word of God, so that things which are seen were not made of things which do appear.

I have read this verse many times over the years, but it was not until last year the understanding was revealed to me. It was like I was reading the verse for the first time. I knew God was saying something to me through this scripture verse. As previously mentioned, I did not know my words were shaping the environment around me, but as I began meditating on this verse, it would change the words I would use daily. There are many scripture verses in the Bible that speaks about the words we speak but let us take a look at these two verses. This is Jesus speaking to the Pharisees as they question Jesus' authority.

Matthew 12:36-37

³⁶But I say unto you, that every idle word that men shall speak, they shall give account thereof in the day of judgment.

³⁷For by thy words thou shalt be justified, and by thy words thou shalt be condemned.

As I was conducting a study on the importance of our words, these two verses triggered something on the inside of me. Jesus said, *"Every **idle** word that men speak, they shall give an account thereof in the day of judgment."* This got me thinking how serious our words truly are. Even though Jesus is speaking to the Pharisees, He is directing His words to "all men."

Jesus was telling the Pharisees; He knew what was in their heart because of the words they spoke. Instead of the Pharisees happily receiving Jesus as the Messiah and being thankful for His arrival, they chose to fight against Him. They were a group of religious leaders who loved walking around demonstrating how important they were. They went around preaching a law, they themselves did not keep. The Pharisees were so caught up in their religious practices and traditions, they were blind to the fact the long-awaited Messiah was there. So, they sought out ways to destroy Jesus any way they could. They constantly questioned Jesus' authority, teachings and healings. Evil was in their heart; therefore, evil came out with every word they spoke. Let us read what Jesus said to them in the next two verses.

Matthew 12:34-35

³⁴O generation of vipers, how can ye, being evil, speak good things? For out of the abundance of the heart the mouth speaketh.

³⁵A good man out of the good treasure of the heart bringeth forth good things: and an evil man out of the evil treasure bringeth forth evil things.

Jesus was basically telling the Pharisees; they had the power to change the course of their lives and how to bring forth this change. But the Pharisees was so caught up in their hatred, they could not hear anything Jesus was saying. They could not see by not accepting Jesus as the Messiah, they were missing out big-time! They could not see, they too, had the opportunity to be set free. And this would put them in the position to help others become free. But they refused. Instead, they chose to hold on to doing things their way which proved to be ineffective and produced nothing.

I had to see exactly what the word idle meant. I had a general idea of its meaning, but I looked it up in the Webster dictionary to get a broader understanding. The word idle means; without effect, pointless, inactive, and useless. Can you see why Jesus said what He said about speaking idle words? Why speak idle words which clearly states in its definition as being, pointless. Which is an absolute waste of time. God did not give us time to waste. God wants us active and bearing fruit for His Kingdom.

If we are speaking non-productive words, what will this accomplish? It will accomplish absolutely nothing. We can see why Jesus was so adamant with the Pharisees, telling them about their words, with the warning they will be judged by them.

You might be asking, "What am I supposed to say?" I am so glad you asked. God gives us words to speak. Words that will bring tremendous changes into our lives. Let us read what the scripture says about God's Word.

Hebrews 4:12 AMPC

12For the Word that God speaks is alive and full of power [Making it active, operative, energizing, and effective]; it is sharper than any two-edged sword, penetrating to the dividing line of the breath of (soul) and [the immortal spirit, and of joints and morrow [of the deepest parts of our nature], exposing and sifting and analyzing and judging the very thoughts and purposes of the heart.

We can see in the verse above; idle words are a total contradiction to the Word of God. The Word of God is powerful, active, and operative. This scripture affirms, when the Word of God is spoken in **Faith,** the Word will go to work in our situation. The Word will work just like it did when God created the earth.

John 1:1-3 MSG

The Word was first, the Word present to God, God present to the Word.
The Word was God in Readiness for God from day one.

Everything was created through Him (the Word); nothing - not one thing! - came into being without Him (the Word).

Can you see how instrumental the Word of God was during the creation process? It clearly states, nothing was created in the earth without the Word. Now that we know, we cannot deny how important the Word of God is to our lives, environment and circumstances. I expressed in the chapter "Where Faith Began" how exciting this scripture was to read in the Message translation. The Message translation emphasizes how the Word of God was ready to go to work, as He waited for God to release Him to create whatever God would speak. Another scripture which ministers the importance of our words is found in the book of Proverbs.

Proverbs 18:21

21Death and life are in the power of the tongue: and they that love it shall eat the fruit thereof.

You might be saying, "Wow, that is a bold statement!" Yes, it is. God is telling us again in this verse how important our words truly are. Look at the two words that are used, death and life. These two words are totally opposite of each other with a major distinction in meaning. It is in this verse, God is saying, "Are you going to speak life over your situation or death? You see, God has given mankind a choice from the beginning. In the book of Genesis, God gave the first human beings on the earth a choice and it was a life and death choice. God forewarned Adam not to eat from the tree of the knowledge of good and evil.

Genesis 2:17

17But of the tree of the knowledge of good and evil, thou shalt not eat of it; for in the day that thou eatest thereof thou shalt surely die.

We can see Adam was explicitly warned not to eat from the tree of the knowledge of good and evil. Even though Adam was warned, when his wife Eve took a bite from the fruit of the tree, she turned to Adam to do the same. Adam could have said (paraphrasing), "Eve this is wrong. God said not to eat from this tree." But Adam did not say anything. Adam and Eve made a conscious choice to eat from the tree, so they had to suffer the consequences of their choices. They lost everything. And because they chose to disobey God, they were evicted from the Garden of Eden. Adam and Eve chose death. Even though they did not die a physical death, they died a spiritual death. It was a spiritual death because that day they were separated from their Creator. And all the provision that was freely given to them. Adam and Eve's actions put them on a path, God never intended for them.

This is the same outcome we can have in our lives if we choose to speak words of death into our situations. When we choose to speak idle or death words, we are unequivocally bringing death into our situations because we are voluntarily separating ourselves from the will of God.

Another example concerning the use of idle words is found in the book of Numbers, chapter 13. Moses sent twelve Israelites to spy out the land God promised to give them. After their deliverance from Egypt, God promised the Israelites, He was going to bring them into a land that flowed with milk and honey. To acquire this land, the Israelites had to dispossess the current inhabitants. God expressed to the Israelites; He was going to undoubtedly deliver the inhabitants of this land into their hands. God was promising them total victory over their enemies.

After the twelve Israelites spies returned, ten of the twelve spies returned with what the Bible calls an evil report. The ten spies brought a death report back to Moses. It was a death report because they did not say what God said. They said the total opposite. The ten spies looked at the people in the land and said, there was no way they could defeat these men because of their huge stature. The inhabitants of the land were giants.

The other two spies responded in **Faith** and said what God said. They brought back a life report to Moses. The two spies eagerly declared, *"Let us go up at once, and possess it; for we are well able to overcome it* (Numbers 13:30)." These two spies were ready to go in and take the land God promised them. So, what happened in this situation? The ten spies and the adult Israelites under the leadership of Moses could not enter the promised land because the words of death they spoke. Because of the words they spoke they caused unbelief to enter the hearts of the others. Only the two spies and the children of the unbelievers would enter the promised land. All the others died in the wilderness. The situation that occurred with the twelve spies demonstrates the importance of our words. This was literally a life and death situation.

Joshua 5:6

⁶For the children of Israel walked forty years in the wilderness, till all the people that were men of war, which came out of Egypt, were consumed, because they obeyed not the voice of the Lord: unto whom the Lord sware that he would not shew them the land, which the Lord sware unto their fathers that he would give us, a land that floweth with milk and honey.

God would not hold us accountable for something if He did not provide us with the correct way of doing what He expects from us. God has given the Body of Christ a book called the "Holy Bible" that is filled with His Word. This book contains His wisdom, knowledge, insight, instructions, blessings, and most importantly, His truth. God's Word is so close and dear to Him that He manifested His Word into the person of Jesus Christ.

Hebrews 10:7

⁷Then said I, Lo, I come (in the volume of the book it is written of me,) to do thy will, O God.

You see, Jesus came to earth to do the Father's will. He came to do what the Father sent Him to do and to speak what the Father gave Him to speak. Jesus said in **John 6:63, *"The words that I speak unto you, they are spirit, and they are life."*** So, we need to do ourselves a favor and speak the Word of God into and over our lives. Do not wait to speak the Word when you have a problem. Do not wait for a problem to surface. Speak the Word of God every day!

God has given us a choice. A choice of life and death. If you did not know before, you have now come into the knowledge of the choices God has laid before you. What God said to the Israelites and Jesus to the Pharisees, God is saying to us today. We will be held accountable for our words. God has provided us with the choice and the answer, so there is no way we can possibly be confused over this. Let us take a look at God's statement to the Israelites spoken by Moses.

Deuteronomy 30:19

¹⁹ I call heaven and earth to record this day against you, that I have set before you life and death, blessing and

cursing: therefore choose life, that both thou and thy seed may live:

And this is what Jesus is saying to us.

John 10:10

10The thief cometh not, but to steal, kill and to destroy: I am come that they might have life and that they might have it more abundantly.

To walk out this life of **Faith** that has been designed for the believer, we must trust and believe God. In trusting God, we need to trust and believe His Word. To see the effects of His Word, we need to speak His Word. When we speak His Word, we need to speak His Word in **Faith** believing it is going to bring life and blessings into our situation. Let me share with you how vital the Word of God and **Faith** is to the Body of Christ. After salvation, these two are the lifeline of the believer and if we do not grab hold of them, we will sink!

If you want to experience an incredible life of **Faith-Style** living you must learn to speak **Faith**-filled words. **Faith-Style** is not a word to be taken lightly, it is the life every believer should be living. By choosing "life" you are taking substantial **Faith** steps into a life which pleases our Heavenly Father!

Hebrews 11:6

6But without Faith it is impossible to please Him: for he that cometh to God must believe that He is, and that He is a rewarder of them that diligently seek Him.

WE ARE THE LENDERS

Have you ever gone to the bank or anywhere else to apply for credit and you filled out the application and after you finished the application you come into a state of worry wondering about the decision that would be made? Or what about how much they would allow you to have or to receive based on your income and debt already incurred by accessing your credit report and scores? How do you feel when you go and purchase something on credit only to have a salesperson tell you, you do not qualify based on your income and/or your credit score? What about when you know you need something, and you go to the store to price what you need and cannot afford to buy them. Every scenario I have described cannot be a good feeling to anyone, especially a believer. I say especially the believer because we go to church on Sundays, watch Christian Television and read the Bible. We hear and read scripture verses that says, I am the head and not the tail, I can do all things through Christ Jesus which strengthens me, all my needs are met and supplied by Christ Jesus, my God owns the cattle on a thousand hills, the earth is the Lord's and the fullness thereof, all the silver and gold belongs to God and I've never seen the righteous forsaken nor His seed begging bread. If we know these promises exists in the Word of God, but they are not quite operating in our lives on a scriptural level, this could bring discouragement and frustration to anyone. This could be the very reason some Christians fall away from their beliefs and stop attending church to figure out how to get everything they need, without God. They eventually incur more and more debt which then begins to take a toll on them and their health.

Sadly, we have so much pressure around us which makes it easy for us to fall into these debt traps. There are constant alluring enticements of buy what you cannot afford, raging around us daily. The pressure to purchase these things are in our world daily in newspaper ads, sales advertisement on websites, sales ads that come to our homes in the mailbox, television commercials, radio advertisement, and an immense amount of credit card offers in practically every store we visit. The pressure to buy is coming through every imaginable outlet possible: It is becoming an inescapable reality.

I was in a store one day picking up some items and afterwards went to the cashier to pay for them. The cashier then asked me, would I like to apply for the store's credit card. She informed me, that if I apply for the store's credit card and get approved, I would only be required to pay a small amount for my items. I smiled at her and said, "No thank you. I will be paying cash." She kept asking me, trying to persuade me and I kept shaking my head no. She was trying so hard to entice me and I tried my best to keep a good attitude about it, but I was getting tired of her saying it. After many attempts she said, "Look at me trying to convince you." I shook my head again and said, "No, I do not need any more debt."

When I walked away from the cash register, I thought the incident was so strange. Many cashiers have approached me about applying for credit, but no one as persistent as this one. She was so persistent like her job was on the line. I knew that it was not. But I later understood the reason for her persistence. You see, when you make a commitment to live God's Word out in your life, the pressure is on! I told my husband when we were leaving the mall what had happened with the cashier. I said to him, it was so strange that she kept pursuing the issue. I know she did not mean any harm, but it was pretty much borderline harassment.

It appears many believe that credit can solve their problems. Ironically, some believe credit is a lifejacket they can use if needed. They believe it will keep them afloat and cover the things their paychecks will not. They believe their credit cards are working for them, as they pay their minimum monthly payments. What they do not realize is, they began to owe more and more money due to the interest rates they incur when you do not pay the debt off completely. It is a vicious cycle that will not end until those credit cards are paid and destroyed.

The world system continues to come up with more and more ways to put consumers in debt. The other day my husband and I were out driving, and I noticed a building that was a pretty decent size building. It had a sign that read "Payday and Auto Loans" on the top of the building. You know, when these kinds of businesses first came on the scene, they started out as spaces usually shared with other businesses like a check cashing place or a rented booth in a store. But now these loan businesses are moving into big buildings which tells me business is indeed booming! I remember a few years ago I was working, and I needed some cash to get me through until my next payday. I went to the check cashing place which shared an office space with a payday loan business. I was so desperate. Of course, they played on my desperation. But I looked at the rates and I saw that if I borrow two hundred dollars against my paycheck. It was only, only, I thought, at the time, forty-nine dollars to pay back. When I went in there, I do not recall needing that amount of money. But when I got there, I thought, "If I am going to do this, I might as well get more." Later, I deeply regretted ever going into that place because every two weeks I was back in that place. I was back in there because when you are living from paycheck to paycheck, you cannot afford to pay two hundred and fifty dollars and just walk away. You must keep reborrowing to make-up for what you lost when you paid them back. So, I was actually losing fifty dollars every two weeks. I basically created another bill for myself, I definitely did not need. So, what did I do in response to my dilemma? I called for help. I called my grandmother and explained my situation to her. I explained to her, I could not stop borrowing because I always needed to re-borrow the money to take care of my bills. So, thank God, she agreed to help me out of this situation I so desperately wanted to get out of. Thank you, Lord!

What I am trying to get you to understand is when you live a life of **Faith** and have full confidence and assurance in God, you do not have to live like what I described. At the time all this was happening, I was a new Christian and did not know much about living by **Faith**. If I had the wisdom then that I have now, I would have never walked into that place. I would have sought out another alternative for my problem. I would have consulted God for the solution, and I am sure He would have led me down a different path.

I know what it is like to have bills due and need money to properly care for your kids. But I also know during that time I could have used a lesson in money management and God knew this as well. It is stated in the book of Hosea, *"My people are destroyed for a lack of knowledge* (4:6)." If we do not spend time in God's Word, how will we get the wisdom to handle life's situations? If we take the time to spend in God's Word and apply what we have learned into our lives, many of us would not suffer the consequences for the difficult circumstances we may find ourselves in. It says in **2 Timothy 3:16-17,** *"All scriptures is given by inspiration of God, and is profitable for doctrine, for reproof, for correction, for instruction in righteousness, that the man of God may be complete, thoroughly equipped for every good work."*

The other day I was listening to a preacher's sermon on television. During his sermon, he spoke about, how many years ago there was an illegal gambling operation called running numbers. He explained how people, mainly people of color, would play the numbers because they could win large sums of money that would take years to accumulate on their jobs. Years ago, this operation was illegal but has been made legal by pretty much taking the same concept and calling it "The State Lottery." As I was thinking about this, I thought about moonshine. Years ago, moonshine was illegal and a few months back I noticed in the store they were selling moonshine. Marijuana was an illegal drug that many states have now made legal. All these things were made legal because the government found a way to make money on them. In the world system everything comes down to money and how the government can benefit from it. As I was pondering all of this, I thought about the difference between the world system and the Kingdom of God. The world system negotiates things no matter the cost. In the Kingdom of God there are no negotiations. God's Word is final! The Bible says God is the same yesterday, today, and forever. He does not change.

Child of God, do not be fooled by the subtly of the enemy. He comes in many different forms and he comes to steal, to kill and to destroy. This reminds me of the situation that transpired in the Garden of Eden. The circumstance may be different, but the culprit is the same. Look at the trap he set for them. It cost them a substantial price. It cost them their provision, their state of peace and tranquility. The same an incurrence of debt can cost us if we allow it. But wait, I have "Good News" for you! Let us take a look at what the Word of God and **Faith-Style** living can do for you!

Deuteronomy 28 is a chapter filled with promises that reveals to us how God sees His children. Although Moses was talking to the children of Israel in these passages of scripture, because of the Blood of Jesus, we are now included in these wonderfully professed blessings. We too, are now the descendants of Abraham!

Verses 1-13 contains some of the promises God through Moses declared over the children of Israel's lives.

Deuteronomy 28:1-13

¹And it shall come to pass, if thou shalt hearken diligently unto the voice of the Lord thy God, to observe and to do all his commandments which I command thee this day, that the Lord thy God will set thee on high above all nations of the earth:

²And all these blessings shall come on thee, and overtake thee, if thou shalt hearken unto the voice of the Lord thy God.

³Blessed shalt thou be in the city, and blessed shalt thou be in the field.

[4]Blessed shall be the fruit of thy body, and the fruit of thy ground, and the fruit of thy cattle, the increase of thy kine, and the flocks of thy sheep.

[5]Blessed shall be thy basket and thy store.

[6]Blessed shall thou be when thou comest in, and blessed shalt thou be when thou goest out.

[7]The Lord shall cause thine enemies that rise up against thee to be smitten before thy face: they shall come out against thee one way, and flee before thee seven ways.

[8]The Lord shall command the blessing upon thee in thy storehouses, and in all that thou settest thine hand unto; and he shall bless thee in thy land which the Lord thy God giveth thee.

[9]The Lord shall establish thee an holy people unto himself, as he hath sworn unto thee, if thou shalt keep the commandments of the Lord thy God, and walk in his ways.

[10]And all people of the earth shall see that thou art called by the name of the Lord; and they shall be afraid of thee.

[11]And the Lord shall make thee plenteous in goods, in the fruit of thy body, and in the fruit of thy cattle, and in the fruit of thy ground, in the land which the Lord sware unto thy fathers to give thee.

[12]The Lord shall open unto thee his good treasure the heaven to give the rain unto thy land in his season, and to bless all the work of thine hand: and thou shalt lend unto many nations, and thou shalt not borrow.

[13]And the Lord shall make thee the head, and not the tail; and thou shalt be above only, and thou shalt not be

beneath; if that thou hearken unto the commandments of the Lord thy God, which I command thee this day, to observe and to do them.

This is good news! These blessings are amazing! God brought the children of Israel out of poverty and blessed them to receive supernatural increase, wealth and abundance. They went from being slaves to becoming extremely wealthy. God was placing His children in the position of not having to borrow anything from anyone again. God was setting them up for life! They were to be the Lenders and not the borrowers and God wants the same for us! We are to be the LENDERS and not the borrowers! You need to receive this by **Faith**!

You know the children of Israel had such a hard time receiving their new identity. Through their wilderness experience Moses was constantly revealing to them who they truly were, which I have discussed in the chapter "Your Identity." God desired to bless the Israelites like He blessed their forefather, Abraham. The Bible declares, Gold blessed Abraham in all things (Genesis 24:1). Let us read what "all things" entailed in the life of Abraham. These are the words of Abraham's servant.

Genesis 24:35

35And the Lord hath blessed my master greatly; and he is become great: and he hath given him flocks, and herds, and silver, and gold, and menservants, and maidservants, and camels, and asses.

God demonstrated what it is like to be the lender and not the borrower in the life of Abraham! You want to know how Abraham received his wealth?

When God instructed Abraham to leave his country, Abraham later encountered a famine. Because of the famine, Abraham and his wife Sarah traveled to Egypt. When they arrived, God used what appeared to be a very challenging situation to bless Abraham beyond his wildest imagination. Abraham departed Egypt with great wealth! From that one trip, God caused Abraham to become the lender and not the borrower, the head and not the tail and above only and not beneath. God did the same thing for Abraham once again, only this time there was no famine involved. Abraham and his wife took another journey to a country named, Gerar. During their time in Gerar, God blessed Abraham again by causing him to prosper under very strange and unusual circumstances. All the wealth God bestowed upon Abraham, took away the need for Abraham to travel to another nation for anything again. Instead, other nations recognized how extremely blessed Abraham was.

God blessed Abraham with such great wealth that he refused the spoil from a battle, he and his people fought. Abraham wanted it to be very clear to everyone, who was directly responsible for his good fortune.

Genesis 14:21-23

21And the king of Sodom, said unto Abram, Give me the persons, and take the goods to thyself.

22And Abram said to the king of Sodom, I have lift up mine hand unto the Lord, the most high God, the possessor of heaven and earth.

23That I will not take from a thread even to a shoelatchet, and that I will not take any thing that is thine, lest thou shouldest say, I have made Abram rich:

You see, Abraham did not allow the king of Sodom to get the faintest idea that he had anything to do with Abraham's fortune. Abraham knew who blessed him and he was not about to let a pagan king take away God's credit. You know, the views of the people then are not much different from the views of the people today. If Abraham would have kept the spoils from the battle, the king of Sodom would have told anybody who would listen it was because of him Abraham accumulated his wealth. Even though he and another king fled from the battle.

Although the spoils were not technically debt, do you see how this king spoke to Abraham. He spoke to Abraham like he had something to do with Abraham receiving the spoils. Why? Because he wanted to have something to bring to Abraham's attention, if there ever was a need to. You know the kind of people that like to stake a claim in your victories even though they had nothing to do with it. This is exactly why God is not a fan of debt and He certainly does not want anybody taking credit for anything He has done in your life. He does not want us owing any man anything but to love them (Romans 13:8). He does not want us to be a servant to the lender (Proverbs 22:7). God desires for his children to take their rightful places as the lender and not the borrower. There have been many going into debt believing it was God who blessed them. But always remember, God's blessings do not bring any sorrow.

Proverbs 10:22 AMPC

22The Blessing of the Lord---it makes [truly] rich, and He adds no sorrow with it [neither does toiling increase it].

Dear believer, do not entertain a life filled with a "lack of knowledge" anymore. Please do not take the Word of God for granted. Getting the knowledge of God takes time and patience.

I heard Gloria Copeland once say, "If you're going to use your **Faith,** you cannot be lazy about it." As it is stated in the book of Joshua, we must get into the Word of God and consistently work the Word.

Joshua 1:8

⁸This book of the law shall not depart out of thy mouth; but thou shalt meditate therein day and night, that thou mayest observe to do according to all that is written therein: for then thou shalt make thy way prosperous, and then thou shall have good success.

If you want to live the life God has purposed and planned for His children, you need to do what Jesus said in Matthew 6:33.

³³But seek ye first the kingdom of God, and his righteousness; and all these things will be added unto you.

Jesus said we are to seek first God's kingdom and His righteousness. Because when we do it God's way, everything He has purposed for us will be added to us. The word seek means, to go in search of, try to acquire or gain, to aim at, or to make an attempt. Out of all the definitions that were provided "to aim at" stood out to me the most. You see, we must take an aggressive stand with the Word of God if we want to see its promised results. The Bible declares in, **Matthew 11:12, *"The kingdom of heaven suffereth violence and the violent take it by force."***

Let us get to work in God's Word, so we can reap the awesome benefits that are outlined in God's Word. What are the benefits and promised results for the believer? There are many, but this scripture is one of my favorites!

Psalm 1:1-3

[1]Blessed is the man that walketh not in the counsel of the ungodly, nor standeth in the way of the sinner, nor sitteth in the seat of the scornful.

[2]But his delight is in the law of the Lord; and in his law doth he meditate day and night.

[3]And he shall be like a tree planted by the rivers of water, that bringeth forth his fruit in his season; his leaf also shall not wither; and whatsoever he doeth shall prosper.

Follow God's lead and you will most assuredly become the person His Word says you are. You will become the Lender you were destined to be! Take your rightful place and reap the God-given benefits of **Faith-Style** living!

FAITH IS A REQUIREMENT

J esus, the Son of God, implemented **Faith-Style** living in His life and ministry during His time in the earth. He lived it every day! Jesus was such an advocate of **Faith**, He traveled from region to region looking for **Faith**-filled believers who wanted to see the supernatural hand of God work wonders in their lives. Jesus was looking for people who wanted a change. People who refused to stay the same. For the believer, seeing Jesus was like seeing a solution to their problems walking by them, they could not afford to let get away. This is probably why Jesus became so excited when He came across believers who cried out for His help to heal and rescue them. Jesus became so excited because they possessed the **Faith** to believe what they were asking, could in fact be done. For example, let us take a look at the story of blind Bartimaeus. Bartimaeus' **Faith** caught Jesus' attention. It stopped Him in His tracks!

Mark 10:46-47

46And they came to Jericho: and as He went out of Jericho with His disciples and a great number of people, blind Bartimaeus, the son of Timaeus, sat by the highway side begging.

47And when he heard that it was Jesus of Nazareth, he began to cry out, and say, Jesus, thou son of David, have mercy on me.

Bartimaeus could not physically see Jesus passing by because he was blind, but the Word of God says, he heard it was Jesus of Nazareth walking by. Bartimaeus story shows us that even a man without sight, who cannot physically see, can perceive spiritually, when an answer to his prayers is passing by. The Bible declares, Bartimaeus began to cry out to Jesus. This sounds like a man who was not going to let anything stop him from receiving his miracle.

You see, Bartimaeus had a desire to be made whole. I am sure he grew tired of sitting at the highway begging day after day for handouts. It was Bartimaeus' desire to receive his sight! As we read further into his story, we can see how the people who were around Bartimaeus, thought they could tell him what to do.

Mark 10:48

⁴⁸And many charged him that he should hold his peace: but he cried the more a great deal, thou son of David have mercy on me.

Bartimaeus was determined to get his miracle. He was not going to let anyone stop him from receiving his healing. When the people tried to stop him, the Bible declares, he cried out even more. The more the people tried to hinder him, the more Bartimaeus cried out. This man had some **Faith**! Jesus responded to his **Faith.** Jesus called for Bartimaeus and asked, what He could do for him.

Mark 10:50-52

⁵⁰And he, casting away his garment, rose, and came to Jesus.

⁵¹And Jesus answered and said unto him, What wilt thou that I should do unto thee? The blind man said unto Him, Lord, that I might receive my sight.

⁵²And Jesus said unto him, Go thy way; thy faith has made thee whole. And immediately he received his sight, and followed Jesus in the way.

We can see in the story of Bartimaeus, how important **Faith** is to the life of the believer. Jesus said to Bartimaeus, it was Bartimaeus' **Faith** that made him whole. His **Faith** restored his sight. He used his **Faith** to get the results he wanted. Thank you, Holy Spirit! This story is speaking to me as well!

Bartimaeus had the **Faith**, Hebrews 11:1 speaks about, *"Now faith is the substance of things hoped for, the evidence of things not seen."* Bartimaeus' story is an incredible example of what **Faith** can do for you, even in the most extreme circumstances.

Jesus was also excited about the Centurion soldier's **Faith**. In Matthew 8:8, the Centurion soldier approached Jesus, asking Him to heal his servant. The servant was sick with what the Bible refers to as the palsy. The servant's condition was tormenting. This Roman soldier had to have **Faith** to even approach Jesus because he was not even an Israelite. He was a soldier from the Roman army. At that time, the Romans were governing the Israelites' country and forcing them to pay taxes to the Roman government. Jesus must have been really impressed with the soldier's **Faith** to come to Him, asking Him for help. Or maybe Jesus was moved by the compassion of this soldier because he sought healing for his servant. This was not even his own biological son. Jesus was impressed with this man's **Faith!** Jesus offered to go to the soldier's home, but the soldier said it was not necessary. The soldier knew Jesus could speak the word and his servant would be healed. This soldier had **Faith** in the Word of God! Let us read what transpired between Jesus and the Centurion soldier.

Matthew 8:8-10

[8]The Centurion answered and said Lord, I am not worthy that thou shouldest come under my roof: but speak the Word only, and my servant shall be healed.

[9]For I am a man under authority, having soldiers under me; and I say to this man, Go, and he goeth; and to another, Come, and he cometh; and to my servant, Do this, and he doeth it.

[10]When Jesus heard it, he marveled, and said to them that followed, Verily I say unto you, I have not found so great faith, no, not in Israel.

I love the response Jesus gave in verse 10. It said, Jesus marveled at the Centurion soldier's response. This reminds me of when my children were young, and they would do something they discovered for the first time. They would shout, "Look mom!" And I would light up like it was the first time I had ever seen it. I am sure you can remember tender moments like this with your children or from your own childhood with your parents. How I felt in those moments caused me to see Jesus in the same way. How pleased and excited He must have been to hear someone profess great **Faith**. This man knew his servant could be healed without Jesus stepping foot in His home. Let us take a look at Jesus' response to the Centurion soldier.

Matthew 8:13

¹³And Jesus said unto the centurion, Go thy way; and as thou hast believed, so be it done unto thee. And his servant was healed in the selfsame hour.

This Centurion soldier was not even an Israelite, but the demonstration of his **Faith** is remarkable! As I reread the story to write about it, the Centurion's **Faith** is totally inspiring!

There is another story in the Bible that demonstrates commendable **Faith.** It is the story of the Syrophoenician woman. This woman was also a non-Israelite. She sought out Jesus, seeking healing for her daughter. Her daughter was in torment because she was possessed by a demon. Let us take a look at Jesus' response to the Syrophoenician woman.

Mark 7:27

²⁷But Jesus said unto her, let the children first be filled: for it is not meet to take the children's bread, and to cast it unto the dogs.

How many of you would have been in tears after hearing Jesus' response? Or how many of you would have been so crushed, you would have just wanted to crawl into a hole and hide? The first time I read this story in the Bible, to be honest, I was a little upset with how Jesus spoke to this woman. But now that I am more mature in the Word, I understand Jesus' response much better. His response says to me, when you are seeking something you need; you may not always get the response you want. When you are desperately in need of something and the person initially says no. You must stand firm until you get what you need. The feeling of the humiliation you may feel can be devastating but you suck it up until you get what you need. It could absolutely feel as if life is crushing you in that moment but once you get what you need, that is all that matters. Let us take a look at the Syrophoenician woman's response to Jesus.

Mark 7:28

28And she answered and said unto him, Yes Lord: yet the dogs under the table eat of the children's crumbs.

Wow, what a response! I like this Syrophoenician woman! We all could learn a lot from her. This was a wisdom filled response she gave to Jesus. She did not get offended and if she did, she did not let it show. She certainly did not allow it to interfere with getting the miracle she needed for her daughter. Jesus was impressed! You can really detect Jesus' enthusiasm in the book of Matthew.

Matthews 15:28

28 Then Jesus answered and said unto her, O woman, great is thy Faith: be it unto thee even as thou wilt. And her daughter was made whole from that very hour.

Look at the similarities between the Syrophoenician woman and the Centurion soldier. Neither one of them were Israelites but they both pursued Jesus for their miracles. What they needed was not for themselves but for their loved ones. They were unselfishly motivated in their requests and they humbled themselves before Jesus. They knew Jesus was able to perform the miracles they needed. Their miracles were performed the minute they released their **Faith** in the Word of God (Jesus)!

Faith-Style living is important because getting caught up in a life solely governed by the world can be hazardous to our Christian walk. When our trust is solely in the world system, it can bring us to a place where all we can think about is accumulating things the wrong way. I believe this is the reason for much of the greed we see. It is the cause of many suicides, and disregard for human life. It is because many want a surreal lifestyle. Instead of living the way God intended for us to live, many take their lives into their own hands which can produce disastrous results.

Satan tried his best to entice Jesus with acquiring wealth in the wrong way. While Jesus was away fasting in the wilderness, Satan showed up to tempt Him. He waited until he thought Jesus was in a weak moment, to entice Jesus with his deceit and lies. Let us read what transpired between Jesus and Satan.

Matthew 4:1-2

1Then was Jesus led up of the Spirit into the wilderness to be tempted of the devil.

2And when He had fasted forty days and forty nights, he was afterward a hungred.

Matthew 4:8-11:

8Again, the devil taketh Him up into an exceeding high mountain, and showeth Him all the kingdoms of the world, and the glory of them;

9And saith unto Him, All these things will I give thee, if thou wilt fall down and worship me.

10Then saith Jesus unto him, get thee hence, Satan: for it is written, Thou shalt worship the Lord thy God, and him only shalt thou serve.

11Then the devil leaveth him, and behold, angels came and ministered unto him.

Did you see how the enemy tried to get into Jesus' head? He tried to convince Jesus to turn away from doing things God's way. The enemy works by deception and this is how he tries to get into the minds of believers. He wants us to listen to him and believe he can give us all these things without any consequences. If we listen to him and allow him to seduce us with his lies, he will leave us high and dry. He will leave us holding the bag of dishonor, guilt, and shame. The enemy does not care one iota for us. He just wants to steal from us. He wants to make a mockery out of us and say to God, "Look God, here is another one I took away from You. They loved what I could give them more than they loved You (paraphrasing)." This might sound harsh, but it is the truth. We can see the enemy's tactics demonstrated in the life of Job. Let us take a look at the Bible's description of Job.

Job 1:1

1There was a man in the land of Uz, whose name was Job; and that man was perfect and upright, and one that feared God, and eschewed evil.

We can see from reading the verse above, why the enemy would want to come after Job. Job loved God. And because of Job's love for God, God blessed Job and his family's life immensely. Job knew it was only because of the goodness of God, he and his family's life were greatly blessed. For this reason, God happily bragged on the faithfulness of Job. Let us take a look at what the Lord said.

Job 1:8

8And the Lord said to unto Satan, Hast thou considered my servant Job, that there is none like him in the earth, a perfect and an upright man, one that feareth God, and escheweth evil?

God sounded like a Father who was well pleased with His child. Satan became so envious he had the audacity to imply, the only reason why Job honored God is because of everything God did for him. And the hedge of protection God put around Job and his family's life.

Job 1:9-10

9 Then Satan answered the Lord, and said, Doth Job fear God for nought?

10 Hast not thou made a hedge about him, and about his house, and about all that he hath on every side? Thou hast blessed the work of his hands, and his substance is increased in the land.

We can really hear Satan's envy in the next verse.

Job 1:11

11 But put forth thine hand now, and touch all that he has, and he will curse thee to thy face.

After God and Satan's conversation, Job did come to suffer some horrible tragedies and losses. Job lost everything. He lost his children. He lost his wealth. And he was afflicted with a horrible illness. Job's situation was dire. It looked so hopeless that even his wife looked to him and said the most **Faith** destroying words anyone could ever say. *"Then said his wife* *unto him, Dost thou still retain thine integrity? Curse God, and die* (Job 2:9)."

Talk about a kick when you are down!

You see, Job's wife wanted him to get mad at God. She wanted him to take an indignant attitude towards life. Even though what she said to her husband was hurtful, through her statement, us readers can learn a lot about how Job was handling the situation. Through her statement, we learn that through everything Job suffered, somehow, he maintained his integrity. Although Job was going through perhaps the worst moment of his life, his love and reverence for God did not falter. Let us take a look at the wisdom filled words Job spoke to his wife. This was a man with true integrity indeed!

Job 2:10

10 But he said unto her, Thou speakest as one of the foolish women speaketh. What? Shall we receive good at the hand of God, and shall we not receive evil? In all this Job did not sin with his lips.

Wow, what amazing **Faith**! After everything Job suffered, which was enough to drive anyone crazy, Job did not lose his **Faith** in God. Job may not have understood what was going on but throughout this whole ordeal he kept professing his love and adoration for God. Job entrusted his life into the hands of God and he never sought to remove his life from those hands! Glory to God!

Job 23:10-12

¹⁰But he knoweth the way that I take: when he hath tried me, I shall come forth as pure gold.

¹¹My foot hath held his steps, his way have I kept, and not declined.

¹²Neither have I gone back from the commandment of His lips; I have esteemed the Words of his mouth more than my necessary food.

Wow, this is so amazing! Now, let us take a look at Job's unprecedented **Faith** in God.

Job 13:15

¹⁵Thou He slay me, yet will I trust in Him..."

Job retained the required **Faith** he needed to get his life back on track. Even though he may have gotten weary throughout the process, he did not lose hope. Let us take a look at what transpired next.

Job 42:12-13

¹²So the Lord blessed the latter end of Job more than his beginning; for he had fourteen thousand sheep, and six thousand camels, and a thousand yoke of oxen, and a thousand she asses.

¹³He had also seven sons and three daughters.

Verses 15-17

¹⁵And in all the land were no women found so fair as the daughters of Job: and their father gave them an inheritance among their brethren.

¹⁶After this lived Job an hundred and forty years, and saw his sons, and his son's sons, even four generations. ¹⁷So Job died, being old and full of days.

Wow, what an example of **Faith** demonstrated in the book of Job! Again, the power pact esteemed words of Job, *"Thou He slay me yet will I trust Him."* How powerful is that? You know, Job is not named in the Hall of **Faith** in the book of Hebrews but after reviewing his story again, he very well should be. It was Job's unprecedented **Faith** that kept him. Job endured extreme hardships, but he persevered to the end. Job never lost **Faith** in God and therefore, he received double for his trouble in his latter days. Praise God!

This is a remarkable example of the benefits and rewards of **Faith-Style** living!

WHERE IS YOUR FAITH?

Where is your **Faith**? This is the key question every believer should ask themselves. Or maybe the question should be, is your **Faith** in the right place? I believe the answer to this question can be found in the book of Matthew in the sixth chapter. The Message translation of this chapter gives us a clear understanding of what God is saying about our lives here in the earth and our position in life as His children. From day to day many of us walk around with the weight of our circumstances on our shoulders. Many of us are burdened with the troubles of life and the troubles of the world around us. There are constant thoughts of provision that bombard our minds daily. Thoughts such as, what will we eat and drink? Where will we live and how will we live? And how will we pay all these bills? Aren't these the thoughts that plague the minds of the believer? But Matthew 6:33 states, *"But seek ye first the kingdom of God, and his righteousness; and all these things shall be added unto you."*

I have read this verse many times and I thought I understood everything the verse entailed until God led me to read it in different translations. One of the translations I read this verse in was from the Good News translation. I will start from verse 31 so we can get a better understanding of what this verse is implying.

Matthew 6:31-33 GNT

³¹So do not start worrying: Where will my food come from? Or my drink? Or my clothes?'

³²(These are things the pagans are always concerned about). Your Father in heaven knows that you need all these things.

³³Instead, be concerned above everything else with the Kingdom of God and with what He requires of you, and He will provide you with all these other things.

Doesn't this sound so simple? To only be concerned with the Kingdom of God and God will provide you with everything you need. When I read this verse in this translation, I was amazed! This really is Good News! You know what really grabbed my attention? It is where it states, "These are the things pagans are always concerned about." I then said to myself, "Wait a minute. I am not a pagan. A pagan is someone who does not know God. That is not me. I am a believer! I am a child of Almighty God!" This statement is what takes me off the hook for my provision and put God on. God has given to us the right to trust Him to provide for us daily. I then began to ponder, why we put this burden on ourselves? I believe one of the reasons why we do this is because it is the way the world teaches us. From the time we were able to comprehend most things, we listened to the adults in our lives have conversations about providing for their families. Some may not have spoken in the manner of God meeting their families' needs. So, their children are left to assume, it is the parents' responsibility to make sure the family needs are met. In a sense this is true, but I believe when our children are young, we need to implement the truth of the matter, especially if we are of the Christian **Faith**. The truth is, we look to God to meet and supply our every human need. Now, whichever way God chooses to do this is up to Him, but we must believe God will make a way. As parents we need to thank God, in front of our children, for every opportunity He has given to us to provide for our families.

When God spoke to Abraham to leave his country, God did not provide Abraham with a mapped-out plan. God did not tell Abraham where he was going or how his needs would be met. Abraham was to trust God and believe, God would get him to his destination. Abraham also needed to trust God to provide for him along the way. Was this journey difficult for Abraham? I am sure it was. In fact, the Bible informs us, Abraham encountered a severe famine while he was traveling. Abraham then decided to continue his journey into Egypt to seek provision until the famine subsided. When Abraham and his entourage was approaching Egypt, Abraham was met with a dilemma. Abraham became fearful because his wife was so beautiful, he knew the Egyptians would kill him and take Sarah. Can you imagine how uncomfortable this trip into Egypt made Abraham? I am sure his mind was bombarded with many thoughts as to what might happen. Abraham was right. As soon as they arrived in Egypt, the Egyptian men instantly noticed Sarah's beauty. They asked Abraham, who Sarah was to him and he said she was his sister. The Egyptians took Sarah and placed her in the king of Egypt's house. Can you imagine how this made Abraham feel? His wife was taken into another man's home. And there was nothing he could do about it. But because Abraham's **Faith** was in the right place, God visited Pharaoh in a dream and commanded him to return Sarah to Abraham. The king also gave Abraham riches beyond measure. This was an overflowing blessing. It was pressed down, shaken together and running over (Luke 6:38).

Genesis 13:1-2

¹And Abram went up out of Egypt, he, and his wife, and all that he had, and Lot with him, into the south.

²And Abraham was very rich in cattle, in silver, and in gold.

In the book of Exodus, when God sent Moses back to Egypt to deliver the children of Israel out of slavery, the children of Israel were so fearful. Even though they cried out to God to be rescued from slavery, when the day finally came for them to be set free, they feared leaving what was familiar to them for so many years. The children of Israel had become so accustomed to their circumstances that when it was time for them to experience the change they prayed for; they became fearful. God was offering them a way out of all the mistreatment and misery they suffered at the hands of the Egyptians. Although they may have wanted freedom badly, it was hard for them to foresee a future outside of Egypt.

The Israelites had become complacent with their surroundings because it was all they knew for over 400 years. This is what happens to many of us today. We cry out to God and moan and groan about our circumstances but when God shows up to deliver us and because it may not be the way we would have chosen to be delivered, we too become fearful. We begin to whine and cry because we are uncomfortable. God has taken us out of what was familiar to us and we cannot handle it. Like the children of Israel, we want the transition to be easy. We expect smooth sailing the whole way. We want to skip the wilderness period and jump straight from the problem to the promised land. To be honest, who wouldn't prefer this option? I know I would. I could speak volumes on this subject from my own personal experiences. Here is one for example.

Some years ago, I was on housing assistance and working for a non-profit organization. God had blessed me with the job, and I was really excited to have it. Although I was glad to be working, there was a dilemma. Because of the amount of money I made, it caused the housing assistance to go down. When I received the letter in the mail explaining the decrease in assistance, I began to panic. I thought, "How am I going to afford to pay this rent, all the bills, and take care of my kids?" It was like I saw no way of getting ahead. I was pretty much back to square one in my finances. Living from paycheck to paycheck and struggling to make ends meet. So, I called the housing authority and spoke to someone about my dilemma. I explained my situation to her, and she said something I have never forgotten. She said, "Although it may seem hard right now, it will pay off in the end." When I hung up the phone with her, I thought, "What is she talking about? That's easy for her to say with her good and well-paying job."

When I looked back over the situation, I realized just how foolish I was. Where was my **Faith**? All I could see was this huge mountain that was in front of me. What I should have done was to get in my Bible and get filled with the knowledge and wisdom of God. I should have been rejoicing over becoming independent from that system. What do I have to say about that whole experience now? She was so right, and I was so foolish. You know I lost that job. You know what I believe to be one of the reasons why I lost the job? It seemed to be for other reasons at the time, but I realized it was because of my mindset. Please here me on this because my situation can be related to several circumstances you may be experiencing in your own life.

After years of receiving housing assistance, it became so familiar to me. Here was God giving me the opportunity to come out of limitation and bondage and what did I do? I murmured and complained. As I look back over the situation with enlightened eyes and understanding, it seems like a slap in the face to God, I deeply regret. God was not trying to cause me or the children of Israel harm, He was delivering us from the poverty mindset we had accumulated over the years.

There was something else about this situation I did not realize at the time. God was granting me another opportunity to exercise my **Faith**. Wasn't this the real lesson behind the wilderness experience for the children of Israel. *"And though shalt remember all the way which the Lord thy God led thee these forty years in the wilderness, to humble thee, and to prove thee, to know what was in thine heart, whether thou wouldest keep my commandments, or no (Deuteronomy 8:2)."*

During the children of Israel's wilderness experience, God wanted them to learn some things throughout their journey. God wanted them to learn some things about Him and He also wanted them to learn some things about themselves. God was showing the Israelites how much He loved them and how special they were to Him. God was taking them off the Egyptian's program and putting them on His program. He was converting their minds from a slave mentality, to the mentality of an owner. God was taking them from a land of scraps and was bringing them into a land of abundance. But He wanted them to know who was providing these things for them. Not Egypt, not Moses and not Aaron but God their creator and true deliverer.

Think about this for a moment. The Israelites had witnessed many miracles God performed on their behalves. You would have thought after witnessing all those miracles, they would have believed God was with them. God even allowed them to depart from Egypt with the Egyptians wealth! In Exodus 12:35, God instructed the children of Israel to go to their taskmasters and borrow silver, gold, and clothes. This was a miracle within itself! God sent the children of Israel to receive the belongings of the people who enslaved them! But wait, the Israelites were not even going directly into the promised land, they were going on a journey in the wilderness. In the wilderness, they did not have anywhere to spend their money. But it did not matter, God loved the children of Israel so much, He wanted to make sure they received compensation for all the years they and their ancestors where enslaved. Everything God did for the Israelites, should have proved to them God was on their side, but no, they continued to murmur and complain like they had it so good in Egypt. The children of Israel had the favor of God and could not even see it.

Hold on. Let us not be so quick to judge them because many of us have behaved in the same way. I know I have. I behaved the same way with the housing situation. Even though I knew God had given me favor to get the job, to get promoted on the job with a nice increase of salary, I did not have **Faith** in Him to get me through the next hurdle. How silly of me. I am going to put it out there because I believe many of you will benefit from my story. Just like the children of Israel, God wanted me to remember how He brought me out before. God also wanted me to know, if He did it then, He would do it again. Glory to God!

Faith in God is perpetual, child of God. Do not ever allow your **Faith** to stagnate. God wants us to use our **Faith** on a continuous basis. When He brings us through one hurdle, always be ready to exercise your **Faith** again. The Bible declares, we are to go from **Faith** to **Faith**.

Romans 1:17 AMPC

¹⁷For in the Gospel a righteousness which God ascribes is revealed, both springing from faith and leading to faith [disclosed through the way of faith that arouses to more faith]. As it is written, The man who through faith is just and upright shall live and shall live by faith.

Always remember, our **Faith** in God should be perpetual while never forgetting the miracles He has already demonstrated in our lives.

I already gave you some Old Testament examples. Now please allow me to provide you with a New Testament example. In the Gospel of Mark chapter 8, it speaks about a religious group called the Pharisees who were always trying to make trouble for Jesus. They would come to Jesus asking Him all kind of questions hoping to find fault in Him. In this story, the Pharisees is asking Jesus questions and challenging Him to give them a sign from heaven (Mark 8:11). After this incident with the Pharisees, Jesus warned the disciples to beware of the leaven of the Pharisees. As Jesus was talking to the disciples about the leaven, the disciples thought Jesus was asking them about not having enough bread. Let us take a look at what transpired.

Mark 8:11-16

¹¹And the Pharisees came forth, and began to question with Him, seeking of Him a sign from heaven, tempting Him.

¹²And He sighed deeply in His spirit, and saith, Why doth this generation seek after a sign? Verily I say unto you, There shall no sign be given unto this generation.

¹³And He left them, and entering into the ship again departed to the other side.

¹⁴Now the disciples had forgotten to take bread, neither had they in the ship with them more than one loaf.

¹⁵And He charged them, saying, Take heed, beware of the leaven of the Pharisees, and of the leaven of Herod.

¹⁶And they reasoned among themselves, saying, It is because we have no bread.

At this point, Jesus had already performed many miracles in front of the disciples. On two different occasions, Jesus fed thousands of men, not including the women and children that were present. And both occurrences happened in the desert place. Meaning this miracle happened in a place where there was nothing physically there to sustain them. Jesus performed these miracles by multiplying a little boy's lunch. So why would the disciples be thinking Jesus was talking to them about not having enough bread when they witnessed the multiplication of the bread and fish. Jesus reminds them of this in the next few verses.

Mark 8:17-21

¹⁷And when Jesus knew it, he saith unto them, Why reason ye, because ye have no bread? Perceive ye not yet, neither understand? Have ye your heart yet hardened?

¹⁸Having eyes, see ye not? And having ears, hear ye not? And do ye not remember?

¹⁹When I brake the five loaves among five thousand, how many baskets full of fragments took ye up? They say unto him, Twelve.

²⁰And when the seven among four thousand, how many baskets full of fragments took ye up? And they said, Seven.

²¹And he said unto them, How is it that ye do not understand?

This is the same situation that was demonstrated with the children of Israel in the Old Testament. Jesus was trying to get the disciples off the world's way of seeking provision, while showing them how to get their needs met by using their **Faith**. The disciples' minds kept going back to the natural while Jesus was constantly teaching and demonstrating supernatural living.

So, what is the lesson here? The Apostle Paul puts it perfectly in Galatians 4:8-9, CEB, *"At the time, when you didn't know God, you were enslaved by things that aren't gods, by nature. But now, after knowing God (or rather, being known by God), how can you turn back again to the weak and worthless world system? Do you want to be slaves to it again?"*

Wow, what a statement! Once you know your God and learn His way of doing and being right, why would you want to turn back to the weak and beggarly systems of this world? This is powerful scripture!

This is what happened to the children of Israel, the disciples and me with the housing situation. Instead of continuing in **Faith** with the Word of God, we turned back. Instead of moving forward in **Faith** we let what we were seeing dictate our circumstances. I personally never want to make this mistake again. This is exactly why we need to keep our **Faith** in God and in His Word! Even though we cannot physically see God's Word at work, we must believe by **Faith** God's eternal Word is at work on our behalves. It is like what Jesus said in Matthew 4:4, *"Man does not live by bread alone but by every Word that proceedeth out of the mouth of God."*

We need more in this life than edible food. We need the eternal Word of God to thrive in this life! God's Word is eternal. It is everlasting! Previously, when I thought about the word eternal, I always tied it to heaven. I now understand, God is showing me when He speaks about eternity, He is not only speaking about heaven, He is speaking of eternity within us right now in this moment. Remember we have a renewed born-again spirit, right now. We are body, soul, mind and spirit right here in the earth. But remember when we are born again our inner man is supposed to grow and mature daily. Our spirit grows by the eternal Word of God and it need to be fed every day. Perishable food does nothing for our spirit, only the eternal Word of God feeds our spirit because our spirits do not die.

1 Timothy 6:12

¹²**Fight the good fight of faith, lay hold on eternal life, whereunto thou art called.**

You see, our flesh likes to contradict our eternal spirit, every step of the way. The Apostle Paul tells us in the verse above, we must fight the good fight of **Faith.** When we fight the good fight of **Faith**, we are laying hold to eternal life. By feeding ourselves with the eternal Word, we are strengthening our inner man. When are inner man is strengthened, we can override fleshly thoughts, desires and behaviors. This can be an ongoing battle for the believer, but we can win it every time! This is a lesson God wants all of us to learn and this is the same lesson God was teaching the children of Israel in the wilderness. He was teaching them no matter the circumstance they encountered in the wilderness, they were to "fight the good fight of **Faith**" by laying hold to His eternal Word. Let us take a look at Deuteronomy 8:3.

³And He humbled thee, and suffered thee to hunger, and fed thee with manna, which thou knewest not, neither did thy fathers know; that He might make thee know that man doth not live by bread only, but by every Word that proceedeth out of the mouth of the Lord doth man live.

You see, God was teaching the Israelites, He could care for them during their wilderness experience. He was teaching them no matter what environment they were in, He would provide for them supernaturally, in ways they could have never dreamed of. God rained bread down from heaven every day that was edible. He caused quail to fall from the sky which fed them for months (Numbers 11:31). He caused water to come out of a rock (Numbers 20:8). All these things were performed by God, Supernaturally!

Do we forget these things, or do we not believe God would or could perform these same miracles today? Whatever the case, God is the same yesterday, today, and forever. Everything God did for every person in the Old and New Testament, God wants to do for us today. This brings me back to the key verses for the Kingdom of God. Let us read them in a different translation. The Message Translation is so good, I am going to start from verse 24.

Matthew 6:24-33 MSG

You can't worship two gods at once. Loving one god, you'll end up hating the other. Adoration of one feeds contempt for the other. You can't worship God and Money both.

"If you decide for God, living a life of God-worship, it follows that you don't fuss about what's on the table at mealtimes or whether the clothes in your closet are in fashion. There is far more to your life than the food you put in your stomach, more to your outer appearance than the clothes you hang on your body. Look at the birds, free and unfettered, not tied down to a job description, careless in the care of God. And you count far more to Him than birds.

Has anyone by fussing in front of the mirror ever gotten taller by so much as an inch? All this time and money wasted on fashion-do you think it makes that much difference? Instead of looking at the fashions, walk out into the fields and look at the wildflowers. They never primp or shop, but have you ever seen color and design quite like it? The ten best dressed men and women in the country look shabby alongside them.

If God gives such attention to the appearance of wildflowers - most of which are never seen - don't you think He will attend to you, take pride in you, and do His best for you? What I'm trying to do here is to get you to relax, to not be so preoccupied with *getting*, so you can respond to God's *giving*. People that don't know God and the way He works fuss over these things, but you know both God and how He works.

Steep your life in God-reality, God-initiative, and God-provisions.

Don't worry about missing out. You'll find all your everyday human concerns will be met.

Let's start with verse 24. How do people end up worshipping money? This is one way I see a possibility of this happening. By not seeing God as your one and only source. Here is an example. Many times, we will believe God for a new job, a new business or even a job promotion. While we are in this believing mode, we will attend church faithfully, attend all the church events and even participate in many of the church activities. Then our situation begins to change. Our situation begins to look a lot brighter when we receive the blessings, we have been believing God for. Then we begin to look at our paychecks as if it is our source. We take the amount of money we earn and try to build our entire lives around this one set amount. We base our every need and want around that paycheck. And if it is not enough, we start thinking, "Maybe I can work some overtime or maybe I can find a second job. This will bring more money in." As we continue thinking about the amount of money we have, we are constantly trying to figure out how we are going to take care of our family on this income? And if we cannot fix it, we become discouraged. We start charging things we cannot afford, taking loans out to get a car or a house we cannot afford and getting every department store credit card we cannot afford. Why? Because we are trying to figure it out all by ourselves. While going through these motions, if we do begin to work the extra hours or find a second job or another job that is more demanding in days or hours, what happens to all the time we once had for God? For some reason, most of the time, God is the first to get put out of the equation when we feel we have gotten our needs met or when we have incurred more needs. We began to miss one Sunday of church, then two. You come home so tired and say, "I do not think I can go to Bible study tonight." The program you were volunteering for becomes too much of a burden because of the overtime you are working to pay your bills. If you have a family, they rarely see you now because you are always working. You were so excited when you got the job, it was such a tremendous blessing but now you have no peace. I am sure many of you can relate to exactly what I am saying.

Then we began to wonder, why are all these things happening? If this job was such a blessing from God, why do it feel like a burden? Then who gets the blame? God does. Can you see what happened here? Someone made their paycheck from their job their source. But the Word of God declares, you cannot serve both God and money. You will love one and hate the other. You see, when you feel like you have to run after money, you begin to resent God. You know why? Because you were not created to be provision minded (in the state of hunting down provision) and our spirits know this. This is why we become so grieved and frustrated when we are looking for other avenues to meet our needs other than God. God wants you to put your trust in Him, so He can provide you with resources besides your paycheck to meet your needs and wants. God does not want to cause you any harm and He surely do not want you to become too busy for Him. He wants to love you, commune with you, and provide for you. After all He did promise these things in His Word.

Philippians 4:19

19But my God shall supply all your need according to His riches in Glory by Christ Jesus.

The bottom line is Jesus instructs us to take no thought for our lives. He reveals to us how God takes care of the birds of the air and that we are much more valuable than them. After all, we were created in God's image and after His likeness. Why wouldn't God want the best for us? We can see Jesus' statement as being true while he lived in the earth. Do we read anywhere in the Bible, where Jesus is found running around stressed out seeking provision? The Bible never mentions anything about Jesus leaving His assignment to seek after provision while He functioned as a man in the earth.

It is God's desire to see His creation living "A life of God worship." A life of God worship is the chapter heading for Matthew 6:19-34 in the Message Translation. So, here is my question for you. Are you living a life of God worship? Are you seeking God? Are you asking God for His purpose and plan for your life? Are you asking God what is your part in the expansion of His Kingdom in the earth? If not, take some time to seek God and inquire of Him, the purpose and plan He has for your life. As believers we should be asking God these questions daily.

The verses below are key factors for **Faith-Style** living. This is so powerful! Please, read them out loud.

Matthew 6:30-32 MSG

If God gives such attention to the appearance of wildflowers - most of which are never seen - don't you think He'll attend to you, take pride in you, do His best for you?
What I'm trying to do here is to get you to relax, to not be so preoccupied with getting, so you can respond to God's giving. People who don't know God and the way He works fuss over these things, but you know both God and how He works.

Take a look at the next verse!

Matthew 6:33 MSG

Steep your life in God-reality, God-initiative, God-provisions. Don't worry about missing out. You'll find all of your everyday human concerns will be met.

When I first read these verses in the Message translation, I was amazed. How much clearer can the message get? This is Jesus talking people! God does not want you to be provision minded! He wants you to be mindful of His agenda.

I perceive this to mean when I steep my life in:
God's **reality** (God's way of doing and being right):

11 But you, O man of God, ...pursue righteousness, godliness, faith, love, patience, gentleness (1 Timothy 6:11).

God's **initiative** (His kingdom, sovereign rule and government):

18 Let them do good, that they be rich in good works, ready to give, willing to share (1 Timothy 6:18).

God's **provisions** (not looking to meet my own needs):

17 Command those who are rich in this present age not to be haughty nor to trust in uncertain riches but in the living God, who gives us richly all things to enjoy (1 Timothy 6:17).

When I do everything stated above, then all my everyday human concerns will be met! Glory to God! This is shouting time once again! The last verse from this chapter confirms what I just said.

Matthew 6:34 MSG

Give your entire attention to what God is doing right now, and don't get worked up about what may or may not happen tomorrow. God will help you deal with whatever hard things come up when the time comes.

Do you see why we as believers need to take time out of our day to commune with God? We can commune with God by spending time in His Word, our prayer time, or just by the acknowledgement of His goodness throughout the day. We need to know on a continuous basis what the Lord requires of us and give our entire attention to it!

God blessed Solomon beyond His wildest dreams! After the death of his father king David, Solomon was appointed the new king of Israel. The most interesting component to Solomon's story for me is, Solomon did not just take the position of king and run with it. He did not say, "I am the new king of Israel and I get to run this kingdom anyway I choose." No, not at all. Solomon took the time to separate himself and seek God for the wisdom he needed to govern God's people. Solomon went to a mountain to pray and to offer sacrifices to God. After Solomon concluded this time of worship and sacrifice, Solomon fell asleep. The Lord then appeared to Solomon in a dream and asked Solomon what is it that He could do for him. Solomon said to God, *"Thou hast shewed unto thy servant David my father great mercy, according as he walked before thee in truth, and in righteousness, and in uprightness of heart with thee; and thou hast kept for him this great kindness, that thou hast given him a son to sit on his throne, as it is this day. And now, O Lord my God, thou hast made thy servant king instead of David my father: and I am but a little child: I know not how to go out or come in. And thy servant is in the midst of thy people which thou hast chosen, a great people, that cannot be numbered nor counted for multitude. Give therefore thy servant an understanding heart to judge thy people, that I may discern between good and bad: for who is able to judge this thy so great a people* (1 Kings 3:6-9)?"

How awesome is that! As I mentioned before, Solomon did not just take the title of king and run with it. Solomon acknowledged he was a young man that lacked the wisdom he needed to govern God's people. Solomon desired to be a good and wise king. He desired to please both his earthly father and heavenly Father. God had to be pleased with Solomon's request. Let us take a look at God's response to Solomon.

1 Kings 3:11-13

11And God said unto him, Because thou hast asked this thing, and hast not asked for thyself long life; neither hast asked riches for thyself, nor hast asked the life of thine enemies; but hast asked for thyself understanding to discern judgement;

12Behold, I have done according to thy Words: lo, I have given thee a wise and an understanding heart; so that there was none like thee before thee, neither after thee shall any arise like unto thee.

13And I have also given thee that which thou hast not asked, both riches and honor: so that there shall not be any among the kings like unto thee all thy days.

Oh my God! Look how God's blessings overtook Solomon when Solomon chose to seek God concerning wisdom for the governing of God's people. Solomon set his heart toward God's initiative and was blessed beyond measure!

God bestowed upon Solomon blessing after blessing. God gave Solomon a wise and understanding heart, along with riches and honor. God even went as far as to tell Solomon; no other king will ever be like him. God blessed Solomon to never have to think about provision, ever. Solomon was set for life!

There are two more things I did not mention concerning God's amazing grace toward Solomon. The first is found in verse 14. God promised Solomon that if he observed His ways, statutes, and commandments as his father David did, He would lengthen the days of his life.

14And if thou wilt walk in my ways, to keep my statutes and my commandments, as thy father David did walk, then I will lengthen thy days.

The other is found in 1 Kings 5:2-4, where Solomon is found telling a Gentile king from another land how God has given him rest from his enemies on every side.

1 Kings 5:2-4

2And Solomon sent to Hiram, saying,

3Thou knowest how that David my father could not build an house unto the name of the Lord his God for the wars which were about him on every side, until the Lord put them under the soles of his feet.

4But now the Lord my God hath given me rest on every side, so that there is neither adversary nor evil account.

You see, God did not leave anything out pertaining to the well-being of Solomon's life. God gave Solomon everything he would ever need to do the job He gave Solomon to do. This included the building of God's house. And this is the same message Jesus is conveying to us in Matthew 6:33. We are to live "A life of God Worship" by seeking first the Kingdom of God and His righteousness with the promise of everything, we would ever need, being added to us. Glory to God!

Dear believer, you are not a pagan. You are the child of the most high God. You know our God is a provider, so why fall into the traps and snares of the world and its ways. Live the life God has blessed you to live from the foundation of the world!

Matthew 6:32 MSG

What I'm trying to do here is to get you to relax, to not be so preoccupied with *getting*, so you can respond to God's *giving*. People that don't know God and the way He works fuss over these things, but you know both God and how He works.

As believers we have been privileged to enjoy an adventurous and fulfilling life of walking by **Faith** and not by sight!

This is indeed **Faith-Style** living!

THERE IS JUSTICE IN FAITH-STYLE LIVING

Now take another look at this chapter's heading. People of God did you get that! There is Justice in **Faith-Style** living! You are probably saying, what are you talking about? I am talking about our Rights and Privileges as born-again believers. When God the Father sent His Son, Jesus into the earth, He came with a specific mission in mind. This mission was to Recover and Restore the Rights of God's children in the earth, by invoking their covenant rights that was stolen from mankind in the Garden of Eden. Jesus came to bring long awaited Justice to the people of God!

If you recall, Adam and his wife Eve disobeyed God and ate from the tree of the knowledge of good and evil, which then created a great injustice toward mankind. Mankind from that point forward had to wrestle with the ground to bring forth provision, which was a tremendous difference from the provision God established in the Garden of Eden. In the chapter "It's Up to You" I discussed how God had given Adam and Eve a life of privilege. God, the Master Architect, created this beautiful, serene place for His creation to live in which contained everything they could possibly need or want. Adam and Eve possessed a massive supply of everything. The word "lack" was never a thought in their mind or a word in their vocabulary! Lack did not exists in the Garden of Eden.

Genesis 1:29

29And God said, Behold, I have given you every herb bearing seed, which is upon the face of all the earth, and every tree, in which is the fruit of a tree yielding seed; to you it shall be for meat.

When God created the Garden of Eden, God intended for man to live in the earth like God lived in heaven. The Garden of Eden was an extravagant place infused with perpetual abundance. In this Garden, Adam and Eve shared a life anyone would dream about. It was exceedingly and abundantly above what any of us could imagine. It was a depiction of the divinely prosperous life God had in store for all His creation. But unfortunately, after that tragic incident took place, Adam and Eve were driven out of the Garden.

Genesis 3:24

24So he drove out the man; and he placed at the east of the Garden of Eden, Cherubims, and a flaming sword which turned every way, to keep the way of the tree of life.

Because of the act of disobedience that transpired, the abundant life Adam and Eve had become accustomed to was now gone. Let us take a look at what God said to Adam.

Genesis 3:17-19

17And unto Adam he said, Because thou hast hearkened unto the voice of thy wife, and hast eaten of the tree, of which I commanded thee, saying, Thou shalt not eat of it: cursed is the ground for thy sake; in sorrow shalt thou eat of it all the days of thy life;

18Thorns and thistles shall it bring forth to thee; and thou shalt eat the herb of the field;

¹⁹In the sweat of thy face shalt thou eat bread, till thou return unto the ground; for out of it wast thou taken: for dust thou art, and dust shalt thou return.

According to the verses above, we can see things became complex for mankind. But thank God, He already had plan B in place. God had a plan to redeem mankind from Adam's transgression. God had a plan to bring **Order** to the chaos, **Restructure** to the breaking, and **Justice** to the injustice.

One night around three o'clock in the morning I could not sleep, so I decided to get up and watch television. There was a preacher on preaching a story from the book of Jeremiah. She spoke about, God speaking to the prophet Jeremiah to buy a piece of land from his cousin, Hanameel. At the time this conversation was taking place, Jeremiah was being held in captivity by the Babylonians. For this reason, Jeremiah could not understand why God was telling him to purchase this plot of land.

Jeremiah 32:6-8

⁶And Jeremiah said, The Word of the Lord came unto me, saying,

⁷Behold, Hanameel the son of Shallum thine uncle shall come unto thee, saying, Buy thee my field that is in Anathoth: for the right of redemption is thine to buy it.

⁸So Hanameel mine uncle's son came to me in the court of the prison according to the Word of the Lord, and said unto me, Buy my field, I pray thee that is in Anathoth, which is in the country of Benjamin: for the right of

redemption is thine; buy it for thyself. Then I knew that was the Word of the Lord.

Although, I believe this was the first time I had ever heard this story preached, for some reason this story resonated with me. I was so excited about the story and I did not have a clue as to why. But as I continued to read the story multiple times, the reason for the fascination of this story became apparent to me.

Remember when I mentioned earlier God always has a Plan B. Although we as God's children may stray away from God's original intended path; God can always get us back on the right course. These mishaps, no matter how big or small, show us how greatly magnificent God truly is and only He deserves all the glory!

During the time of Jeremiah's story, things were chaotic with the children of Israel. The Israelites were backsliders, they were involved in every possible sin you can imagine. God detested this lifestyle for His children. Why? Because God only wanted the best for them like any parent would want for their child. God knew the life they were living would only bring them harm. All God wanted the children of Israel to do was to acknowledge their misconduct and return to Him and His ways. God loved the children of Israel so much that He enlisted Jeremiah as His representative. Jeremiah was a prophet of Israel who was frequently referred to as the "weeping prophet." Jeremiah was to cry out to the Israelites concerning their reckless behavior and get them to return to the perfect will of God for their lives. A life where they would continue to live the amazingly blessed life, God was providing for them. Let us take a look at what God said to Jeremiah.

Jeremiah 3:12-14

¹²**Go and proclaim these words toward the north, and say, Return, thou backsliding Israel, saith the Lord; and I will not cause mine anger to fall upon you: for I am merciful, saith the Lord, and I will not keep anger forever.**

¹³**Only acknowledge thine iniquity, that thou hast transgressed against the Lord thy God, and hast scattered thy ways to the strangers under every green tree, and ye have not obeyed my voice, saith the Lord.**

¹⁴**Turn, O backsliding children, saith the Lord; for I am married unto you: and I will take you one of a city, and two of a family, and I will bring you to Zion.**

Can you see in this verse God's loving plea to Israel?

Jeremiah 4:1

¹**If thou wilt return, O Israel, saith the Lord, return unto me: and if thou wilt put away thine abominations out of my sight, then shalt though not remove.**

God did not want to bring wrath upon His children, therefore He sent Jeremiah to warn them. Through the words of Jeremiah God would display His mercy and forgiveness for their transgressions. But Israel refused the goodness of God, they had more **Faith** in their idols. The Israelites wanted to do what they wanted to do, and

Revelation Point:

Here is another glorious picture of salvation right here. All we have to do is to repent and through the blood of Jesus the right of redemption is ours: We then have access to the wealth of promises in the Bible.

they wanted to live the way they wanted to live. Adversely to the ways of God. The Israelites felt they could live a better life by worshipping idols. In this way they would not be obligated to live God's way. They believed their idols would provide for them and protect them.

Although the Israelites were thoroughly warned of their transgressions, they continued to be stubborn. Because of their defiance they would be taken into captivity, given over to the Babylonians.

Jeremiah 5:19

19And it shall come to pass, when ye shall say, Wherefore doeth the Lord our God all these things unto us? Then shalt thou answer them, Like as ye have forsaken me, and served strange gods in your land, so shall ye serve strangers in a land that is not yours.

Do you see how the children of Israel went off the intended path God had for them, due to their own treachery? Do you know God in His mercy, did not abandon them? God had a plan of redemption in place. Glory to God! What amazing grace! They did eventually go into captivity, but God never intended to leave them in the hands of a pagan nation forever. Thank You, Lord!

For this reason, God spoke to Jeremiah to purchase his cousin's field. God had plans to bring the Israelites back to the land He had given to them. God had already initiated His plan B in the midst of the children of Israel's rebellion. God already had a plan to redeem and restore them.

Jeremiah 32:15

15For thus saith the Lord of hosts, the God of Israel; Houses and fields and vineyards shall be possessed again in this land.

The most significant part of this story for me is Jeremiah's "Right of Redemption." Jeremiah was most likely the next of kin to Hanameel. So, because Hanameel was still living, the property could not yet pass to Jeremiah through inheritance. By law Hanameel had to offer the property to Jeremiah first, before offering to sell it to anyone else.

We can also see this "Right of Redemption" principle exercised in the story of Ruth. When Boaz wanted to marry Ruth, he could not just run off and marry her. There was a protocol that needed to be followed. Boaz was the kinsman of Naomi's husband Elimelech. Because Elimelech and his two sons were deceased, neither one of his sons were able to receive their inheritance from their father. So, this put their next of kin in the position to redeem the dead men's property and to marry his widow. Because Ruth was a young woman and the daughter-in-law of Elimelech and Naomi, the kinsman would have to marry Ruth. But there was a kinsman who was next in line before Boaz. So, Boaz approached his kin to ask him if he would be exercising his right as kinsman redeemer. If this relative chose to redeem the property of his deceased kin, he would then have to marry Ruth as well. This kinsman wanted the property, but he did not want to marry Ruth. So, thankfully the kinsman turned down the property which moved Boaz into position to redeem the property and to marry Ruth.

So, we can see in both stories Jeremiah and Boaz exercised their "Right of Redemption" privileges as kinsman redeemers.

Child of God, I said all of this to tell you, "There is Justice in **Faith-Style** living!"

One day I was meditating on what it actually means to "possess the land" as a born-again Christian. So, I decided to look up the word possessor. I wanted to know in detail what it meant to be a possessor of the promises of God. As I was reading the definition I had found on a site on the internet, I saw the words "Right of Redemption." I immediately thought about the story of Jeremiah buying the field. As I referred back to the story of Jeremiah, it became clear what the "Right of Redemption" privilege meant to me as a born-again Christian. All I could see from that moment was a little demon sitting on my land (the promises of God) and that he was occupying my land illegally.

Jesus came to destroy the works of the devil and to recover what was stolen from the hands of God's people. The only way the enemy can steal from us today is if we allow him to do so. We were given covenant rights the day we became born again. The day we made Jesus our Lord and Savior was the day we were adopted into the family of God. When we became a part of God's family, we gained the "Right of Redemption" to His promises. Jesus is our kinsman redeemer. Through His *Death, Burial and Resurrection* we gained an inheritance. And that inheritance gave us our rights and privileges as Kingdom citizens.

John 1:12

12But as many as received Him, to them gave He power (the right or privilege) to become the sons of God, even to them that believeth on His name.

I know we just left the Old Testament but let us revisit it again for a moment. In the book of Exodus, when God was getting ready to set the children of Israel free from their enslavement by the Egyptians, the Passover of the Lord was initiated.

Exodus 6:6

⁶Wherefore say unto the children of Israel, I am the Lord, and I will bring you out from under the burdens of the Egyptians, and I will rid you out of their bondage, and I will redeem you with a stretched out arm, and with great judgments.

Exodus 12:11-13

¹¹...It is the Lord's Passover.

¹²For I will pass through the land of Egypt this night, and will smite all the firstborn in the land of Egypt, both man and beast; and against all the gods of Egypt I will execute judgment: I am the Lord.

¹³And the blood shall be to you for a token upon the houses where ye are: and when I see the blood, I will pass over you, and the plague shall not be upon you to destroy you, when I smite the land of Egypt.

In the Old Testament God used the Passover to redeem the children of Israel from the grips of slavery. The children of Israel were descendants of Abraham and because of the covenant God made with Abraham, God promised to bring Abraham's descendants into the promised land. It was a land that flowed with milk and honey. A land that was as delightful and provision filled as the Garden of Eden. It was a land where they would never hunger or thirst again. All their needs would be met. There would be nothing lacking, missing or broken in their lives.

In the Old Testament the "promised land" consisted of physical land that was occupied by physical enemies. The book of Numbers illustrates the children of Israel getting ready to enter the land God promised them. Prior to them entering the land, Moses dispatched twelve men from the tribes of Israel into the land to see:

1. If it was a good and fertile land.

2. To size up their enemies (to see if they were able to beat them).

To answer question number one, this was the report the twelve spies brought back to Moses and Aaron.

Numbers 13:25-27

[25]And they returned from searching of the land after forty days.

[26]And they went and came to Moses, and Aaron, and to all the congregation of the children of Israel, unto the wilderness of Paran, to Kadesh; and brought back word unto them, and unto all the congregation, and shewed them the fruit of the land.

[27]And they told him, and said, We came unto the land whither thou sentest us, and surely it floweth with milk and honey; and this is the fruit of it.

As we can see here the twelve spies agreed with the condition of the land. It was not so with the answer to the second question. Let us take a look at what ten of the spies had to say.

Numbers 13:32

³²**And they brought up an evil report of the land which they had searched unto the children of Israel, saying, The land, through which we have gone to search it, is a land that eateth up the inhabitants thereof; and all the people that we saw in it are men of a great stature.**

Joshua and Caleb shared a different viewpoint than their counterparts. Let us take a look at what they had to say.

Numbers 13:30

³⁰**And Caleb stilled the people before Moses, and said, Let us go up at once, and possess it; for we are well able to overcome it.**

Did you hear the confidence and enthusiasm Caleb had? Caleb seen this beautiful and fertile land and was ready to go in and clear those enemies out of the land.

Do you know the Israelites that left Egypt as adults did not enter this land? They forfeited this fruitful land because they could not wrap their minds around their true identity as the head and not the tail, above only and not beneath and the lender and not the borrower. They could not see themselves as owners of anything. They saw themselves as mere little slaves that did what they were told to do, went where they were told to go, and ate what they were told to eat. They could not see past their lives in Egypt, even after all the miracles they witnessed. Even after all the wars they had already fought and won. They were victorious in possessing the cities and houses of other nations. But sadly, they still could not see themselves as God saw them.

God even made it easy for them to enter the land by promising to deliver all their enemies into their hands. God had done it before with the Amorite kings, Sihon and Og. So why did the Israelites refuse to believe He could do the same with these inhabitants. It makes you wonder did the children of Israel really want to be set free from slavery. If they did, why did they continue to keep Egypt in their hearts? They should have left Egypt, and everything associated with Egypt behind the day they departed and walked out free? Let us take a look at the Israelites response to Moses.

Numbers 14:1-4

¹And all the congregation lifted up their voice, and cried; and the people wept that night.

²And all the children of Israel murmured against Moses and against Aaron: and the whole congregation said unto them, Would God that we had died in the land of Egypt! Or would God we had died in this wilderness!

³And wherefore hath the Lord brought us unto this land, to fall by the sword, that our wives and our children should be a prey? were it not better for us to return into Egypt?

⁴And they said one to another, Let us make a captain, and let us return into Egypt.

Does this sadden you? I know it saddens me. The children of Israel were then referred to as being, *"Children in whom is no Faith* (Deuteronomy 32: 20)."

The bottom line is, God very well expected the Israelites to take possession of this land, no matter who was in it. It was a land described in Deuteronomy 11:12, as a land that God Himself cared for. A land where they would forget the days of their hardships in Egypt.

Deuteronomy 11:10-12

¹⁰For the land, whither thou goest in to possess it, is not as the land of Egypt, from whence ye came out, where thou sowedst thy seed, and wateredst it with thy foot, as a garden of herbs:

¹¹But the land, wither ye go to possess it, is a land of hills and valleys, and drinketh the water of the rain of heaven:

¹²A land which the Lord thy God careth for: the eyes of the Lord thy God are always upon it, from the beginning of the year even unto the end of the year.

Do you see how Israel's concern for the enemy kept them out of the fruitful land God prepared for them? They did not have to pay for this land, it was given to them free and clear. The land was debt-free! It did not matter how big and numerous the enemies in the land were, all they had to do was to believe God and enter the land God had given to them. It was their inheritance, through the covenant God made with their deceased ancestor Abraham.

Once we discover this truth, we can no longer tolerate the lies of the enemy. This is exactly why the enemy works incessantly to keep us out of the truth of God's Word. Let me share with you some of the tactics of Satan. He wants to keep our lives plagued with problems and distractions. He wants to get into our minds and thoughts to make us think the promises of God are not for us. Remember, he comes to steal, to kill and to destroy and he will use any method he can to keep us out of the will of God. He will use shame, condemnation, fear, illness, financial issues, confusion and strife. He will use anything to keep you tense, distracted and overwhelmed.

As believers we must invest our time wisely and make it our life's mission to learn about God's supreme benefits package. As previously mentioned, God sent His Son to bring **Justice** to every injustice we have suffered. Not only did God promise the believer Salvation, He has also promised us total deliverance from the enemy.

In the book of Ephesians, we can find our inheritance. Let us take a look at our supreme benefits package we have received through our "Right of Redemption" privileges.

Ephesians 1:7

⁷In whom we have redemption through His blood, the forgiveness of sins, according to the riches of His grace;

As born-again believers this is our promised land. Our promised land consists of salvation and deliverance, according to the riches of God's grace. All these benefits became our inheritance when our Kinsman Redeemer died for us on the Cross. Do you know how hard it had to be for God to see His Son suffer such a horrific death for us? This was not the lamb that was sacrificed during the Passover in the Old Testament which was a shadow of what Jesus was going to do on the Cross. This was the real deal! This was the Son of God suffering in a way we could never imagine. Therefore, God fully expects us to use our **Faith** to possess every promise He has made available to us. Come on believer, His Son died for us to have them.

I looked up the words; salvation, riches and grace in the Hebrew and Greek dictionaries to get a broader understanding of the words. Salvation in the Hebrew dictionary means a present or gift. If this were the only benefit available to us it would certainly be enough because our sins have been paid for in full. It is not because of anything we have done but for everything Jesus has done for us. But thank God He did not stop there. Let us see what riches entail. Riches means, wealth, possessions, money, abundance, richness, and valuable bestowment. Are you excited, child of God? Well, we are not done yet. Grace means, unmerited and undeserved favor. It is God's grace that allows us to possess all these things.

I will say this, and I am sure you would agree; this is an excellent benefits package! As believers we must read and study God's Word to receive His promises. Not knowing your rights and privileges as a believer can cost you dearly. It is like having the most excellent benefits package available to you on your job and not being aware of it. What a waste that will be!

Dear believer, our Heavenly Father has set us up for life! He has given to us richly all things to enjoy (1 Timothy 6:17). Seize every opportunity that has been made available to you through the Blood of Christ, which gives us (ALL BELIEVERS) the "Right of Redemption" privilege to inherit every promise in the Word of God!

There is Justice in **Faith-Style** living!

TAKE THE LIMITS OFF!!!

I regret to start this chapter on what may be perceived as on the downside, but there is something that weighs heavy on my heart. One of the things that saddens me greatly is when a Christian does not take God's Word literally. What I mean by this is many Christians go to church every Sunday, watch Christian television regularly, attend weekly Bible studies, go to prayer meetings, read their Bibles, have Christian decoration all over their homes and clothes, but have very little to no **Faith** in God. You may be saying, what would make you say a thing like that? I say it because it is true. There are so many Christians that do not take the Word of God in the Holy Bible literally. They just read the words on the pages the same as they would read any other book. Let me give you some examples.

The other day my husband and I were out, and we came across an elderly lady with a brace on her arm. It appeared as if she needed the brace to help keep her balance. As she walked into the store, we noticed she had on a hat which read GOD in huge letters. She looked like she needed some help, so my husband went over to assist her. My husband asked her what church did she attend? She replied, she did not currently attend church but watched certain preachers on television in her home. So, I continued to listen as my husband spoke to her. She began to name some of the preachers she listened to and every name she called out; we were very familiar with. The next question my husband asked is, "Do you believe God for your healing?" The lady immediately began shaking her head in a no pattern, she then said, "No. I am alright," and began to murmur other words. By the words she murmured, it seemed as if she was saying, "That is taking it too far!" This lady accepted her condition and did not want to hear anything about being healed. As I previously mentioned, she called out the names of some very well-known televangelists. Every one of the preachers she named has taught many Bible based messages on healing and having the **Faith** for healing. When she, in my opinion minimized God's ability to heal her, I just dropped my head down. I dropped my head down because I thought, here is another person walking around displaying I am a child of God but when she opened her mouth her words were a total contradiction to what she was displaying. Now I do not know why this lady responded in the way she did and I really did not want to impute judgment because what I was seeing at this point was just a moment out of the many years of her life. I do not know what she may have been through that brought her to this point but it was sad to hear someone express such little interest in one of the greatest benefits God has made available through His Son.

Another incident I experienced was through an encounter with my husband and a fellow church member. During the conversation between the two, she began to express the burden of paying the mortgage on her home. My husband then conveyed to her, "Maybe God will present a way for you to own your home debt-free." She replied, "I don't know how He would do that." My husband insisted the reply she gave was full of doubt and unbelief, as if she believed there was absolutely no way this could happen. I said to my husband, "Did she really say this to you?" Now, I was in disbelief and again I just dropped my head down. This lady is also an elderly woman. She goes to church every week and is very active in the church.

She is very nice and compassionate and has a beautiful personality. What I could not understand is, why a woman that has been in church for so many years could not believe or in any way perceive that the God she has faithfully served for years, could bless her to pay her mortgage off.

As we look at both stories, we can see one rejected the healing power of God and the other rejected the financial abilities of God. Both ladies viewed their situations as impossible situations. But the true question is, where was the **Faith** of these two women? Why did they think their situations were too much for God to handle? Did they not know, God specializes in conditions that we deem impossible and makes them possible? This reminds me of the words my grandmother spoke, when she said, "People do not have **Faith** like they used to."

Suppose you wanted to do something nice for your child and your child did not believe you could do it. How would this make you feel that your child did not take you seriously? Would you be a little heartbroken? I know I would. As a mother, I would want my children to know how much I love them and to believe me when I have something for them. I want them to be able to count on me and to rest assure it would be waiting for them when they needed it. God feels the same way about us. I believe many of us try to limit God to only what our minds can handle. This is a tremendous mistake. If God were on the same level as us, how would this make Him God? Sure, He created us in His image and after His likeness. And He has given us dominion in the earth, but God is the Supreme Being with Supreme Rule. Therefore, how can the Maker be on the same level as His creation? He cannot. God is the Sovereign Head over us.

God loves us dearly, and this is proven all throughout the Bible. As I have discussed in many chapters already, we know God created the earth for a dwelling place for mankind. As we read the book of Genesis, we can see God filled the earth with everything man would need to live. God was so concerned about Adam having everything he needed, He even thought about a companion for Adam. God created many animals looking for a suitable companion for His son. When God saw that none of the animals would do, He thought about a helpmeet for Adam. God put Adam to sleep and then took a rib from his side and formed Eve. You see, God took pleasure in meeting Adam's every need. God then blessed Adam and his wife and gave them access to everything in the Garden of Eden, all except for the tree of the knowledge of good and evil.

There is a story in the Bible that led me to write this chapter for the book. When I first read the story, it was something about it that would not allow me to let it go. Although it is not exactly what we would call a story but rather a mention of an occurrence that took place between a father and daughter. This is what I believe to be a revelation of the relationship between God and His children.

It is the story of Caleb and his daughter Achsah. In these times most inheritances usually went to the sons of the family. If there were no sons and there were only daughters, the inheritance would then pass to the daughters' husbands. In the book of Joshua, Achsah tells her husband to ask her father, Caleb for a piece of land. Once Caleb gives his son-in-law the land, Achsah then feels impressed to ask Caleb for a blessing.

Joshua 15:18-19

[18]And it came to pass, as she moved him to ask of her father a field: and she lighted off of her ass; and Caleb said unto her, What wouldest thou?

[19]Who answered, Give me a blessing; for thou hast given me a south land; give me also springs of water. And he gave her the upper springs, and the nether springs.

Achsah asked her husband to ask Caleb for a field and he granted his request. But what made Achsah hop off her mule and ask her dad for the springs of water? Why didn't she have her husband to ask for the springs also? The Bible declares, she lighted off her mule. This causes me to think she approached her dad boldly and was not looking to take no for an answer. Like I previously mentioned, there was something about this story that has caused me to *Selah* several times as I have read it. This story illustrates to me, that although it was not the custom for women to ask their fathers for inheritances, Achsah decided she was going to approach her dad to ask for the blessing she wanted. She approached her dad boldly not looking to be denied. She knew the springs on the land belonged to Caleb and as his daughter, she wanted him to bless her with them. Caleb did not refuse Achsah, he blessed her with both springs: the upper and the lower springs.

Hebrews 4:16

[16]Let us therefore come boldly to the throne of grace, that we may obtain mercy, and find grace to help in the time of need.

God wants to bless His children whether we think we deserve it or not. God desires for His children to come to Him confidently and make our request known to Him.

John 15:16

16that whatsoever ye shall ask of the Father in my name, He may give it you."

Another story that gives me revelation of how God takes pleasure in blessing his children is found in the story of Jacob and Esau. Jacob tricked his brother Esau a couple of times. The first time, Jacob tricked Esau into giving him his birthright. Jacob then tricked Esau out of receiving their father's blessing. While their father Isaac was on his deathbed, their mother Rebekah plotted with Jacob to fool Isaac into believing Jacob was Esau, so that Isaac could pronounce the blessing he intended for Esau onto Jacob. When Esau discovered that Isaac had already pronounced the blessing over Jacob, Esau became livid and begged Isaac to bless him as well.

Genesis 27:34

34And when Esau heard the words of his father, he cried with a great and exceeding bitter cry, and said unto his father, Bless me, even me also, O my father.

Once Esau learned only one son could receive the blessing and it was irrevocable, Esau vowed to kill Jacob. When Rebekah was informed of Esau's intentions, she quickly made up an excuse for Isaac to send Jacob away. They sent Jacob away to go and live with Rebekah's brother Laban. After Jacob spent many years with Laban, Jacob desired to return to his homeland. But Jacob was fearful to return because of Esau's earlier threats on his life. Jacob then thought to bring his brother some gifts so he could soften Esau's heart towards him.

Genesis 32:13-15

13And he lodged there that same night; and took of that which came to his hand a present for Esau his brother;

14Two hundred she goats, and twenty he goats, two hundred ewes, and twenty rams,

15Thirty milch camels with their colts, forty kine, and ten bulls, twenty she asses, and ten foals.

When Jacob returned home, Esau traveled to meet his brother on the road. And all that Jacob imagined happening when the two crossed paths again, did not happen. Esau ran to his brother and embraced him. They were so excited to see each other that they wept on each other's necks. Once they were done greeting each other, Esau asked Jacob why he had so much stuff. Jacob conveyed to his brother, he brought him gifts. Esau replied to Jacob that it was not necessary to give him anything, he had plenty already. But Jacob refused to take no for an answer. Jacob wanted to bless his brother, so much so, he insisted Esau take everything he brought for him.

Genesis 33:8-11

8And what meanest thou, by all this drove which I met? And he said, these are to find grace in the sight of my lord.

9And Esau said, I have enough brother; keep that thou hast unto thyself.

10And Jacob said, Nay, I pray thee, if now I have found grace in thy sight, then receive my present at my hand: for

therefore I have seen thy face, as though I had seen the face of God, and thou wast pleased with me.

¹¹Take, I pray thee, my blessing that is brought to thee; because God hath dealt graciously with me, and because I have enough, And he urged him and he took it.

This is what I perceive to be the Father's message to us. He longs to bless His children. It does not matter what we have or what we do not have, He is the God of more than enough. He takes pleasure in seeing that His children are well provided for.

These are remarkable examples of **Faith-Style** living! This is what God was trying to demonstrate in the children of Israel's lives. The children of Israel departed Egypt with the wealth of Egypt. They left Egypt with silver and gold, expensive jewelry, and expensive clothes. But despite everything they were carrying, God had a land He already prepared for them. Remember the promised land was not given to them contingent upon their possessions. God prepared this place for them before the foundation of the world! It was only by **Faith** they were going to possess this land and not by the material possessions they were carrying. The wealth of Egypt was a bonus! Glory to God!

God wants to do the miraculous in our lives. He wants us blessed in every area of our lives. God desires for unbelievers to look at our lives and ask what can they do to have a prosperous life like ours? This is what God wanted to do in the lives of the children of Israel. God wanted the Israelites to have such a full and prosperous life that the pagan nations would become jealous and turn to Him to make Him their God. This is what God wants to do in the lives of every believer today. He wants your unsaved loved ones, friends and anybody you encounter to know you serve the one and only true God. He wants them to know it is your God who has given you the blessed life you now possess. God said in His Word, He has given to us all things to richly enjoy!

1 Timothy 6:17

17Charge them that are rich in this world, that they be not high minded, nor trust in uncertain riches, but in the living God, who giveth us richly all things to enjoy;

This is why I said in the beginning of the chapter it saddens me when God's people are not representing the goodness of God to the fullest. Instead of walking around looking like weak and defeated Christians, let us be a painted portrait of what Christianity should look like.

This brings me to another story I read in the Bible which spoke to me in volumes as I read it. All these stories are snippets of what we would actually consider a story, but they are power packed in illustration and meaning.

This story comes from the book of Ezra in the Old Testament. Child of God listen carefully. You are going to hear **Faith, Faith**, and more **Faith**! This is the **Faith** every Christian should come to possess at some point in their walk with God.

In the book bearing his name, we learn that Ezra was a skilled priest and scribe who was recognized as a faithful man of God. The king of Persia recognized that the hand of God was upon Ezra and because of this, the king granted Ezra his every request. Out of all the scribes and priest that may have been around in those days, the king of Persia issued a decree for

Ezra to orchestrate and govern the return of the Jews to their homeland. The decree also stated for the Jews to carry valuable possessions to place in the house of God. Because they would be carrying valuable items on their journey, Ezra knew there would be thieves looking to steal from them. Ezra would be traveling with a company of Israelites that were just coming out of captivity. Their families would be traveling with them as well, so they were not looking to get into fights with the thieves. The Israelites were just looking to return to their homeland safely and to deliver the items they would be carrying to the house of God. So, what did Ezra do to ensure the safety of the people that would be traveling with him? Let us read the verses below.

Ezra 8:21-23

²¹Then I proclaimed a fast there, at the river of Ahava, that we might afflict ourselves before our God, to seek of Him a right way for us, and our little ones, and for all our substance.

²²For I was ashamed to require of the king a band of soldiers and horsemen to help us against the enemy in the way: because we had spoken unto the king, saying, The hand of our God is upon all them for good that seek Him; but His power and His wrath is against all them that forsake Him.

²³So we fasted and besought our God for this: and he was entreated of us.

When I read this passage for the first time, I was absolutely blown away. I want to repeat this part right here so hopefully you are receiving from this exactly, what I am receiving.

Verse 22

[22]For I was ashamed to require of the king a band of soldiers and horsemen to help us against the enemy in the way: because we had spoken unto the king, saying, The hand of our God is upon all them for good that seek Him..."

We as Christians go to church every Sunday to hear and speak the greatest accolades toward our God as we continuously shout out the many names for God such as:

- El Shaddai (Lord God Almighty)
- El Elyon (The Most High God)
- Adonai (Lord, Master)
- Yahweh (Lord, Jehovah)
- Jehovah Nissi (The Lord My Banner)
- Jehovah-Raah (The Lord My Shepherd)
- Jehovah Rapha (The Lord That Heals)
- Jehovah Shammah (The Lord Is There)
- Jehovah Tsidkenu (The Lord Our Righteousness)
- El Olam (The Everlasting God)
- Elohim (God)
- Jehovah Jireh (The Lord Will Provide)
- Jehovah Shalom (The Lord Is Peace)
- Jehovah Sabaoth (The Lord of Hosts)

And we quote scriptures and sing songs about the Bigness and **Faith**fulness of our God but cannot muster up enough **Faith** for God to meet our simplest need. Why is that?

Ezra most likely bragged to the king of Persia about the goodness of God, as he should have. It is just like what we do today. So, if you are bragging on God and telling whoever that will listen how great and powerful God is but turn around and ask for the person's help, would you somewhat feel ashamed or embarrassed?

Isn't this what happen in our lives today? We go to church on Sundays, we hear the preacher preaching on how big God is. We talk about all His supernatural abilities. We say He can do anything. We clap and yell with excitement for the message being preached. We quote scripture after scripture and sing song after song praising God but as soon as we come across a problem, we are running to everybody for help but God. Why is this? Is it because we do not believe God can do it, will do it, or will take too long to do it?

Isn't this the truth? I am not just getting on you; I have been guilty of this behavior myself.

Let us take another look at what Ezra said. *"I was ashamed to require of the king a band of soldiers and horsemen, because of what we have spoken to the king* (Ezra 8:22)." So, what does this say about us as believers when we say our God owns the cattle on a thousand hills or I have never seen the righteous forsaken or his seed begging bread, but we are broke. Or what about when we quote scriptures like, we are the lender and not the borrower and we owe no man anything but to love them, but we owe everybody that would lend us money or extend us credit. What about when we declare promises such as, by Jesus stripes we are healed, but we embrace the sickness as if it belonged to us. Instead of us going to God, fasting and praying and laying out before Him for a solution to our problems. We are running to the banks, to family, friends, doctors or anybody we feel can help us quickly, without running to God and entreating of Him first.

Are you ashamed child of God?

Instead of running to the king to seek protection, Ezra and his travel companions fasted and besought God for His wisdom in the matter and God heard them! Let us take a look at what transpired next in verse 31.

³¹Then we departed from the river of Ahava on the twelfth day of the first month, to go unto Jerusalem: and the hand of our God was upon us, and he delivered us from the hand of the enemy, and of such as lay in wait by the way.

Ezra and company had a dilemma that could have cost them their lives, but Ezra refused to ask the king for help. Ezra examined the situation and determined the best thing they could do was to fast and call out to the God he magnified. God heard their prayers and intervened in their situation. God protected them as they traveled to Jerusalem and they arrived at their destination safely.

Ezra put his trust and confidence wholly in the God he bragged upon. Ezra used his **Faith** to get the results he wanted. It was according to Ezra's **Faith** in God, the request he made for safe travel was met.

Matthew 9:29

²⁹According to your Faith be it unto you."

I believe God took pleasure in the fact Ezra sought Him out for help instead of going to the king of Persia. Ezra put his **Faith** and confidence in the true King of kings and Lord of lords. I am sure this was not an easy decision for Ezra, his life and the life of the people with him was on the line. Although he could not see the help God would provide, he believed by **Faith** God would provide the help they needed to arrive to their destination safely. And God came through. Glory to God!

Hebrews 11:6

⁶But without Faith it is impossible to please Him: for he that cometh to God must believe that He is, and that He is a rewarder of them that diligently seek Him.

Faith is so important to Christian living. What Ezra did is a tremendous example of **Faith-Style** living. Ezra did not look to the left or to the right, his eyes looked straight to God, the Author and Finisher of his **Faith**!

You see, I am at the point in my life where I will not look to anyone but God to help me with my problems. I think highly of my God, I speak highly of my God and I expect what I need from my God. When I put my **Faith** in the right place, He will send me or lead me to the help I need. Thank you, Jesus!

You see, I cannot continue to read the Bible and not take God's Word literally. What would be the point? It all boils down to whether I believe God or not. I choose to believe Him, and it is my prayer that you will too!

Turn off the characteristics and the meaning of a lifestyle that holds no foundation to truth. Instead, grab hold of the true life of the believer and this is a life dedicated to **Faith-Style** living. A life that is rooted and grounded in the Word of God and attributed to having **Faith** in God.

Mark 11:22-24

²²And Jesus answering saith unto them, Have Faith in God.

[23]For verily I say unto you, That whosoever shall say unto this mountain, Be thou removed, and be thou cast into the sea; and shall not doubt in his heart, but shall believe that those things which he saith shall come to pass; he shall have whatsoever he saith.

[24]Therefore I say unto you, What things soever ye desire, when you pray, believe that ye receive them, and ye shall have them.

Like Ezra, believe you receive what you are seeking, child of God. Believing you receive is a significant key to **Faith-Style** living!

FAITH AND HONOR IN GOD

There are many components to **Faith-Style** living but this one I believe has caused a major rift amongst believers. There is so much talk amongst believers when it comes to the issue of tithing in the church. I have even noticed myself in recent social gatherings how the issue of tithing comes up and how immediately it seems people get so intense about the subject. I then began to wonder and inquire of God, is this something that you are bringing to my attention purposely? The reason why I asked God this question is because I was so surprised by the conversations and wondered of all the things to talk about in these particular group settings, why the subject of tithing?

Child of God let me tell you this. I am not a pastor and I do not have a church. I am just a person who loves God and His Word. As a Christian and as a child of God, it is my prayer that I am living a life that is pleasing to my Father by honoring Him and His Word. As an earthly parent I love my children whether they are obedient or not. But when my children listen to me and obey me without gripe and hesitation it makes me feel really good inside. If you are a parent, teacher, someone who works with children or someone one in a leadership position, I am sure you can appreciate what I am saying. What could be more pleasing to a parent than an obedient child?

In the book of Exodus, Numbers, and Deuteronomy, we can see the many trials of the children of Israel. And we can also see how their continuous acts of disobedience grieved God. Even after the Israelites witnessed the many miracles God performed on their behalves, they chose to murmur and complain over the simple things compared to the miracles they had already witnessed. What was the contributing factor to the Israelites disobedience? The contributing factor was indeed fear. The Israelites called out to God so many times over the years because of their condition. Generations of Israelites were enslaved by Egyptian taskmasters for over four hundred years, so there were possibly four or more generations who succumbed to this life of poverty and bondage. So, when it was time for God to deliver them, we could see by their actions how their lives as slaves affected them. Every time the Israelites encountered a situation, they would become fearful and their hearts would turn back to Egypt. The Israelites were so fearful that it totally clouded their judgment. It got to the point they wished they were still in Egypt working as slaves. They had become so accustomed to the mistreatment they were receiving in Egypt which made it hard for them to appreciate the new life God was preparing for them. From the time their deliverance process began the Israelites complained about everything, so much so, that when it was time for them to possess their promised land, they had the nerve to say they would rather return to Egypt.

Numbers 14:3-4

3And wherefore hath the Lord brought us unto this land, to fall by the sword, that our wives and our children should be a prey? were it not better for us to return into Egypt.

4And they said one to another, Let us make a captain, and let us return into Egypt.

The constant rebellious acts of the children of Israel grieved God. All God wanted to do was to give them a better life. He wanted to take them from a life of scarcity and bring them into a land with plenty of everything they would need. And God still desires this life for believers today.

In my opinion, I truly believe that the superfluous incessant arguing over giving tithes grieves God. I say this because look at what God conveys about tithes and offerings to the Israelites in the Old Testament. *Malachi 3:7-8, "Even from the days of your fathers ye are gone away from mine ordinances, and have not kept them. Return unto me, and I will return unto you, saith the Lord of hosts. But ye said, Wherein shall we return? Will a man rob God? Yet ye have robbed me. But ye say, Wherein have we robbed thee? In tithes and offerings.*

After reading all of chapter three in the book of Malachi over and over again, I wondered out of all the things God could have said the Israelites robbed Him of, why would God choose tithes and offerings? God could have said love, worship or their time, but He said they robbed Him of tithes and offerings. This tells me tithes and offerings are important to God.

Now, this is where I believe the rift over tithes and offerings in the church comes in. Some argue that tithing is an Old Testament requirement that is no longer required today. Some say tithing was a requirement through the Law and is no longer a requirement for the New Testament church. The first thing I would like to point out concerning tithing in the Old Testament is that the Law did not exist until the book of Exodus. God issued the conditions of the Law to Moses after the Israelites departed Egypt and were living in the wilderness. Second, from what I have read in the Bible; I have not read anywhere tithing is no longer required. But honestly, I believe many are seeing the practice of giving tithes and offerings in the wrong way.

A couple of years ago I was reading a book by Kenneth Copeland. As I was reading his book, it spoke about the event that transpired in the Garden of Eden where God announces to Adam, he could eat from any tree, except for the tree of the knowledge of good and evil. How the author singled this one tree out, I looked over to my husband and said this sounds like the tithe. As I kept reading further the author confirmed what I had just said. The tree of the knowledge of good and evil was the 10% that was holy and devoted to God and the other trees were the 90% God gave to them to do with as they pleased. God had given Copeland the revelation of the tithe dating all the way back to the Garden of Eden. Glory to God!

This was absolutely amazing to me because I had read this story many times, but it was not until I read Copeland's book, that I saw this tree as the tithe. Picture this. There was this huge garden filled with a variety of trees, plants and animals. God says to Adam, I am paraphrasing, "Adam, you see all this beauty and abundance that is surrounding you? Okay, you can have everything you see. The trees, the plants, the animals, the rivers of water, the gold and all the precious stones. You can have it all! Except for this one tree I choose to reserve for Myself."

This sounds like the deal of the century to me! Look how generous God was. Everything belonged to God anyway, but He gave it to Adam and Eve to manage and enjoy. You know what I believe to be God's message to Adam and to believers today?

Obedience, Reverence and Honor

I believe these were the three main things God wanted to teach His children. Not only these three things, which we can learn a lot from, but God was also establishing some boundaries in the Garden of Eden. Even today we cannot just go around doing whatever we want and taking things that do not belong to us. Therefore, we have the laws of the land in place because boundaries must be established. So, just like we have physical laws, there are spiritual laws we need to observe as well. This is what God was teaching Adam and Eve in the Garden of Eden.

As a parent I know when I tell my children not to do something, it is for their own good. When Adam and Eve decided to eat from the tree of the knowledge of good and evil, they made the worst mistake they could ever make.

Genesis 2:17

17But of the tree of the knowledge of good and evil, thou shalt not eat of it: for in the day that thou eatest thereof thou shalt surely die.

Because I have discussed this many times already, we know that after Adam and Eve ate from the tree of the knowledge of good and evil, they were immediately driven out of the Garden. They also died a spiritual death in which they were no longer connected spiritually to their Creator. God warned Adam what would happen if he ate from this tree but when Satan showed up with his deception and lies, Adam ignored God's warning and put his **Faith** in Satan's lies.

Did Adam and Eve show God any reverence when they ate from the tree, God specifically instructed them not to eat from?

159

No, they did not. So, they had to suffer the consequences of their choices. They did not suffer because God wanted them to suffer, they suffered because of their own choices. Adam and Eve was given the choice to follow God's instruction and they chose not to.

You know what is so remarkable about the God we serve? It is the fact that He has blessed us with free will. God has given us the privilege to make our own choices. God has issued commands about many things, but He leaves us with the decision to make the right choices (Just like He did with Adam and Eve in the Garden). God has also given us a choice when it comes to salvation through His son Jesus Christ. God does not force us to accept Jesus as our Lord and Savior, but we will not come to Him unless we do. But still, the choice is ours to make.

Let us take a look at another example of tithing from the book of Genesis. This example was also conducted before the Law was issued in the book of Exodus. This example derives from the story of Abraham. When we read the story of Abraham in the book of Genesis, we can clearly see how Abraham **Reverenced, Honored and Obeyed** God in so many ways during his walk with God. It was because of Abraham's reverence for God, he was called a friend of God (James 2:23). As I have mentioned many times already, God spoke to Abraham to leave his country after living there for many years to journey to a land God promised to give to Abraham and his descendants. Abraham trusted the voice of God and in an act of **Obedience,** he left the country he was very familiar with.

Another phenomenal thing I noticed about Abraham while reading his story is how he **Reverenced** God during his journey. In Genesis 12:7 it says, *"The Lord appeared unto*

Abraham, and said, unto thy seed will I give this land: and there builded he an altar unto the Lord, who appeared unto him." So, you see after God confirmed to Abraham what God had previously spoken to him, Abraham built an altar to God, reverencing God as an act of worship. Abraham did the same in verse 8 and again in Genesis 13:18.

Now, let us take a look at how Abraham **Honored** God in the giving of tithes. Abraham had just returned from a battle against five wicked kings that had captured the people of Sodom including his nephew Lot and Lot's family. Abraham and his people, who were fewer in number, supernaturally defeated all five kings and their armies. As the king of Sodom was on his way to meet with Abraham in the king's dale, before the meeting could take place, Melchizedek the king of Salem, the priest of the most high God appeared to Abraham.

Genesis 14:17-18

¹⁷And the king of Sodom went out to meet him after his return from the slaughter of Chedorlaomer, and of the kings that were with him, at the valley of Shaveh, which is the king's dale.

¹⁸And Melchizedek king of Salem brought forth bread and wine: and he was the priest of the most high God.

Let us take a look at what Melchizedek said to Abraham.

Genesis 14:19-20

¹⁹And he blessed him, and said, Blessed be Abram of the most high God, possessor of heaven and earth.

²⁰And blessed be the most high God, which hath delivered thine enemies into thy hand. And he gave him tithes of all.

Abraham knew this man was sent from God! Abraham knew it was God who had blessed him to win the battle against his enemies, making it possible to deliver Lot and his family out of the hands of those wicked kings. God gave Abraham the victory and Abraham honored God by presenting the tithes to the high priest God sent to bless him.

We can see here; Abraham had a choice to either honor God or not to honor God. Now, does it say anywhere in those verses of scripture, God commanded or asked Abraham to give tithes to Melchizedek? No, it does not. Abraham made a choice to honor God because he knew if it were not for God, there was no way he would have prevailed over his enemies. Just as we should honor God by acknowledging He is the one who has blessed us with everything we have, including our lives. Contrary to what many may think, we only exist as human beings because of God. Abraham knew this. Therefore, when God gave Abraham the victory, to acknowledge God's hand in his victory, Abraham made the choice to tithe to Melchizedek. Abraham placed the tithes in the hand of Melchizedek as if he were placing it in the hands of God himself!

As previously mentioned, God is an awesome God and I truly believe some believers are looking at giving tithes and offerings in the wrong way. Have you read the verses in Malachi concerning tithes and offerings? Have you seen the promises that are connected to giving tithes and offerings? Let us read them together.

Malachi 3:10-12

10Bring ye all the tithes in to the storehouse, that there may be meat in mine house, and prove me now herewith, saith the Lord of hosts, If I will not open you the windows

of heaven, and pour you out a blessing, that there shall not be room enough to receive it.

¹¹And I will rebuke the devourer for your sakes, and he shall not destroy the fruits of your ground; neither shall your vine cast her fruit before the time in the field, saith the Lord of hosts.

¹²And all the nations shall call you blessed: for ye shall be a delightsome land, saith the Lord of host.

I don't know about you, but I believe this is something to shout about! Do you see how wonderful God is? Look at the results we can have when we choose to be faithful in giving our tithes and offerings. Why would anyone refuse to tithe? God said He would open you the window of heaven and pour you out a blessing you do not have room enough to receive! How amazing is that! God also said, He will rebuke anything that will try to destroy our blessings. And He promises not to allow the vine to cast its fruit before the time. This means, God is going to make sure our blessings come to maturity. They are going to be full and ripe before they come into our hands! Hallelujah! Glory to God! I am getting so excited about this.

This reminds me of the beautiful Garden God prepared for Adam and Eve. It also reminds me of the rich and fertile land God established for the children of Israel. Sadly, Adam, Eve and the Israelites were talked out of their blessings. The serpent tricked Adam and Eve out of their blessing by causing them to forfeit the Garden of Eden. He talked the Israelites out of their promised land by causing them to fear their enemies. Child of God please do not let this happen to you. The enemy is subtle, and he wants you to forfeit the blessings of God for your life. For this reason, he wants to get into your minds and make you question tithing so he can keep stealing from you. Come on believer! Come out of your natural thinking and open up your spiritual eyes and ears!

Matthew 11:15

15He that has ears to hear, let him hear.

What I have already covered regarding the blessing of tithing is amazing enough, but God also said another benefit of tithing is, *"All nations shall call you blessed: for you shall be a delightsome land* (Malachi 3:12)." Meaning, people are going to look at you and know you are blessed, you and your household! This is amazing! I write these scriptures on my tithing envelope mostly every time I give tithes and offerings. I do this because I am saying to God, "Lord I believe you and your promises. And I know everything you said in your Word concerning tithes and offerings is for me." Glory to God!

I believe, tithing for the believer today is saying: **God I honor you and I trust you with my life. I trust you with every aspect of my life including my finances. By presenting my tithes and offering to you, I am showing you how much I need you by inviting you into all my circumstances. By giving my tithes and offerings, I am sowing in Faith believing for your supernatural intervention in every area of my life! Glory to God!**

Do not let the enemy steal from you another day. Give joyfully of your tithes and offerings. Honor God, and then recognize and celebrate His supernatural intervention in every area of your life.

I would like to share a testimony regarding the first time God began talking to me about tithing. Prior to this, I was already giving offerings and sowing into the Kingdom, but then God began to deal with me in the area of tithing alone. God did not just come out and say, "Sherrelle, I will like for you to start paying your tithes." No, He did not. Although He has spoken to me about sowing seed into specific ministries before, this time it was different. From what I can recall, I kept hearing sermons about tithing. I never thought about it before until now, but it seemed like I was hearing it differently this time. It was like the word tithing was much notable than any of the other words. Do you understand what I am saying? It was like I was hearing the word tithe from a different dimension. I guess you can say I was hearing it with my spiritual ear. The word tithe was coming to me when I wasn't watching or hearing any sermons on tithing. Tithing would just come into my thoughts. So, I said to God, "It seems as if You want me to do this. When I get paid from my job and go to church on Sunday, I will write my first tithe check."

I do not recall if I was nervous about it at the time, I just wanted to obey God. I read the scriptures pertaining to tithing and even though I did not fully understand what it all entailed. What I did know is what I read and did understand sounded good to me. I went to church that next Sunday and I was late. They already collected the tithes and offerings. I then thought to myself, "It's okay; I will just give it next week." I left the church and while I was driving, I looked over to my passenger seat and noticed my Bible was missing. I pulled over to search the car and could not find it. I headed back to the church, hoping and praying it was still open. When I reached the church, I was thankful the doors were unlocked. When I walked inside, there was a lady in the foyer speaking to someone. She looked over to me and with a big smile she asked, "Can I help you?" I replied, "I believe I left my Bible in the sanctuary." She said it was okay to go in and look for it. When I entered the sanctuary, I walked over to the seat I was sitting in during the service, my Bible was there! I was so relieved. Since I was back at the church, I decided to write out my tithe check. So, I did. When I finished, I walked back over to the foyer and asked the lady, where should I leave it. She said to drop it in the bucket under the seat and the ushers will get it. As I was leaving, she asked did I find my Bible? I answered, "Yes, I did. I guess it was a good thing it was left behind because it gave me an opportunity to return and give my tithes." She smiled and nodded in agreement. And we exchanged our goodbyes.

Driving home, I thought about the events that transpired and I was feeling really good. I was so happy I left my Bible at the church. It gave me the opportunity to go against my fear and leave the tithe check just like I told God I would. When I arrived home, I decided to listen to some music as I was getting ready to prepare dinner for my family. When I left the kitchen, as I was approaching the hallway this feeling came over me. A feeling I have never felt before. All I know is, it was not of this world. It felt so good, it was absolutely phenomenal! I did not want it to go away. It felt as if I was enraptured in the Glory of God. I have never forgot it and I have been longing to experience it again ever since that day.

It may have been a day or two later, I received a call from my supervisor asking me to come into the office. She did not give me a reason why she wanted to see me, so I just assumed the worst. If memory serves me right, the meeting was scheduled two or three days from when I received the phone call. My mind kept performing different scenarios as to what this meeting could be about. Many times, I was tempted to call her to inquire the reason for the meeting. The pressure was on! I just wanted for that day to come so I could know what this meeting was all about.

The day of the meeting finally arrived, and I was so relieved. I went to the office and sat down in the lobby to wait for her to call me into her office. My heart was beating so fast. As I was waiting, I was thinking, "Did she make me wait all this time just to fire me?" As I continued pondering the reason for the meeting, she finally came out and invited me into her office. As I sat down, she began to talk and explain the reason she wanted to see me. She informed me that my immediate supervisor was leaving her position as shelter manager. I was totally shocked. I had no clue of this. She continued and said she would like to offer me the position. She said the days and hours would be better and it was a salary position. She also said it paid hundreds of dollars more a month than I was currently making which meant thousands of dollars more annually. I was so excited! I sat in the chair marveling over what was happening. I could not believe this conversation was taking place. Tears began to roll down my face while I sat there thinking about the goodness of God. I said, "Yes. Of course, I will take the position!" As we continued to talk, I just sat there in amazement, marveling at the goodness of God!

It was no doubt in my mind it was God who had given me the promotion. First of all, I did not have much of a work history because I was a full-time parent for most of my children's lives. Second, I had just started working for the company less than a year before this had taken place. Third, when I was first hired, I read in the company's policy and procedures booklet, the company did not promote from within. For any open positions, they would hire from the outside. Fourth, there was a couple of ladies that worked there for many years before me. Out of fairness, they approached one of them for the position and she declined. So, I knew this was definitely God! He had given me favor, with this supervisor! Thank You Jesus!

As I was pondering these events, I remembered the incident that happened at the church. When God was speaking to me about tithing, He was looking to bless me! When I left my Bible at the church, this was not an accident, God had a blessing scheduled for me already and I had no clue! This blessing was contingent upon my **Faith** in God. When I was at church during the service, I could have asked one of the ushers if they could take my tithe check, but I admit I became a little fearful and decided to put it off until the next week. So, the question was, was I going to look at the money and miss out on the blessing or was I going to trust God and be obedient to His Word? What is amazing about this experience is, I could have left church that day with my Bible in hand and that would have been it. Listen, my Bible being left behind was no accident, God had a blessing for me, and He wanted to be sure I received it! Glory to God! Look at God's hand in this. My Father promised me according to Malachi 3:10, He would open me the windows of heaven and pour me out a blessing. This blessing was contingent upon me being obedient to His Word by bringing His tithes into His storehouse. Glory to God! There is no other explanation for this, and I refuse to see it any other way. God is so good!

So, we have talked about tithing on the obedience part. Let us take a look at tithing on all three fronts: **Obedience, Reverence and Honor.** Let us revisit a portion of the Malachi Scripture again.

Malachi 3:10

¹⁰Bring ye all the tithes into the storehouse, that there may be meat in mine house.

According to the scripture verse above, we can see the Lord desires for His storehouse to be filled and He gives us the responsibility of doing so. We also know everything already belongs to the Lord, Psalm 24:1 confirms this.

¹The earth is the Lord's and the fulness thereof, the world, and they that dwell therein.

Now, do God really need us to fill His storehouses? Probably not. But this is the method He has chosen and put into place. You see, God has given every one of us an assignment, which is primarily to be a vessel He can use. Why does God need His storehouses filled? First, so that believers can have a place to gather and receive His Word administered by His appointed earthly shepherd. Second, God wants His storehouses filled so the church would be amply supplied to help the poor. If the institution of the church is not abundantly supplied, how can the church help anyone? Therefore, God blesses us financially, so we can bring the first fruits of our increase and fill His storehouses.

Proverbs 3:9-10

⁹Honour the lord with thy substance, and with the firstfruits of all thine increase:

¹⁰So shall thy barns be filled with plenty, and thy presses shall burst out with new wine.

You may be saying, "This is not my responsibility." Yes, it is. Jesus administered the command to take the Gospel into the world. And we know we cannot do this for free. The churches we sit in on Sundays and any other day, has a cost of operation. As the children of God, we should be honored to contribute into the causes of God. Let us take a look at the verse below.

Psalm 35:27

27Let them shout for joy, and be glad, that favour my righteous cause: yea, let them say continually, Let the Lord be magnified, which hath pleasure in the prosperity of His servant.

We should be excited for the opportunity to dedicate our time, treasure and talent into the work of God. The scripture verse above illustrates to us when we give into the causes of God, we cannot go wrong!

When it comes to giving, we need to take the attitude of King David. David realized the importance of honoring God. David knew without a shadow of doubt God's hand was upon him. For this reason, David spent all his days glorifying His Heavenly Father and proof of this is available to us in the book of Psalms, in which king David is the author of many of them.

I want the understanding of these verses to be so clear to you, that I have cited them from the Message Translation. I want you to see the dedication king David expresses as he glorifies God and the importance of giving into the causes of God.

1 Chronicles 29:10-14 MSG

David blessed God in full view of the entire congregation: Blessed are you, God of Israel, our Father from of old and forever.

To you, O God, belong the greatness and the might, the glory, the victory, the majesty, the splendor; Yes! Everything in heaven, everything on earth; the kingdom all yours!
You've raised yourself high over all.
Riches and glory come from you, you're ruler over all; You hold strength and power in the palm of your hand to build up and strenghthen all.
And we are, O God, our God, giving thanks to you, praising your splendid Name.
But me – who am I, and who are these my people, that we should presume to be giving something to you? Everything comes from you; all we're doing is giving back what we've been given from your generous hand.

This is the attitude of a true worshipper! I am getting so excited while writing this! David is expressing incredible worship right here. In these words, David is demonstrating **Honor, Reverence and Obedience** to the will of God. David gladly gave of his material substance. David happily acknowledged that everything he owned came from God. David enthusiastically dedicated an immense amount of his wealth for the building of God's house, his son Solomon was given charge to build.

Let us look at another example of the people of God bringing their tithes and offerings into the house of God. This illustration comes from 2 Chronicles 31:4-10. King Hezekiah gives a command to the people of Jerusalem to take part in providing for the priest.

2 Chronicles 31: 4-10

⁴Moreover he commanded the people that dwelt in Jerusalem to give the portion of the priests and the Levites, that they might be encouraged in the law of the LORD.

⁵And as soon as the commandment came abroad, the children of Israel brought in abundance the firstfruits of corn, wine, and oil, and honey, and of all the increase of the field; and the tithe of all things brought they in abundantly.

⁶And concerning the children of Israel and Judah, that dwelt in the cities of Judah, they also brought in the tithe of oxen and sheep, and the tithe of holy things which were consecrated unto the LORD their God, and laid them by heaps.

⁷In the third month they began to lay the foundation of the heaps, and finished them in the seventh month.

⁸And when Hezekiah and the princes came and saw the heaps, they blessed the LORD, and his people Israel.

⁹Then Hezekiah questioned with the priests and the Levites concerning the heaps.

¹⁰And Azariah the chief priest of the house of Zadok answered him, and said, Since the people began to bring the offerings into the house of the LORD, we have had enough to eat, and have left plenty: for the LORD hath blessed his people; and that which is left is this great store.

This is amazing! Do you see what transpired here? Because the people responded so generously, there was a great abundance brought in. The people brought in so much, they had to build additional storehouses to store all the goods. The people brought heaps upon heaps of everything the priests would need. It was such an abundance, even king Hezekiah questioned the number of offerings, even though it was him who issued the command. It was amazing! It is amazing to me and I was not even there to witness it, but my spirit rejoices wholeheartedly at the obedience of the people. The people did this in honor of the Lord. They may have received the command from king Hezekiah, but they did it in honor of the Lord. Can you imagine how happy the Lord must have been seeing His people honor Him in such a way?

Let us look at another example that was given in the book of Exodus. While the Israelites were in the wilderness, God instructed them to build a tabernacle, where they could spend time with Him and store the ark of the covenant. Moses then requested for the Israelites to bring offerings from their material possessions to assist with the building of the tabernacle. Moses said to the Israelites, *"Take ye from among you an offering unto the Lord: whosoever is of a willing heart, let him bring it, an offering of the Lord; gold, and silver, and brass* (Exodus 35:5)."

Exodus 35:29

29The children of Israel brought a willing offering unto the Lord, every man and woman, whose heart made them willing to bring for all manner of work, which the Lord had commanded to be by the hand of Moses.

Let us read the result. It was nothing short of amazing!

Exodus 36:5-7

[5]**And they spake unto Moses, saying, The people bring much more than enough for the service of the work, which the Lord commanded to make.**

[6]**And Moses gave commandment, and they caused it to be proclaimed throughout the camp, saying, Let neither man nor woman make any more work for the offering of the sanctuary. So the people were restrained from bringing.**

[7]**For the stuff they had was sufficient for all the work to make it, and too much.**

You see, Moses called upon the people with a willing heart and those people showed up. They gave such an abundance, Moses had to order them to stop. It was too much! Can you believe it? This sounds like excellent teamwork to me! But wait, we are not done yet. There is another great example of giving provided in the book of Nehemiah.

There was deception going on in the house of God. A priest named Eliashib and his accomplice Tobiah invaded the house of God and they were stealing. Their detestable acts caused the temple's storehouse to be empty and the priests to go without their daily provisions.

Nehemiah, who was a significant leader at that time, was away when all this treachery was taking place. When he returned home, he noticed Eliashib moved Tobiah into the temple. He also noticed all the other things that were missing as well. Nehemiah was furious. Let us take a look at what transpired when Nehemiah confronted Eliashib and Tobiah concerning their wicked schemes.

Nehemiah 13: 7-13

⁷And I came to Jerusalem, and understood of the evil that Eliashib did for Tobiah, in preparing him a chamber in the courts of the house of God.

⁸And it grieved me sore: therefore I cast forth all the household stuff of Tobiah out of the chamber.

⁹Then I commanded, and they cleansed the chambers: and tither brought I again the vessels of the house of God. With the meat offering and the frankincense.

¹⁰And I perceived that the portions of the Levites had not been given them: for the Levites and the singers, that did the work, were fled everyone to his field.

¹¹Then contended I with the rulers, and said, why is the house of God forsaken? And I gathered them together, and set them in their place.

¹²Then brought all Judah the tithe of the corn and the new wine and the oil unto the treasuries.

¹³And I made treasurers over the treasuries, Shelemiah the priest, and Zadok the scribe, and of the Levites, Pedaiah: and next to them was Hanan the son of Zaccur, the son of Mattaniah: for they were counted faithful, and their office was to distribute unto their brethren.

In reading the verses above, we can see the active role Nehemiah took in bringing restoration to the house of God. He wanted to make sure the house of God was operating in the way it was designed to operate. Nehemiah called on the people in the land to bring their tithes and offerings into the storehouse. After the temple's treasuries were filled, Nehemiah then assigned faithful men to oversee the distribution of its goods. This is the responsibility of every church and ministry.

Some of you may be thinking, "Here we go again with these Old Testament stories." It makes no difference; it is all Bible. But unless I offend thee, let us take a look at this powerful New Testament story. This story is phenomenal! I was amazed when I first read it. This is the perfect example to base funding the Gospel on.

Jesus performed many miracles in the earth. He turned water into wine, He directed Peter to a part of the sea where he was able to catch an abundance of fish and He sent Peter to the sea to retrieve money from a fish's mouth. So, we can clearly see Jesus never had to carry a wallet with cash or credit cards. He could manifest abundance wherever He went! Therefore, I do not understand how so many people are under the impression that Jesus was poor. How could He be poor when He knew where every resource of the earth was. He could manifest abundance even in the desert place. Jesus did not become poor until He went to the Cross. And the only reason He became poor was so that through his poverty, we would be made rich (2 Corinthians 8:9). Jesus encounter with poverty was not for long because everything was restored to him when He defeated hell, sin and death and was elevated to sit at the right hand of the Father.

The verses below illustrate what happens when we come to love the Lord so much, we want to be a part of what He is doing.

Luke 8:1-3

¹And it came to pass afterward, that he went throughout every city and village, preaching and shewing the glad

tidings of the kingdom of God: and the twelve were with him,

²And certain women, which had been healed of evil spirits and infirmities, Mary called Magdalene, out of whom went seven devils,

³And Joanna the wife of Chuza Herod's steward, and Susanna, and many others, which ministered unto him of their substance.

You see, these women had a powerful encounter with Jesus. They were set free from all their infirmities! And after they witnessed such an amazing transformation in their own lives, they wanted to see this change in the lives of others. These women desired to help Jesus in any way they could. And this meant helping to fund His missions in the earth. They desired to stay close to Him and be a blessing to Him. These women became such an integral part of Jesus' life and ministry that their names are recorded in the Bible documenting the good they did.

You are probably thinking, "It did not mention anything about tithing." It did not have to. Do you really want to miss a move of God by getting hung up on a word and not honoring Him? These women gave of their substance because they were honoring Jesus and everything He was doing in the earth. They wanted to make sure He had what He needed to get the job done, so much so, they became willing participants to help fund His work. It was their custom to give tithes and offerings. As I have discussed previously, it was their custom to provide for the priests and the temples. So, they were already accustomed to giving into the work of the Lord, but this time it was different. These women were able to give to the Messiah personally!

When we give our tithes and offerings, we are doing the same as those women. It allows us to become willing participants in the Lord's work. Can you imagine if these women debated over helping the Messiah because they were hung up on tithing? They would have missed out big-time! But thank God these women were smart; they were not about to let that happen. These women knew helping Jesus to fund His mission, would be the greatest thing they could have ever done in their lifetime. Giving into the Lord's work should really be a matter of the heart. When you give into the Lord's work, you should take great pleasure in doing so. It is recorded in 2 Corinthians 9:7, *"Every man according as he purposeth in his heart, so let him give; not grudgingly, or of necessity: for God loveth a cheerful giver."*

You know why I believe God expects us to be cheerful givers? Because it shows us that we too have the heart of our Father. God loves to give to His children, and He wants us to experience all the joy giving brings.

From what I have read in the Bible, I have not read anywhere God does not require the giving of tithes and offerings. When Jesus was in the earth, He never said to stop tithing. On the contrary, Jesus encouraged tithing. But He put the matter of tithing in its right perspective. There are a couple of stories where Jesus addresses tithing. Let us take a look at the first story.

The Pharisees noticed Jesus did not wash His hands before eating dinner which was a custom of the Law. When they noticed this, they immediately began to criticize Him. When Jesus noticed their reaction, Jesus pretty much said to them (paraphrasing), "How dare you worry about the outside of the body, when your insides are in need of much work." Let us take a look at what Jesus said to the Pharisees.

Luke 11:42

⁴²But woe unto you, Pharisees! For ye tithe mint and rue and all manner of herbs, and pass over judgment and the love of God: these ought ye to have done, and not to leave the other undone.

Let us take a look at the book of Matthew's account.

Matthew 23:23

²³Woe unto you, scribes and Pharisees, hypocrites! For ye pay tithe of mint and anise and cummin, and have omitted weightier matters of the law, judgement, mercy, and faith: these ought ye have done, and not to leave the other undone.

Let us read it in the Amplified Translation.

²³Woe to you, [self-righteous] scribes and Pharisees, hypocrites! For you give a tenth (tithe) of your mint and dill and cumin [focusing on minor matters], and have neglected the weightier [more important moral and spiritual] provisions of the Law: justice and mercy and faithfulness; but these are the [primary] things you ought to have done without neglecting the others.

So, we can see Jesus never communicated to the Pharisees not to tithe. Jesus was putting tithing into its true perspective.

Jesus was saying to the Pharisees, do not sit here and make a religious act out of tithing thinking you are doing something grand when you sit around passing judgment on others and do not have the love of God in your heart. Jesus was basically telling them to get their priorities straight! What good is tithing if your heart is not right! Jesus was saying, yes, tithe! But instead of doing it as a ritual, making it mechanical, do it because you want to **Honor** God. Now, let us take a look at the second story.

In this story, the same religious group as before, is found trying to trap Jesus with His own words. The Pharisees approached Jesus about paying taxes to the Roman king, Caesar, who ruled over Jerusalem in those days. Let us take a look at what transpired.

Mark 12:14

14And when they were come, they say unto him, Master, we know that thou art true, and carest for no man: for thou regardest not the person of men, but teachest the way of God in truth: Is it lawful to give tribute to Caesar, or not?

Jesus was already aware of the schemes of the Pharisees. He already knew what they were up to before they could even propose the question. You see, what the Pharisees did not realize was, when you are real about who you are, you do not have to search for answers to please man. The response you give is going to be genuine no matter what. When Jesus did respond to their question, He presented them with a wisdom filled answer, delivered as always in eloquence of speech. But before Jesus answered, He asked them to bring Him a coin. Jesus then asked them whose face and name did they see on the coin. The Pharisees responded, Caesar. Let us read Jesus response.

Mark 12:17

¹⁷And Jesus answering said unto them, Render to Caesar the things that are Caesar's, and to God the things that are God's. And they marveled at him.

I believe there were two important lessons Jesus was demonstrating in His answer to the Pharisees. First, Jesus was communicating to them and us, to honor the laws of the land by paying our taxes. Second, Jesus was also communicating to them and us, to honor God by giving our tithes and offerings. I believe Jesus was talking about tithes, even though He did not mention it by name. In a nutshell, Jesus was saying (paraphrasing), "Give God what belongs to Him and Caesar what belongs to him. Honor both your spiritual and earthly obligations." God is such a great Dad; He gives us the opportunity to do what is right. He gives us the choice to tithe. The government does not give you a choice on paying taxes, they automatically deduct it from your paycheck before it even gets into your hands!

Let us take a look at God's promises concerning giving in the scripture verses below.

Malachi 3:10-12

¹⁰Bring ye all the tithes into the storehouse, that there may be meat in mine house, and prove me now herewith, saith the LORD of hosts, if I will not open you the windows of heaven, and pour you out a blessing, that there shall not be room enough to receive it.

[11]And I will rebuke the devourer for your sakes, and he shall not destroy the fruits of your ground; neither shall your vine cast her fruit before the time in the field, saith the LORD of hosts.

[12]And all nations shall call you blessed: for ye shall be a delightsome land, saith the LORD of hosts.

Matthew 6:33

[33]But seek ye first the kingdom of God, and his righteousness; and all these things shall be added unto you.

Luke 6:38

[38]Give, and it shall be given unto you; good measure, pressed down, and shaken together, and running over, shall men give into your bosom. For with the same measure that ye mete withal it shall be measured to you again.

2 Corinthians 9:6-11

[6]But this I say, He which soweth sparingly shall reap also sparingly; and he which soweth bountifully shall reap also bountifully.

[7]Every man according as he purposeth in his heart, so let him give; not grudgingly, or of necessity: for God loveth a cheerful giver.

[8]And God is able to make all grace abound toward you; that ye, always having all sufficiency in all things, may abound to every good work:

9(As it is written, He hath dispersed abroad; he hath given to the poor: his righteousness remaineth for ever.

10Now he that ministereth seed to the sower both minister bread for your food, and multiply your seed sown, and increase the fruits of your righteousness;)

11Being enriched in everything to all bountifulness, which causeth through us thanksgiving to God.

Every one of these scriptures have amazing blessings attached to them. Did God have to promise anything in these verses? Of course, He didn't, but He did because He is an awesome God! In these promises God is showing us He is not trying take from us, He wants to bless us. Having a giving heart is a blessing. It keeps us from becoming stingy and selfish. Let us make an effort to trust our Heavenly Father, He knows what He is doing.

Acts 20:35

35It is more blessed to give than to receive.

We are all members of the Body of Christ and every one of us has a functioning part in this ensemble. We need to work together to get the will of God done in the earth. My dear brothers and sisters do not begrudge giving. Do not miss out on the chance of a lifetime! God has blessed us with the amazing opportunity, to be an active participator in the Body of Christ!

John 4:23

23But the hour cometh, and now is, when the true worshippers shall worship the Father in spirit and in truth: for the Father seeketh such to worship Him.

Have the heart of a true worshipper! Being a giver is an essential element to **Faith-Style** living!

FAITH TO BE LED; FAITH TO BE SENT

There are so many amazing stories in the Bible which illustrates the use of **Faith** which made it really hard to pinpoint the ones to use for this book. Can you imagine if every **Faith** encounter was recorded in the Bible? We probably could not read them all in one lifetime. Jesus' **Faith** encounters alone were pretty massive! The book of John reveals, if all the miracles Jesus performed during His time in the earth were documented, the world itself could not contain them.

John 21:25

25And there are also many other things which Jesus did, in which, if they should be written every one, I suppose that even the world itself could not contain the books that should be written, Amen.

As previously mentioned, the Bible declares, "The Just shall live by **Faith**!" There is just no other way for the believer to live. The Bible also declares, without **Faith** it is impossible to please God!

Hebrews 11:6

6But without Faith it is impossible to please Him: for he that cometh to God must believe that He is, and that He is a rewarder of them that diligently seek Him.

That one verse says a whole lot but what about this passage of scripture.

Hebrews 10:38

38Now the just shall live by Faith: but if any man draw back, my soul shall have no pleasure in him.

Both scriptures clearly suggest how important the use of our **Faith** is to God. I considered myself to be finished with the chapters of this book but during a study on this subject, I knew I had to include this chapter.

Many times, God is trying to send or lead us into places as His representatives but because of our obligations we are sometimes reluctant to obey the voice of the Lord. As I was conducting further study and meditating on this, this is what I perceive the Lord was saying to me: **Many Christians are dying off today because they are not entering into My rest due to spiritual blindness (unbelief and hardened hearts).**

I can see this as being true and I am sure you can too. We can also see proof of this in the lives of many throughout the Bible. Like for instance Adam and Eve, the children of Israel and the ones who refused to accept Jesus as the Messiah.

It also reminds me of a story in the Bible, when Jesus was speaking to the people of His hometown, Nazareth. While Jesus and the people were in the synagogue, Jesus stood up and quoted scripture from the book of Isaiah and the people were excited about the words He spoke. But then later, they began to question who Jesus was by saying, *"Is not this Joseph's son* (Luke 4:22)?" Let us read Jesus' response to them.

Luke 4:24-27

[24]And he said, Verily I say unto you, No prophet is accepted in his own country.

[25]But I tell you of a truth, many widows were in Israel in the days of Elijah, when the heaven was shut up three years and six months, when great famine was throughout all the land;

[26]But unto none of them was Elijah sent, save unto Sarepta a city of Sidon, unto a woman that was a widow.

[27]And many lepers were in Israel in the time of Elisha the prophet; and none of them was cleansed, saving Naaman the Syrian.

So, what was Jesus saying here? Jesus was pretty much telling the people of His hometown (paraphrasing), "If you want to worry about who I am related to and disregard my words and authority, you will miss out on your miracle!"

You see in those days; the prophets were sent to the people who were believing God for a miracle. The ones who would receive and adhere to the Word of the Lord. God will use the lives of people who are not tied to religion and tradition to perform some of His greatest miracles through. In the verses above, Jesus was speaking about two non-Israelites who received great miracles performed in their lives. The widow of Sidon who was sustained during a drought because her meal and oil multiplied supernaturally. And Naaman the Syrian who was miraculously cured from leprosy, which was an incurable disease. Jesus was also communicating to them, how they, His own people, the Israelites, would not receive Him because of their own spiritual blindness and hardened hearts. These people refused to believe He was the Messiah they had been waiting for. They disregarded the massive amounts of healings He performed for countless people, setting them free from the bondage they suffered for many years. But they refused to believe. And because of their unbelief, they were stuck trying to serve a Law they were constantly breaking the rules of everyday. As Jesus was speaking, telling them all of this, the people in Nazareth became so angry. Let us read what transpired next.

Luke 4:28-29

²⁸And all they in the synagogue, when they heard these things, were filled with wrath,

²⁹And rose up, and thrust him out of the city, and led him unto the brow of the hill whereon their city was built, that they might cast Him down headlong.

We can see the same defiance of the people demonstrated in the Old Testament. We have discussed the children of Israel many times already but let us take another look at their story.

After God delivered the children of Israel out of captivity, God would then lead them into the promised land. They had to travel through the wilderness to get to their destination. Deuteronomy 1:2 reveals, their journey to the promised land was only supposed to be an eleven-day journey. God had everything planned for them to get to their destination, including their route to it. All the Israelites had to do was to trust God and adhere to His Word. To ensure their safety throughout their journey, God directed them on a path where they would not encounter any immediate wars and regret leaving Egypt.

Exodus 13:17-18

[17]And it came to pass, when Pharoah had let the people go, that God led them not through the way of the land of the Philistines, although that was near; for God said, Lest peradventure the people repent when they see war, and they return to Egypt.

[18]But God led the people about, and through the way of the wilderness of the Red Sea and the children of Israel went up harnessed out of the land of Egypt.

Unfortunately, their presumed eleven-day journey turned into a forty-year stay in the wilderness. During their time in the wilderness, they murmured and complained about everything. Every situation they encountered they became fearful. They complained about what I would call the little things compared to the great miracles God had already performed on their behalves.

Deuteronomy 8:2-3

[2]And thou shalt remember all the way which the Lord thy God led thee these forty years in the wilderness, to humble thee, and to prove thee, to know what was in thine heart, whether thou wouldest keep his commandments, or no.

[3]And He humbled thee, and suffered thee to hunger, and fed thee with manna, which thou knewest not, neither did thy fathers know; that he might make thee know that man doth not live by bread only, but by every Word that proceedeth out the mouth of the Lord doth man live.

God allowed the Israelites to go on a journey through the wilderness for a reason. God wanted to reveal what was in their hearts. And because of their constant murmuring and complaining, God saw exactly what was in their hearts.

You see, there was a lesson for the children of Israel to learn on their journey. God was not trying to harm them or starve them. This is not what this verse is implying. God was simply trying to grow them up. Think about it. For generations they were enslaved for over four hundred years. They were only allowed to do what the Egyptians told them to do. Can you imagine the affect this treatment had on their minds and self-esteem? Can you imagine how unworthy they must have felt because of all the mistreatment they suffered? As previously mentioned in another chapter, God was trying to get them off the Egyptian's program and put them onto His program. He was delivering them from a life of fear and bringing them into a life of **Faith.** God was changing the trajectory of their lives! He was bringing them into their inheritance, a place where they were no longer slaves but heirs of the promise, God gave to the forefathers of their nation.

You see, the children of Israel did not even depart Egypt looking like slaves, they walked out looking like the blessed people of God they were! They departed Egypt as royalty! And God had a beautiful place waiting for them. Let us take a look at the description of the promised land given in the book of Deuteronomy.

Deuteronomy 11:10-12

¹⁰For the land, whither thou goest in to possess it, is not as the land of Egypt, from whence ye came out, where thou sowedst thy seed, and wateredst it with thy foot, as a garden of herbs:

11But the land, whither ye go to possess it, is a land of hills and valleys, and drinketh of the water of the rain of heaven:

12A land which the Lord thy God careth for: the eyes of the Lord thy God are always upon it, from the beginning of the year even unto the end of the year.

Isn't this amazing! This reminds me of the beautiful provision-filled Garden God created for Adam and Eve. All God wanted the children of Israel to do was to stay in **Faith**. He wanted their total trust and confidence in Him. God wanted the children of Israel to believe He was going to bring them into the land He promised them. This was their lesson in the wilderness, they needed to learn how to trust God and His Word.

The Israelites entered the wilderness with the wealth they received from Egypt and had no place to spend it. The Israelites would not be using their newfound wealth to purchase the land, it was a land that was going to require their **Faith** to enter. It was their God given inheritance! It was through God's solemn oath to Abraham they were going possess this land. God reminds the Israelites of His covenant with Abraham in this next verse.

Deuteronomy 8:18

18But thou shalt remember the Lord thy God: for it is He that giveth thee the power to get wealth, that He may establish his covenant which He sware unto thy fathers, as it is this day.

And God was letting the Israelites know in this next verse, they would in no way to take credit for anything He had done for them.

Deuteronomy 8:17

17And thou say in thy heart, my power and the might of mine hand hath gotten me this wealth.

So, we can see God wanted the children of Israel to have total trust and confidence in Him. God wanted them to know He would take care of them no matter what obstacles they faced on their journey. It did not matter what dilemma they found themselves in, God had a solution for them all! God fed them, clothed them, kept them in perfect health and protected them from every danger. These were the things God wanted embedded on the inside of them.

Deuteronomy 8:15-16

15Who led thee through that great and terrible wilderness, wherein were fiery serpents, and scorpions, and drought, where there was no water; who brought the forth water out of the rock of flint;

16Who fed thee in the wilderness with manna, which thy fathers knew not, that he might humble thee, and he might prove thee, to do thee good at thy latter end;

While I was studying the Bible, I noticed how Deuteronomy chapter 8 and Luke chapter 10 are almost synonymous in their teachings. I say this because we can see in both chapters the fruitful results we can have when we step out on the Word of God.

In Deuteronomy 8:3, God conveys to the Israelites, ***"Man doth not live by bread alone but by every Word that proceedeth out the mouth of the Lord doth man live."*** As previously mentioned, God wanted the children of Israel to trust Him to get them through every situation they encountered. He wanted them to know He was with them every step of the way.

In Luke chapter 10, Jesus teaches the same lessons to His disciples, God was teaching the Israelites in the Old Testament. When Jesus was preparing to send Seventy preachers away to different regions to preach the Kingdom of God, Jesus gave them specific instructions to follow for when they arrived in these cities. Let us take a look at what Jesus said to the Seventy preachers.

Luke 10:3-4, 8

³Go your ways: behold, I send you forth as lambs among wolves.

⁴Carry neither purse, nor, scrip, nor shoes: and salute no man by the way.

⁸And into whatsoever city ye enter, and they receive you, eat such things as are set before you:

I am sure we can all agree this sounds a little scary. This probably would have been most people's reaction, "Jesus, why are you sending us away into this dangerous situation? These people may want to hurt us. And you are sending us away without any money or extra clothing. What if are needs are not met as you said? What will we do then?"

You see why these Seventy preachers would need to receive Jesus' instructions by **Faith**. They had to know if Jesus were sending them away under these circumstances, they would be provided for just like He said. Jesus confirms this in the next few verses.

Luke 10:5-7

⁵And into whatsoever house ye enter, first say, Peace be to this house.

⁶And if the son of peace be there, your peace shall rest upon it: if not, it shall turn to you again.

⁷And in the same house remain, eating and drinking such things as they give: for the labourer is worthy of his hire. Go not from house to house.

When the Seventy arrived at their destination, they did exactly what Jesus instructed them to do and they were well taken care of. When they completed their mission and returned home, they returned with such joy and excitement. *"**And the seventy returned again with joy, saying, Lord, even the devils are subject unto us through thy name (Luke 10:17)."*** You see, not only were their needs met but the Seventy preachers also realized, that nothing could hurt them. Again, the Seventy said to Jesus, *"Even the devils are subject unto us through thy name!"* And Jesus responded by declaring to them, ***"Behold, I give unto you power to tread on serpents and scorpions, and over all the power of the enemy; and nothing shall by any means hurt you (Luke 10:19)."***

You see, the Seventy did not return with an evil report. They did not say they went where Jesus sent them and they were in danger nor did they say they were cold or hungry. No, not at all. They were excited! They were telling Jesus about the wonderful time they had. They went into those cities, preaching the Kingdom of God and witnessing all the miracles that were taking place! Why did these Seventy preachers have such a great experience? They had such a great experience because they stepped out in **Faith** at the Word of God! This is the same **Faith** the children of Israel should have had in the wilderness.

God was trying to teach the children of Israel to have **Faith** in Him. He was saying to the Israelites (paraphrasing), "Have **Faith** in me. I will provide for you. I will protect you. I will give you the land." God reminded them of this time and time again.

We can see in both cases the Israelites and the Seventy were being taught a lesson in **Faith-Style** living. The children of Israel needed **Faith** to enter their promised land and the Seventy needed **Faith** for their safety and provisions. The only difference between the two is one succeeded and the other did not. I am sad to say, the adult Israelites under Moses' leadership did not go into the promised land, due to their unbelief and hardened hearts.

Hebrews 3:17-19

[17]But with whom was He grieved forty years? Was it not with them that had sinned, whose carcasses fell in the wilderness?

[18]And to whom sware He that they should not enter into His rest, but to them that believed not?

[19]So we see that they could not enter in because of unbelief.

Again, let me express the importance of living by **Faith** for the believer. We do not want to be like the Israelites who died in the wilderness without taking possession of our promised land. You see the children of Israel could not see how they would be provided for. They became so accustomed to receiving from the hands of the Egyptians. They knew if they worked, they would receive something. So, when they went into the wilderness, they did not understand how God would provide for them. For this reason, they believed they had it better in Egypt because they knew what to expect from the Egyptians. But in the wilderness, they saw no possible way of getting their needs met.

Acts 7:25

25For he supposed his brethren would have understood how that God by his hand would deliver them: but they understood not.

2 Corinthians 5:7 declares, *"For we walk by Faith and not by sight."* We can no longer hold an excuse for not trusting God. We have the Holy Bible filled with His Word, we can pick up and read anytime to be reminded of His promises. The Israelites may not have possessed the written Word of God, but they did hear the spoken Word of God delivered by Moses and God very well expected them to adhere to his Word.

If you ever find yourself in a situation you cannot see any possible way of getting out of do not panic and lose heart. God has a solution for any problem we could ever have! In our wilderness experience we need to trust God; learn the lessons He is teaching us and thank Him for leading us into our promised land. Our land that flows with milk and honey! The land He took time to prepare for us before the foundation of the world!

The children of Israel had plenty of money in the wilderness and Jesus sent the Seventy away without any provision to sustain them and they both were expected to use their **Faith**. You see, man seek out physical provision (food, material things) for sustainment. But we can see in both cases the true sustainment came from the Word of the Lord. The Word of God received and acted upon by **Faith** would provide them with everything they needed.

Yes, we need money to live in the earth, but our **Faith** must be in God as our total source of supply. We must believe God will meet and supply our every need (Philippians 4:19). You are probably saying, "Yea right!" But it's true. Look at the abundantly blessed life God was providing for the children of Israel in the promised land. God was supplying them with cities they did not build, houses full of all good things they did not fill, and an unending amount of whatever they needed.

Deuteronomy 6:10-12

[10]And it shall be, when the Lord thy God shall have brought thee into the land which he sware unto thy fathers, to Abraham, to Isaac, and to Jacob, to give thee great and goodly cities, which thou buildest not,

[11]And houses full of all good things, which thou filledst not, and wells digged, which thou diggedst not, vineyards and olive trees, which thou plantedst not: when thou shalt have eaten and be full;

[12]Then beware lest thou forget the Lord, which brought thee forth out of the land of Egypt, from the house of bondage.

Remember, the children of Israel had plenty of money but were not expected to spend any. The only thing God expected them to use to acquire all these amazing things was their **Faith.**

There are so many miracles attributed to **Faith** in the Bible, they are too numerous to count! When we utilize our **Faith** and step out on the Word of God, we too, can experience miraculous results!

Let us take a look at some of the people in the Bible who used their **Faith** and received amazing results!

- **Noah listened to the voice of God when no one else would and was led by God to build a boat that would save him and his family from the flooding of the earth.**
- **Abraham stepped out on the Word of God, left his homeland of seventy-five years and became extravagantly rich and a father of many children in his old age.**
- **Isaac was led by God to sow seed during a famine and he reaped a hundred-fold harvest in the same year.**
- **Peter after toiling all night was instructed by Jesus to go into deep waters to let down his nets and he caught a huge draught of fish.**
- **Jesus sent the twelve disciples away to preach the kingdom of God just like the Seventy, without provision, and they were provided for.**
- **Jesus sent Peter to the sea with the instructions to get money out of the fish's mouth, they needed to pay their taxes.**

Do you see all the examples of God taking care of His children? Do you see what can happen when you step out in **Faith** at the

Word of Almighty God? Everything God said to everyone He led and sent came to pass. Jesus confirms this truth in the verse below with the disciples He sent away.

Luke 22:35

35And he said unto them, When I sent you without purse, and scrip, and shoes, lacked ye anything? And they said, Nothing.

Here it is out of the mouths of the disciples! They were well provided for during their stay in the cities they were sent to. They lacked nothing! This is the confidence we should all eventually have in God. When God tells you do something just do it! You do not know what great blessing could be behind His instructions.

Since we are talking about stepping out in **Faith** at the Word of God, I must share this testimony! Some years ago, I had started a new job and I was really excited to have it. One of the requirements for the position was, you needed your own transportation because you could not be dropped off or picked up from work. When I first started the job, I did have a car but later had some problems with it. So, I rented a car for a couple of weeks until I could decide what I was going to do. Well, renting a car added even more pressure to the problem I had because the car rental was so expensive. When I thought about my options, they certainly did not look too good. To tell you the truth, I did not have the money to buy a car at all and the thought of making payments on another used car was not appealing to me. A few years prior to this incident, I had a couple of not so good experiences with used cars. You would buy the car, pay the note on the car, pay the car insurance and pay for any repairs the car might have needed. In my opinion, it was just too much! The whole time I was considering what to do about my situation, the option of paying a car note was causing me so much grief but I just didn't see any other way.

As I was pondering what to do about my situation, one night I had a dream where the Lord impressed upon me to sow a specific seed amount into a specific ministry. At the time, this ministry was doing their annual back to school program where they helped disadvantaged children with the essentials they needed for school. When I saw the program on television, I thought, I would love to participate in this but at the time my kids needed back to school clothing as well. So, the thought was well intentional but there was no way I was able to contribute at that time. When God spoke to me to sow the seed, I did not remember the ministry was conducting their back to school program. But when God spoke to me to do it, I woke up that morning and just did it. Looking back, I now realize, I was being led by the Holy Spirit to sow this seed. Remember, I needed everything but nevertheless, I was obedient to the Lord and did what the Lord instructed me to do.

When the time was approaching for me to return the rental car, I called my mother and asked her to ask my father, if he would go with me to look for a car. After this, every time I thought about paying a car note, a feeling of heaviness would come over me. I would not only have to pay the car note but I would have to borrow the money for the down payment as well! This whole situation was really depressing me.

On my day off, I had everything arranged. My kids and I headed down to my parents' home to celebrate my brother's birthday and later we would be going to look for a car. When we arrived at my parents' home, I sat there in disgust as I was waiting for my father. People are usually excited when they are going shopping for a car, but I wasn't. As I sat there talking with my family, I thought to myself, "Where is he, it is getting late and I am ready to go get this over with!" When he finally came down the stairs, he and my mother approached me and handed me an envelope. I opened the envelope and it was a letter with a key inside of it. To be honest, I did not even notice the key. This is how discontent I was. When I unfolded the letter to read it, it said (It's been a while since it happened so I will paraphrase), "We know you have been going through a rough time lately, so hopefully this will help."

Do you know, I still did not get it? My parents had to literally pick the key up and put it in my face. They took me outside; I could not believe it! They had a car sitting in the driveway for me. I was in shock! I could not believe it! I was not expecting them to buy me a car!

My parents bought me a car, paid for in full, with no car payments! Glory to God! I was totally amazed! The Lord had blessed them just in time to be a blessing to me. Oh...what a burden lifted!

But wait, there is more! My aunt called me not too long after and asked me to come to her house because she wanted to give me some money to purchase my kid's school clothes. When I arrived at her house, I not only received the one check from her, but I received two checks! She and her husband blessed us with two checks! Now, I was able to go buy my kids everything they needed for school! Glory be to God! You see, what happens when you step out in **Faith** at the Word of God! Do you see what will happen when you have the **Faith** to believe God? Therefore, God does not want our trust in anyone or anything but Him. If I were totally dependent on the money instead of His Word, I would have missed out on the blessing God had for me. I am so grateful that God helped me to put my **Faith** in the right place!

Take confidence in the Word of the Lord! Have **Faith** He will provide for you wherever He is sending you or leading you. Even if you cannot see where He is taking you, always trust Him to bring you out better off than you were before!

THE POWER IN BELIEVING

I truly believe the title of this chapter is powerful within itself. Just thinking about these four little words make me think of all the unlimited possibilities in life. I remember when I first started reading the Bible, I was truly amazed at all the awesome stories it contained. They really ignited something within me. When you think about it, most of the greatest Bible stories with the greatest outcomes are all centered around people who dared to believe. The people who chose to put their **Faith** in an unseen God and believed for the impossible to be made possible in their lives. There are many stories I have read personally in the Bible and wondered, wow, how did this happen? Reading those stories made me feel anything is possible and the God who performed all those awesome miracles in their lives is the same God who could do the same in my life. It all comes back to the bigness of our God and what can happen when we choose to believe in Him. These stories were **Faith** builders for me, and through them all God is demonstrating to all Bible readers the power we can possess in life, if we only believe.

Believing is also an essential element to **Faith-Style** living. You really cannot have **Faith** without it. Believing is the precursor of **Faith**. Let us take a look at the scripture verse below, so we can see the importance of believing and its connection to **Faith-Style** living.

Hebrews 11:6

⁶But without Faith it is impossible to please Him; for he that cometh to God must believe that He is, and that He is a rewarder of them that diligently seek Him.

We can see how believing and **Faith** goes hand and hand? We can also see in this verse for our **Faith** to work, we must first believe our unseen God exist. When we adhere to this verse, we know our **Faith** is in the right place, which then puts us in the position for the miraculous to be demonstrated in our lives.

There are many stories in the Bible that ascribes to the power of believing but there are a couple that really amplifies my **Faith** in God. In these two stories we can see how God made the impossible possible and caused the unseen to become seen. Isn't this the purpose of these stories, for us to read them and know that the same God who performed these mighty acts in the past is the same God that can perform these mighty acts today? After all it is stated in the Bible that God is the same, yesterday, today and forever (Hebrews 13:8). Let us look at some of the people who believed God despite their natural circumstances and were given totally undeniable miracles for the world to see.

I love reading Genesis the fifteenth chapter where it talks about God promising Abraham, he would have a child. Not only did God promise Abraham that he would have a child, God also promised Abraham he would have as many descendants as there are stars in the sky. This was a totally impossible situation because as I have discussed in previous chapters, we know Abraham's wife was barren, and she was declared barren from her youth.

Genesis 11:30

30But Sarai was barren; she had no child.

This confirms that even when Abraham and Sarah were younger, it was clearly impossible for them to conceive a child together in the natural. You know what really amazes me about the story of Abraham and Sarah? It is the fact that God waited until their situation was totally impossible in the natural. Sarah was already barren, so we know she could not have any children, but God even went beyond this physical challenge and waited until they were too old to even think about conceiving a child together.

Genesis 18:10-11

10And He said, "I will certainly return unto thee, according to the time of life; and lo, Sarah thy wife shall have a son. And Sarah heard it in the tent door, which was behind him.

11Now Abraham and Sarah were old and well stricken in age; and it ceased to be with Sarah after the manner of women.

What God was proposing to Abraham and Sarah seemed totally impossible in the natural, so much so, Abraham and Sarah laughed at the possibility of them having a child together. They knew the condition they were in. They knew they were now infertile and incapable of producing children.

Genesis 17:17

17Then Abraham fell upon his face, and laughed, and said in his heart, Shall a child be born unto him that is an hundred years old? And shall Sarah, that is ninety years old, bear?

Genesis 18:12

¹²**Therefore Sarah laughed within herself, saying, After I am waxed old shall I have pleasure, my Lord being old also?**

In the next couple of verses, God asked Abraham two astounding questions. First, God asked, "Why did Sarah laugh?" Second, He asked, "Is there anything too hard for the Lord?" These questions would help both Abraham and Sarah to get their **Faith** in the right place. It would help them to get their minds off their abilities and physical conditions and focus on the God that makes the impossible possible.

Genesis 18:13-14

¹³**And the Lord said unto Abraham, Wherefore did Sarah laugh, saying, Shall I of a surety bear a child, which am old.**

¹⁴**Is anything too hard for the Lord? At the appointed time I will return unto thee, according to the time of life, and Sarah shall have a son.**

Despite Sarah and Abraham's laughter, we know God had already performed some mighty acts in their lives. And now, for them to hear, they were going to have a child at their age, was nothing short of amazing! In Genesis 15, a few chapters prior to this, God told Abraham he would indeed have a child, but Abraham did not laugh at that time.

Genesis 15:4-5

⁴**And, behold, the Word of the Lord came unto him, saying, This shall not be thine heir; but he that shall come forth out of thine own bowels shall be thine heir.**

⁵And he brought him forth abroad, and said, Look now toward heaven, and tell the stars, if thou be able to number them: and he said unto him, So shall thy seed be.

The next verse declares, *"And Abraham believed in the Lord; and he counted it to him for righteousness* (Genesis 15:6)." So, we can see Abraham believed God about having a child in this chapter when it was still physically possible for him to produce a child. We also know that Abraham did not gain the title of "Father of **Faith**" for nothing. Abraham's belief in God is the most amazing aspect of his story. Even though it is recorded Abraham laughed at the thought of having a child a few chapters later, I believe the Lord wanted us to see this for a reason. I believe the Lord was showing us in this later chapter that Abraham was a human being just like us and God did not want to portray Abraham as being superhuman. It only shows us, Abraham thinking within himself, "How will this be possible?" Just like when God gives us a promise that may be unimaginable to us when we first hear it. The first thing we may do is look at ourselves and wonder the same thing. Why? Because we wonder, how can anything like it happen for us.

I do not believe Abraham doubted God's ability, but Abraham doubted his own ability to have a child. But just like us, God had to work with Abraham's **Faith**. Abraham had to be reminded not to look at himself but to believe the Word of Almighty God.

Romans 4:18-21

¹⁸Who against hoped believed in hope, that he might become the father of many nations, according to that which was spoken, So shall thy seed be.

¹⁹**And not being weak in faith, he considered not his own body now dead, when he was about an hundred years old, neither yet the deadness of Sarah's womb:**

²⁰**He staggered not at the promise of God through unbelief; but was strong in faith, giving glory to God;**

²¹**And being fully persuaded that, what he had promised, he was able also to perform.**

When Abraham's **Faith** in God was magnified, God delivered the promised child into their hands!

Genesis 21:1-2

¹**And the Lord visited Sarah as he had said, and the Lord did unto Sarah as he had spoken.**

²**For Sarah conceived, and bare Abraham a son in his old age, at the set time of which God had spoken to him.**

When we put our **Faith** in God, God will make His promises a physical reality! Although we may sometimes forget about God's miracle working power, God is always here to remind us, all things are truly possible when we choose to believe Him!

Another story that demonstrates the power in believing in such an amazing way, is the story of a young girl named Mary. Mary's story is undeniably remarkable in every way. Now this is what you would call a totally impossible situation.

An Angel appeared to Mary, to announce a miracle that was getting ready to happen in her life. Let us read the conversation that took place between the Angel and Mary.

Luke 1:28-33

²⁸And the angel came unto her, and said, Hail, thou that art highly favored, the Lord is with thee: blessed art thou among women.

²⁹And when she saw him, she was troubled at his saying, and cast in her mind what manner of salutation this should be.

³⁰And the angel said unto her, Fear not, Mary: for thou hast found favor with God.

³¹And, behold, thou shalt conceive in thy womb, and bring forth a son, and shalt call his name JESUS.

³²He shall be great, and shall be called the Son of the Highest: and the Lord God shall give unto Him the throne of His father David:

³³And He shall reign over the house of Jacob for ever; and of his kingdom there should be no end.

After the Angel spoke to Mary about getting pregnant and having a baby, Mary asked a question many of us would have asked in her situation. Mary said to the Angel, *"How shall this be, seeing I know not a man (Luke 1:34)?"* The Angel then explained to Mary, how this epic event would transpire in her life.

Luke 1:35

³⁵And the angel answered and said unto her, The Holy Ghost shall come upon thee, and the power of the Highest shall overshadow thee: therefore also that holy thing which shall be born of thee shall be called the Son of God.

Even though the Angel did answer Mary's question, can you imagine what she must have been thinking? Mary was a virgin! This defied all human logic! But this was not the only miracle in the making. When the Angel communicated to Mary the miracle she would be participating in, the Angel revealed another miracle to Mary which had already taken place. The Angel informed Mary that her cousin Elisabeth, who was barren all her life and was well past child-bearing age, was now pregnant!

Luke 1:36

36And, behold, thy cousin Elisabeth, she hath also conceived a son in her old age: and this is the sixth month with her, who was called barren.

The Angel of the Lord reminded Mary just like God reminded Abraham in what appeared to be an impossible situation: *"For with God nothing shall be impossible (Luke 1:37)."*

Mary could have asked the Angel many more questions, in hopes of getting a more realistic answer, but she did not. Mary was excited! She was excited to learn about Elisabeth's pregnancy, as well as her own. In fact, Mary welcomed the Angel's news despite any consequence she may have to face as a result.

Luke 1:38

38And Mary said, Behold the handmaid of the Lord; be it unto me according to thy word. And the angel departed from her.

Mary was so excited to receive the news regarding Elisabeth's pregnancy that she decided to pay Elisabeth a visit. Mary was convinced if what the Angel had spoken to her about Elisabeth's pregnancy was true, then what the Angel had spoken to her about her pregnancy would be true as well. Let us read what happened when Mary went to Elisabeth's home.

Luke 1:39-45

³⁹And Mary arose in those days, and went into the hill country with haste, into a city of Judah;

⁴⁰And entered into the house of Zacharias, and saluted Elisabeth.

⁴¹And when it came to pass, that, when Elisabeth heard the salutation of Mary, the babe leaped in her womb; and Elisabeth was filled with the Holy Ghost:

⁴²And she spake out with a loud voice, and said, Blessed art thou among women, and blessed is the fruit of thy womb.

⁴³And whence is this to me, that the mother of my Lord should come to me?

⁴⁴For, lo, as soon as the voice of thy salutation sounded in mine ears, the babe leaped in my womb for joy.

⁴⁵And blessed is she that believed: for there shall be a performance of those things which were told her from the Lord.

We can see Mary did not have to say a word to Elisabeth about anything the Angel said. Elisabeth began to confirm everything the moment Mary stepped into her home! I love what Elisabeth said to Mary in the last verse, *"Blessed is she that believed; for there shall be a performance of those things which were told her from the Lord (Luke 1:45)."*

Mary believed the Word of the Lord emphatically! And this put her in the most astounding position, ever! Mary was going to be the mother of the Savior of the world! Mary was so amazed by Elizabeth's words, she immediately began to praise God, commemorating this monumental event.

Luke 1:46-55

[46]And Mary said, My soul doth magnify the Lord,

[47]And my spirit hath rejoiced in God my Saviour.

[48]For He hath regarded the low estate of His handmaiden; for, behold, from henceforth all generations shall call me blessed.

[49]For He that is mighty hath done for me great things; and holy is His name.

[50]And His mercy is on them that fear Him from generation to generation.

[51]He hath shewed strength with His arm; He hath scattered the proud in the imaginations of their hearts.

[52]He hath put down the mighty from their seats, and exalted them of low degree.

[53]He hath filled the hungry with good things; and the rich He hath sent empty away.

[54]He hath holpen His servant Israel, in remembrance of His mercy;

[55]As He spake to our fathers, to Abraham, and to his seed forever.

Glory be to God!!! I was not even there but I can feel Mary's excitement by reading the words of her praise! Mary praised God emphatically without her seeing any visible signs of her pregnancy! So, we can see there is truly power in believing! Abraham and Mary believed God when everything around them said no, not possible. But their **Faith** in God said yes! God took their impossible situations and made them possible! It was not by their might or power, but it was truly by God's Spirit which brought all these wonderful things to pass in their lives (Zechariah 4:6)!

In the book of John, Jesus addressed the importance of believing after He was resurrected from the grave and appeared to His disciples.

John 20:19

¹⁹Then the same day at evening, being the first day of the week, when the doors were shut where the disciples are assembled for the fear of the Jews, came Jesus and stood in the midst, and said unto them, Peace be unto you.

When Jesus came back to show His resurrected body to His disciples, a disciple named Thomas was not present to see Him. Therefore, Thomas did not believe what the other disciples conveyed to him about Jesus' return. Let us read the conversation that transpired between Thomas and the other disciples.

John 20:24-25

²⁴But Thomas, one of the twelve, called Didymus, was not with them when Jesus came.

²⁵The other disciples therefore said unto him, We have seen the Lord, But he said unto them, Except I shall see in

his hands the print of the nails, and put my finger into the print of the nails, and thrust my hand into his side, I will not believe.

Do you see the last statement Thomas made to the disciples? Thomas said, *"Except I shall see in his hands the print of the nails, and put my finger into the print of the nails, and thrust my hand into his side, I will not believe."* Thomas believed what the other disciples said was totally impossible. Even after all the miracles Thomas witnessed when he walked with Jesus. Thomas said there was no way he would believe unless he saw Jesus with his own eyes. The Lord did not disappoint, He made another appearance to the disciples and gave Thomas exactly what he wanted, just as he requested.

John 20:26-27

26And after eight days again his disciples were within, and Thomas with them: then came Jesus, the doors being shut, and stood in the midst, and said, Peace be unto you.

27Then saith he to Thomas, Reach hither thy finger, and behold my hands; and reach hither thy hand, and thrust it into my side: and be not Faithless, but believing.

Wow, what a powerful statement Jesus made! And what Jesus was voicing to Thomas, Jesus is voicing to every believer today. Jesus said, *"Be not Faithless but Believing."* I am getting so excited as I am writing this! Can Jesus' Words be any plainer? Again, **Faith** is not contingent upon what you can see with your natural eyes, if it were there would be no need for it. Let us take a look at the next powerful statement Jesus made to Thomas.

John 20:29

29Jesus saith unto him, Thomas, because thou hast seen me, thou hast believed: blessed are they that have not seen, and yet have believed.

Jesus' statement to Thomas brings us back to the scripture verse I have discussed many times already.

Hebrews 11:6

6But without Faith it is impossible to please Him; for he that cometh to God must believe that He is, and that He is a rewarder of them that diligently seek Him.

As believers, we need to get back to a life governed by the Word of God and **Faith**. Many of us are missing out on the benefits of **Faith-Style** living because we are too focused on what we can see opposed to the unseen. We are looking at our natural circumstances as if it has the final authority over our lives. Instead, we should be looking to, Jesus, the Author and Finisher of our **Faith**.

God has gifted every one of us with "the measure of **Faith**" to change every pre-existing circumstance in our lives that is contrary to His Word. God used His Word and **Faith** to change the pre-existing conditions of the earth and He wants us to know, we too, possess the same power. Before Jesus performed some of the miracles He did, He would ask the question, *"Do you believe I am able to do this?"* And they responded, *"Yes, Lord* **(Matthew 9:28).***"* We must also believe God is able!

Do not be dismayed about any situations in your life which are contrary to the Word of God. Believe God and put your **Faith** in

214

Him. Let us be like Abraham, Sarah, Mary and so many others and watch the impossible become possible in our lives.

The greatest component to **Faith-Style** living is believing our unseen God exist and that He truly desires the best for His children.

Faith-Style living is a life predicated on trusting God as we step into the unseen world of **Faith**!

HAVE FAITH IN GOD

Mark 11:22-23

And Jesus answering saith unto them, Have Faith in God.

For verily I say unto you, That whosoever shall say unto this mountain, Be thou removed, and be thou cast into the sea; and shall not doubt in his heart, but shall believe that those things which he saith shall come to pass; he shall have whatsoever he saith.

While meditating on the Word of God this morning, I believe the Holy Spirit was revealing to me the excitement all believers should have in being "People of **Faith**." For this reason, I started this chapter with these particular scripture verses. It is in these powerful, dynamic scripture verses we can see the astronomical results our **Faith** can produce when we as believers put our **Faith** in God. It is in these scripture verses Jesus is illustrating to us the power we can have when our **Faith** is in the right place. It shows us our **Faith** in God can indeed move mountains, meaning the removal of what may appear to be the most severe, impenetrable circumstances. Therefore, we as "People of **Faith**" need to get excited about the precious gift of **Faith-Style** living because it is by and through our **Faith** in God that any condition we may deem impossible, are all subject to change!

When God began to show me this my spirit rejoiced, and I became so excited because I knew this was the truth. We can see several examples of this truth frequently demonstrated in the Bible. Look at the life of Peter for example. There were two occasions in the Bible where Peter needs were met, supernaturally. On one occasion, Peter who was a professional fisherman, was fishing all night and had caught nothing. Peter was a professional. He knew when it was the best time for him and his partners to go fishing. This was how he made his living. It was important for him to know these things. So, when Jesus instructed Peter to go back into the sea and let down his nets for a huge catch, initially Peter hesitated. Peter said to Jesus, *"Master, we have toiled all the night, and have taken nothing... (Luke 5:5)."* Peter was basically saying to Jesus (paraphrasing), "Look Jesus, I am a pro at this fisherman thing, this is how I make my living. I was out there all night, and nothing happened. I did not catch anything! But if you insist, I will go back out there to prove to you I know what I am talking about."

We can see Peter's initial hesitation by the words he spoke and later by the actions he took. When Peter and his partners came back from fishing, they went to wash their fishing nets (plural). When Jesus instructed Peter to go back into the sea, Jesus instructed Peter to let down his nets (plural) for a huge catch. But when Peter went into the sea, Peter did not follow Jesus' instructions completely. Instead of Peter letting down his nets (plural), he let down a net (singular). So, Peter was pretty much saying to Jesus (paraphrasing), "Okay Jesus, I will go back out there but I am only taking one net this time because as I have already explained, I have tried this, and nothing happened."

So, we can see in the natural, Peter's efforts yielded no results. Although Peter was initially hesitant about going fishing again, he said to Jesus, *"Nevertheless at thy Word I will let down the net*

(Luke 5:5)." Peter exercised his **Faith** in the Word of God and because he did, his **Faith** produced incredible results.

Luke 5:6-7

⁶And when they had this done, they inclosed a great multitude of fishes: and their net brake.

⁷And they beckoned unto their partners, which were in the other ship, that they should come and help them. And they came, and filled both the ships, so that they began to sink.

This is so exciting! Can you see why God was encouraging me to get excited about being "People of **Faith**?" It was through Peter's **Faith;** his condition was subject to change! Peter caught so many fish, his net broke and he had to call for help! Peter beckoned for his partners to come help him with the huge load of fish. Peter put his **Faith** in the Word of the Lord and it produced miraculous results! This huge catch of fish was exceedingly above what Peter could ask or think (Ephesians 3:20).

In this story, God is showing believers that our lives are not contingent upon the natural conditions of this world. For believers, our **Faith** in God is what brings supernatural results into our lives. Our **Faith** says to the systems of this world, I am not constrained or limited by the methods of this world system. My **Faith** in God can take me above and beyond this limited system anytime and anywhere.

Here is another story that proves my point. After Peter caught the draught of fish, Jesus instructed him to leave his job of being a professional fisherman to become His disciple. Instead of Peter being a fisherman, he became a fisher of men. After Peter had been Jesus' disciple for a while there came a time when Jesus and Peter needed to pay their tax bill. Jesus then says to Peter, *"Go thou to the sea, and cast a hook, and take up the fish that first cometh up; and when thou hast opened his mouth, thou shalt find a piece of money: that take and give unto them for me and thee (Matthew 17:27)."* This instruction Jesus gave to Peter went beyond all the natural methods of the world. Jesus did not say to Peter (paraphrasing), "Okay Peter, I want you to take a job and work 8 hours a day, for ten days, to accumulate the money we need to pay our tax bill." No, not at all. In fact, Jesus did allow Peter to use his fisherman skills when he sent him to the sea, but this fishing experience was totally different from the days Peter used his fisherman skills to earn a living. Jesus did not send Peter to the sea to earn a living. No, those days were over. Peter was only sent to the sea to retrieve (not earn) the money to pay their tax bill. You see, Peter did not have to worry about how many fish he would need to catch to pay their taxes. Peter did not have to sit out all night in a panic, wondering if he would obtain the money he needed. All Peter had to do was to step out by **Faith** on the instructions Jesus gave him to follow, no matter how inconceivable they may have seemed. Peter only had to catch one fish, the first fish, which would have the money he needed inside of it. Oh my God, I am getting so excited over this story! Again, this is amazing! Jesus and Peter's ability to pay their tax bill was not contingent upon the natural method of operation of this world system. Peter did not have to spend his whole day fishing, hoping he would catch enough fish to sell, to get the money he needed. Instead he used God's modus operandi. Peter stepped out in **Faith** and obtained the money he needed in a supernatural, unconventional way!

These are stupendous examples of the results we can achieve when we operate by the principles God has established for us.

It is in these two examples we as believers can see the benefits of putting our **Faith** in God. In these two occurrences with Peter, we can see why God does not want his children being provision minded. Because it is when we are provision minded and in the state of chasing down provision, we find it hard to put our trust in God. We become engulfed with trying to make a way for ourselves, this is a way of life God never intended for His children. Let us take a look at the next scripture verse. This is Jesus speaking people!

Matthew 6:31 MSG

What I'm trying to do here is to get you to relax, to not be so preoccupied with getting, so you can respond to God's giving.

This is the very verse that was demonstrated in Peter's experience when he toiled all night trying to catch fish. Can you sense a little frustration in Peter's words when he spoke to Jesus?

Luke 5:5

⁵And Simon answering said unto him, "Master, we have toiled all the night, and have taken nothing:"

Jesus was teaching Peter a lesson from *Matthew 6:31, "What I'm trying to do here is to get you to relax, to not be so preoccupied with getting, so you can respond to God's giving."* When Jesus instructed Peter to launch out into the deep and let down his nets for a draught, Jesus was not asking Peter what happened the first time he went fishing. Jesus already knew Peter did not catch anything. Jesus was saying to Peter (paraphrasing), "Relax Peter. I know you were fishing all night and you didn't get the results you wanted. But put your **Faith** in me and I will show you the benefits in doing so."

Peter was stunned by the results he received! Let us take a look at what transpired after Peter witnessed the huge catch of fish. The Bible states, *"When Simon Peter saw it, he fell down at Jesus' knees, saying Depart from me; for I am a sinful man, O Lord. For He was astonished, and all that were with him, at the draught of the fishes which they had taken (Luke 5:8-9)."* This verse indisputably testifies to Peter's reaction to the huge catch of fish. Peter witnessed first-hand the astounding results he obtained by stepping out at the Word of the Lord.

So, you see child of God, God wants our **Faith** in Him and not in the systems of the world. God will use these systems to bless us, but He wants our **Faith** in Him. As we can see on both occasions, God did use Peter's ability as a fisherman to bless him. The "good news" is Peter's blessings was not limited to the natural conditions around him nor to his abilities alone. God caused Peter to prosper, supernaturally!

Sometimes we can become so panicked and frantic about getting our needs met but this is the reason we have the Bible. God desires to show us what will happen when we put our trust and confidence in Him. I am really getting excited about my **Faith**! The operation of **Faith** is amazing to me because it takes the limits off my life. No longer do I have to look at a situation and think, "That's it. It won't get no better than this." No, not all. That is a lie from the pit of hell. With my **Faith** in God, it can and will get better. Let us revisit the definition of **Faith, *"Now Faith is the substance of things hoped for, the evidence of things not seen (Hebrews 11:1)."***

Contained in the definition of **Faith** is God giving us the divine right to believe for better. It is God saying to us, we do not have to settle for the circumstances we are seeing with our natural eyes. In the Bible, God demonstrates **Faith** in Him is a proven dynamic force that can produce in any situation. Whether it be a famine, a failed economy, a wilderness, a desert place, a drought, a barren place or a barren womb with God the conditions do not matter. **Faith** in God can produce miraculous results anytime and anywhere!

For this reason, Jesus taught His disciples about **Faith** and how to use their **Faith.** The disciples' **Faith** would be essential to their assignment in the earth. They too had to get accustomed to **Faith-Style** living! This is what the illustration of Jesus speaking to the fig tree was all about (Matthew 11:13-23). Jesus was teaching the disciples not to worry about futile conditions because their **Faith** in God could override any preexisting circumstance or condition. Whether it was an unfruitful tree, a storm, sickness, disease or insufficiency of any kind it did not matter. **Faith** in God could override anything!

We must remember, ***"The earth is the Lord's and the fullness thereof; the world, and they that dwell therein (Psalms 24:1)."*** God knows where every source of provision is in the earth. God should know where every source of provision is because He put it there. This reminds me of the remarkable story told about creation. In the book of Genesis, Moses outlines every amazing detail of creation. Moses tells the story of every provision God placed in the earth to sustain the needs of mankind. Moses speaks about the abundance of trees and herb bearing seeds, the vast variety of animals, the rivers of water, the gold and all the precious stones. God created and placed in the earth, everything man would ever need, want or desire. In the Garden of Eden, everything Adam and Eve needed was within their reach. They did not have to worry about a thing! They did not even know what worry was. I believe this is the life God wants us to believe Him for once again. It is the life God has made available to us in His Son, Jesus Christ.

Philippians 4:19 ERV

My God will use His glorious riches to give you everything you need. He will do this through Christ Jesus.

Jesus encouraged His disciples not to worry about provision. Jesus taught His disciples many lessons on using their **Faith** to acquire what they needed, as well as, to meet the needs of others. Jesus wanted the disciples to complete their assignments without having to worrying about anything. Let us read these verses again.

Matthew 6:24-34

24No man can serve two masters: for either he will hate the one, and love the other; or else he will hold to the one, and despise the other. Ye cannot serve God and mammon.

25Therefore I say unto you, Take no thought for your life, what shall ye eat, or what ye shall drink; nor yet for your body, what shall you put on. Is not the life more than meat, and the body than raiment?

26Behold the fowls of the air: for they sow not, neither do they reap, nor gather into barns; yet your heavenly Father feedeth them. Are ye not much better than they?

27Which of you by taking thought can add one cubit unto his stature?

28And why take ye thought for raiment? Consider the lilies of the field, how they grow; they toil not, neither do they spin:

29And yet I say unto you, That even Solomon in all his glory was not arrayed like one of these.

30Wherefore, if God do clothe the grass of the field, which today is, and tomorrow is cast into the oven, shall he not much more clothe you, O ye of little Faith?

31Therefore take no thought, saying, What shall we eat? or, What shall we drink? or, Wherewithal shall we be clothed?

32(For after all these things do the Gentiles seek:) for your heavenly Father knoweth that you have need of all these things.

33But seek ye first the kingdom of God, and his righteousness; and all these things shall be added unto you.

34Take therefore no thought for the morrow: for the morrow shall take thought for the things of itself. Sufficient unto the day is the evil thereof.

These verses have been discussed many times already because I believe it is in these verses Jesus is imploring us to have **Faith** in Him. If Jesus met the needs of others, cannot He do the same for us? Think about it. If God created a provision filled Garden for Adam and Eve to live in and enjoy, why do we think it is so hard for Him to meet our needs. He is the same God who created the Garden of Eden, He is the same God that made Abraham extremely rich, He is the same God that prepared a land flowing with milk and honey for the children of Israel, He is the same God that directed Peter to a huge catch of fish and He is the same God telling us in Matthew 6:24-34 to "take no thought" for our provision today!

Do you still need convincing? Okay, let us explore the story of Abraham's son, Isaac. In the country Isaac was living in there was a severe famine. During this famine God spoke to Isaac, instructing him not to go to Egypt, which was considered a type of world system. Instead, God wanted Isaac to stay in the region he was living in. God's instructions may not have made any sense in the natural, but Isaac chose to put his **Faith** in God and did exactly what God instructed him to do. The Bible states, *"Isaac sowed in the land during the famine and received a hundredfold harvest in the same year (Genesis 26:12)."* Isaac put his **Faith** in the Word of the Lord and God prospered him during a severe famine!

Everyone else was most likely running to Egypt to get their needs met. When Isaac's father Abraham encountered a famine, Abraham traveled to Egypt to dwell there temporarily until the famine subsided. In the story of Isaac's son Jacob, during the famine he experienced in Canaan, Jacob sent his sons to Egypt to obtain provision and later relocated to Egypt. It may have been God's plan for Abraham and Jacob to go to Egypt, but it was not God's plan for Isaac. God was showing Isaac what happens when we trust Him no matter what the current situation looks like. Sometimes God may not want us to do what may seem to be the obvious solution to our problem. This is how God shows us who He is during whatever daunting situation we are going through. When we put our **Faith** in God, He will prosper us in unusual ways. In sometimes under the most unusual circumstances.

God demonstrated this in the lives of the children of Israel. When they were in the wilderness, God provided for them in unusual ways. God fed them with manna something the Israelites never seen or eaten before. It was something they did not have to prepare or bake. God caused the manna to rain down from heaven. It was enough to feed them every day! God caused water to flow from a rock, not from a spring or well in the ground. God caused quail to fall into their camp without them having to hunt for them or catch them. Isn't this amazing! God not only took care of their food needs; He took care of their clothing needs as well. God kept their clothes in excellent condition. God also kept them in perfect health! I am getting so excited about this! This is what happens when you rehearse the miraculous acts of God. Does this not increase your **Faith**? It is increasing mine and there is no way I want my life to be limited or restricted to the natural methods of this world system, ever again!

God want us to be "People of **Faith**" who gets excited about our **Faith**. And God gets excited about our **Faith** as well. We can see examples of this illustrated in the Old and New Testaments. When God communicated to Abraham, he was going to have a child, the Bible states, *"And Abraham believed in the Lord and it was counted to him for righteousness* (Genesis 15:6). You see, righteousness is a big deal to God. Righteousness represents, "God's way of doing things and being right (Matthew 6:33, AMP)." So, this verse conveys to me, God was well pleased with Abraham's **Faith** because it was Abraham's **Faith** that brought him into right standing with God. Mankind being in right standing with God was God's original plan for mankind because we were created in God's image and after His likeness.

Ecclesiastes 7:29

Lo, this only have I found, that God hath made man upright (Righteous):

Jesus also got excited over the people's **Faith**. We can see examples of this illustrated in the stories of the Centurion soldier and the Syrophoenician woman. I have already discussed their stories in another chapter but let us take a look at Jesus' response to their **Faith**.

Luke 7:9

9When Jesus heard these things, he marveled at him, and turned him about, and said unto the people that followed him, I say unto you, I have not found so great Faith, no, not in Israel.

Matthew 15:28

28Then Jesus answered and said unto her, O woman, great is thy faith: be it unto thee even as thou wilt. And her daughter was made whole from that very hour.

So, we can see Jesus marveled over the **Faith** of the Centurion soldier and He praised the Syrophoenician woman for hers. Because they put their **Faith** in the Word of God, they received miraculous results! Take comfort in these two verses below and know that when you put your **Faith** in God, your **Faith** is undoubtedly in the right place!

Numbers 23:19

19God is not a man, that he should lie; neither the son of man, that he should repent: hath he said, and shall he not do it? Or hath he spoken, and shall he not make it good?

Isaiah 46:11

¹¹Yea, I have spoken it, I will also bring it to pass; I have purposed it, I will also do it.

You better hear what I am saying child of God! Get excited about your **Faith** and put your **Faith** in God! Trust God, so you can live the victorious life you were re-created in Christ Jesus to live!

Faith-Style living is the right way of living for the believer!

FAITH IN "RENEWING YOUR MIND" TO THE WORD OF THE LORD

As Christians it is imperative we realize how significant **Faith** is to the life of the believer. When you think about it, we cannot even become a Christian without it. When we become born-again, it is based on what we believe and not what we can see. When we recite the prayer of salvation, salvation is granted unto us. We are saying we believe by **Faith** Jesus Christ is the Son of God. We believe He died for our sins and on the basis of His *Death, Burial and Resurrection*, we become the children of God and receive eternal life. Now, we have not witnessed any of the things I mentioned with our own natural eyes. But we, as believers, must believe them to be true. The Bible also states that one day Jesus will return to earth. This is what we refer to as His second coming. We have never witnessed His first coming and yet we believe He is coming again. Why do we believe these things without seeing them? We believe them because we have **Faith in God.** And because of our **Faith in God** we believe what His Word says.

Hebrews 11:1 MSG

The fundamental fact of existence is that this trust in God, this faith, is the firm foundation under everything that makes life worth living. It's our handle on what we can't see.

What is really interesting about the subject of **Faith** is, the Bible says you cannot please God without it.

Hebrews 11:6

⁶But without Faith it is impossible to please Him: for he that cometh to God must believe that He is, and that He is a rewarder of them that diligently seek Him.

Another scripture which illustrates to me how relevant the life of **Faith** is to the believer is found in **Luke 18:8 NLT.**

⁸...But when the Son of man returns, how many will he find on the earth who have Faith?

Wow, what a statement! This tells me, if we are to have **Faith** at the onset of becoming born-again, and Jesus is telling us in the verse above, it is **Faith** He is looking for upon His return. This means, from the time we become Christians and until Jesus' return, we are to continue in **Faith**! God confirms this in His Word from Genesis to Revelation.

From the beginning of time, I believe God had only one desire for His creation. It was for us to simply believe Him. God wants His children to believe, He is who He says He is, and He will do what He says He will do!

I believe this is a download from the heart of God!

To prove my words, let us take a look at the book of Genesis. We can see God's desire for us to believe Him demonstrated in the story of Adam and Eve.

Genesis 2:15-17

¹⁵And the Lord God took the man, and put him into the Garden of Eden to dress it and to keep it.

¹⁶And the Lord God commanded the man, saying, Of every tree of the garden thou mayest freely eat:

¹⁷But of the tree of the knowledge of good and evil, thou shalt not eat of it: for in the day that thou eatest thereof thou shalt surely die.

Simply believing the Word of God would have been so beneficial for Adam and Eve. They could have lived all their days in the Garden, God personally prepared for them. All their days would have been like heaven on earth with not a worry in the world. But unfortunately, they chose to listen to another voice which cost them the amazing life that was afforded to them.

The situation with Noah was different. The Bible states, *"Noah was a just man and perfect in his generation, and Noah walked with God (Genesis 6:9)."* Noah walking with God meant Noah fellowshipped with God. He had a relationship with God. During the time Noah lived in, the earth was corrupt. God was on the verge of destroying everything He created. But because Noah found grace in the eyes of the Lord, God presented Noah with an opportunity to save him and his family. God then informed Noah of His plan to flood the earth. God instructed Noah to build an ark. God even provided Noah with the knowledge he needed to build the ark and what to fill the ark with. During these conversations with God, Noah could have said to himself, "I must be hearing things, there is no way this can happen." And been just as unbelieving as the rest of the people in the land. But no, not a chance! Noah believed God and because of his **Faith** in God, Noah and his family were saved from the flood and did not perish along with the unbelievers.

Hebrews 11:7 MSG

By faith, Noah built a ship in the middle of dry land. He was warned about something he couldn't see, and acted on what he was told. The result? His family was saved. His act of faith drew a sharp line between the evil of the unbelieving world. As a result, Noah became intimate with God.

The Amplified Bible gives you an even better perspective on Noah's **Faith.**

[Prompted] by faith Noah, being forewarned by God concerning events of which as yet there was no visible sign, took heed and diligently and reverently constructed and prepared an ark for the deliverance of his own family. By this [his faith which relied on God] he passed judgment and sentence on the world's unbelief and became an heir and possessor of righteousness (that relation of being right into which God puts the person who has faith).

Let us take another look at the story of Abraham. I have discussed Abraham many times already, but it is difficult not to mention Abraham when it comes to the subject of **Faith**, after all he is the father of **Faith.**

God defied all the odds in Abraham's life. During a conversation between God and Abraham, we can see how Abraham was feeling a little distraught because he did not have a child of his own. God spoke to Abraham in a vision, assuring

Abraham, he will have a child. Let us take a look at what God said to Abraham.

Genesis 15:1-6

¹Fear not, Abram: I am thy shield, and thy exceeding great reward."

²And Abram said, Lord God, what wilt thou give me, seeing I go childless, and the steward of my house is this Eliezer of Damascus?

³And Abram said, Behold, to me thou hast given no seed: and, lo, one born in my house is mine heir.

⁴And, behold, the Word of the Lord came unto him, saying, This shall not be thine heir; but he that shall come forth out of thine own bowels shall be thine heir.

⁵And he brought him forth abroad, and said, Look now toward heaven, and tell the stars, if thou be able to number them: and he said unto him, So shall thy seed be.

⁶And he believed in the Lord; and he counted it to him for righteousness.

It was Abraham's relationship with God that put him in right standing with God. God loves for His children to be in relationship with Him. Not just one generation, God wants a relationship with you and your children. God is a generational God! God demonstrates this in the lives of Abraham and his descendants. God established a relationship with Abraham's son, Isaac and with his grandson son, Jacob. God did not want to stop with Abraham. No, not a chance! God wanted to build a perpetual bond with all of Abraham's descendants. There are many places in the Bible, showing God, introducing Himself as, the God of Abraham, Isaac and Jacob. In this introduction, God is showing us, He had a relationship with all three men. Their stories clearly demonstrate, all three men reverently adhered to the Word of the Lord. And all three of them had different encounters and experiences with God. God blessed all three of them and made them wealthy in their own right. Abraham, Isaac and Jacob may have been heirs of the same promise, but God dealt with each of them differently. How did these great men of God accumulate their wealth? They accumulated their wealth, by doing what God instructed them to do when God instructed them to do it.

God instructed Abraham to leave his country and because of Abraham's willingness to obey God, God made Abraham a very wealthy man. God had two pagan kings to load Abraham up with riches! Abraham lacked nothing!

Genesis 24:1

¹And Abraham was old, and well stricken in age: and the Lord had blessed Abraham in all things.

Isaac, of course inherited his wealth from his natural father, but God had so much more in store for Isaac. God wanted Isaac to receive from his earthly and heavenly father. When Isaac encountered a famine, God instructed him not to go to Egypt but to remain in the land of Gerar. The Bible states, *"Isaac then sowed in that land, and he received in the same year a hundredfold: and the Lord blessed him (Genesis 26:12)."*

Isaac became so wealthy, the natives of the land ordered him to leave. They became so jealous of Isaac because Isaac became mightier and wealthier than them.

Genesis 26:13-14, 16

¹³**And the man waxed great, and went forward, and grew until he became very great:**

¹⁴**For he had possession of flocks, and possession of herds, and great store of servants: and the Philistines envied him.**

¹⁶**And Abimelech said unto Isaac, Go from us; for thou art much mightier than we.**

This is amazing! God is an awesome God! Isaac was so blessed the people in the land could not stand to have him around. They were so envious.

Jacob was also blessed by God in a remarkable way! Jacob's uncle was taking utter advantage of Jacob while Jacob worked for him. Laban cheated Jacob out of his wages by deceiving him and changing his wages ten times. God gave Jacob an idea in a dream that would turn the tides for Jacob and make him a wealthy man. Let us take a look at what Jacob said to his wives concerning their father's treachery.

Genesis 31:4-9

⁴**And Jacob sent and called Rachel and Leah to the field unto his flock,**

⁵**And said unto them, I see your father's countenance, that it is not toward me as before; but the God of my father hath been with me.**

⁶**And ye know that with all my power I have served your father.**

⁷**And your father has deceived me, and changed my wages ten times; but God suffered him not to hurt me.**

⁸If he said thus, The speckled shall be thy wages; then all the cattle bare speckled: and if he said thus, The ringstraked shall be thy hire; then bare all the cattle ringstraked.

⁹Thus God had taken away the cattle of your father, and given them to me.

This God-given instruction caused Jacob to accumulate an abundance of wealth!

Genesis 30:43

⁴³And the man increased exceedingly, and had much cattle, and maidservants, and menservants, and camels, and asses.

So, there you have it! God worked great miracles in the lives of Abraham, Abraham's son and grandson. The Word of the Lord received and acted upon made a huge impact in their lives. Again, God is a Generational God!

Psalms 33:11 HCSB

¹¹The counsel of Lord stands forever, the plans of His heart from generation to generation.

There are many genealogies recorded in the Bible. In some of the genealogies the ones who walked with God are recognized. People who had special relationships with God. These people had extraordinary trust in God, which made them people of extraordinary **Faith**. The genealogies also exist to show us something even more remarkable. They illustrate, God's love for His creation. God loves us so much that He keeps a record of all of us, chronicling the life of every human being beginning with Adam.

God desires for us to be people of **Faith**. This is why God chose Abraham because He knew Abraham would teach his descendants everything he learned about the ways of God. God confirms this in the verse below. This is God speaking people!

Genesis 18:19

¹⁹For I know him, that he will command his children and his household after him, and they shall keep the way of the Lord.

It was God's desire for Abraham's descendants to learn the ways of God and to live God's way. The Just shall live by **Faith** (Romans 1:17)!

In Genesis 15, God not only tells Abraham he will have a child from his own loins, but his descendants would be innumerable like the stars in the sky. God did not stop there; God also gave Abraham a glimpse into the future of his descendants.

Genesis 15:13-14

¹³And he said unto Abram, Know of a surety that thy seed shall be a stranger in a land that is not theirs, and shall serve them; and they shall afflict them four hundred years;

¹⁴And also that nation, whom they shall serve, will I judge: and afterward shall they come out with great substance.

What an amazing promise God made to Abraham concerning his descendants! God not only promised Abraham he would have a child of his own, God promised him a multitude! When you look at Abraham's story, it does not seem like what God promised him would ever come to pass. Around 15 years later, Abraham had only one son with his wife Sarah. Even though Abraham had other children, it would only be through the promised child, Isaac, that the nation of Israel would be established. When Isaac had children, it is not like he had a bunch. Isaac only had two kids with his wife Rebecca: twin boys, they named Jacob and Esau. Jacob went on to have twelve children. It was not until Jacob's (Israel) descendants (the children of Israel) went to live in Egypt, that they multiplied and grew into a nation of people. It was just as God promised Abraham hundreds of years preceding the actual event. Seventy people went into Egypt, and four hundred years later, they came out a nation of people!

Genesis 46:27

²⁷...All the persons of the house of Jacob who went to Egypt were seventy.

God's promise to Abraham came to pass! Even though Abraham was not alive to witness it, Abraham believed the Word of the Lord. Abraham along with many others died in **Faith** believing what God had promised them would become a physical reality.

Hebrews 11:13

¹³These all died in Faith, not having received the promises, but having seen them afar off, and were persuaded of them, and embraced them.

Are you beginning to understand how important **Faith** in God is to the believer? God wants for all His children to be in **Faith**.

Even Abraham's descendants had to learn this truth. You know what I love most about the Bible when I am reading it, it is the direct correlation of the Old and the New Testament teachings. I love the way God has taught some of the same lessons in the Old Testament in the New Testament. Writing this book has me so excited about the subject of **Faith**. I have learned **Faith** has always been an extremely essential element for God and His creation. From the book of Genesis God has showed us through many stories in the Bible, how important trust and confidence in Him truly is. As previously mentioned in the introduction, **Faith** is the dividing factor between the godly and the ungodly and between the seen and the unseen in this physical material world. It is **Faith** in God which makes the difference between the lives of the believer and the unbeliever.

When the time came for the children of Israel to be delivered from captivity, they had to learn who God was for themselves. Surely, they heard many stories about what God did in the lives of their ancestors, that were passed down from generation to generation. But now it was time for them to have their own relationship with God. It was time for them to get a lesson in **Faith-Style** living. Let us take a look at what was going on, prior to the Israelites deliverance from captivity.

Exodus 2:23-25

²³And it came to pass in process of time, that the king of Egypt died: and the children of Israel sighed by reason of the bondage, and they cried, and their cry came up unto God by reason of the bondage.

²⁴And God heard their groaning, and God remembered his covenant with Abraham, with Isaac, and with Jacob.

²⁵And God looked upon the children of Israel, and God had respect unto them.

God heard the children of Israel's cry, pleading for Him to release them from captivity. God then appeared to Moses instructing him to return to Egypt and be a part of the Israelites deliverance.

Exodus 3:7-8

⁷And the Lord said, I have surely seen the affliction of my people which are in Egypt, and have heard their cry by reason of their taskmasters; for I know their sorrows;

⁸And I am come down to deliver them out of the hand of the Egyptians, and to bring them up out of that land unto a good land and a large, unto a land flowing with milk and honey; unto the place of the Canaanites, and the Hittites, and the Amorites, and the Perizzites, and the Hivites, and the Jebusites.

God enlisted Moses to be His spokesperson. Moses would be speaking to the Israelites and Pharaoh on God's behalf. God then communicated to Moses, His plan to deliver the Israelites from out of the grips of Pharaoh. God also communicated to Moses, the land He had waiting for the children of Israel after their departure from Egypt. God never intended to deliver the Israelites from Egypt and leave them to figure everything else out on their own. No, not a chance! God had a plan for their deliverance, transition, health and wealth.

The greatest benefit of the promised land for the Israelites was, they did not have to work for or pay for the promised land. It was a land God was giving to them! A land they would only obtain by their **Faith** in the Word of the Lord! Don't believe me? Read it for yourself.

Deuteronomy 8:1-3

¹All the commandments which I command thee this day shall you observe to do, that ye may live, and multiply, and go in and possess the land which the Lord sware unto your forefathers.

²And thou shalt remember all the way which the Lord thy God led thee these forty years in the wilderness, to humble thee, and to prove thee, to know what was in thine heart, whether thou wouldest keep his commandments, or no.

³And He humbled thee, and suffered thee to hunger, and fed thee with manna, which thou knewest not, neither did thy fathers know; that he might make thee know that man does not live by bread only, but by every Word that proceedeth out of the mouth of the Lord doth man live.

I love what the Lord was doing in the lives of the children of Israel. He was taking them from a life of slavery and was bringing them into a life of freedom and abundance!

We know the Israelites were enslaved for over four hundred years and we can only imagine the mindset that was developed on the inside of them. They were mistreated and abused for all those years. Their self-esteem was so damaged that when Moses came to deliver the "good news" of their deliverance and the promised land, they probably could not even perceive how this would be possible.

I noticed while reading Leviticus, Numbers, Deuteronomy and Joshua, how many times Moses and then later Joshua, had to remind the children of Israel of God's promise. And I know I did not come across this by accident. I believe God was pointing this out to me for a reason. Moses was God's spokesperson. So, Moses would leave the Israelites for a time and go spend time with God. When Moses returned, he would share what God said with the Israelites. God through Moses was constantly telling the children of Israel, "I have given you the land to possess it." After seeing this numerous times, I immediately took out my pen and began to mark the top of the pages of my Bible with the words "Possess the Land" for every page I had seen the promise.

Why did God have Moses to constantly remind the Israelites of His promise? God did this because He was teaching them how to live by **Faith.** God was teaching them to believe Him without physically seeing Him or the land themselves. A New Testament scripture verse declares, *"So then **Faith** cometh by hearing, and hearing by the Word of God* (Romans 10:17)." So, the Israelites had to keep hearing the promise to magnify their **Faith** in God.

For so many years the Israelites were under the care of taskmasters, people who despised them and did not value their worth. So, the children of Israel's journey, was not to be spent in vain. No, not at all. God was using their time in the wilderness to "renew their minds" to the Word of the Lord. God wanted every negative behavior and thought pattern, such as bondage, fear and idol worship uprooted from their minds and hearts.

Ephesians 4:22-23 ESV

22To put off your old self, which belongs to your former manner of life and is corrupt through deceitful desires,

²³And to be renewed in the spirit of your minds,

God was also using their time in the wilderness to restore them to their rightful position in the earth.

Ephesians 4:24

²⁴And to put on the new self, created after the likeness of God in true righteousness and holiness.

God was also using their time in the wilderness to usher them into a loving Father and child relationship. He wanted to be their God and for them to be His people.

Leviticus 25:38

³⁸I am the Lord your God, which brought you forth out of the land of Egypt, to give you the land of Canaan, and to be your God.

For the children of Israel to know God, they had to spend time with God. They needed to learn God's ways. Everything they learned in Egypt needed to be uprooted out of their minds and hearts. When God told them the land was theirs, they were supposed to believe it no matter the obstacles they encountered. But instead this generation of Israelites rebelled against the Lord and forfeited their entrance into promised land. Let us take a look at what Moses said to the Israelites.

Deuteronomy 9:23

²³Likewise when the Lord sent you from Kadesh-barnea, saying Go up and possess the land which I have given you; then ye rebelled against the commandment of the Lord

your God, and ye believed him not, nor hearkened to his voice.

During their journey in the wilderness, the children of Israel should have been willing to learn everything they needed to learn. And they should have been saying what God said. They should have taken the promise and meditated on that promise, day and night. They should have meditated it until their situation lined up with God's promise. If they would have done this, they would have prospered and had good success (Joshua 1:8). Instead, they were labeled as *"Children in whom is no **Faith** (Deuteronomy 32:20)."*

This is what the Woman with the issue of blood did. She heard about Jesus, and all the people He healed. What Jesus was doing for so many others, gave her **Faith** for her situation. She said to herself (paraphrasing), "If Jesus did it for them, He can do it for me!" Let me translate this for you, ***"If the Word of God did it for them, the Word of God can do it for me!"*** This woman took the Word of God and meditated it. The Amplified translation says, *"For she kept saying to herself, If I only touch His garment, I shall be restored to health (Matthew 9:21)."* This woman had **Faith!** She kept declaring the results she wanted, and she received exactly what she was believing for!

Matthew 9:22 AMPC

[22]Jesus turned around and, seeing her, He said, Take courage, daughter! Your Faith has made you well. And at once the woman was restored to health.

This Woman took hold of the revelation of what God's Word could do for her situation. She "renewed her mind" to the Word of God and her body was immediately transformed! She was made whole!

I have a powerful testimony to share concerning "renewing your mind" to the Word of the Lord. Only God could help me in this situation. A situation arose in my life where I had to defend myself because of an allegation that was made against me. I must admit I was so scared. This meeting involved something that was very important to me and my family's livelihood at the time. I was nervous because every person I knew who had gone to this meeting did not have a chance at winning nor did they even have a chance to defend themselves. When I had received the letter in the mail stating I had to attend this meeting, my heart dropped. I was expecting to get the letter, but receiving it was something altogether different.

One day I was reading a devotional, and I came across an article that spoke to my situation. At the end of the article was this scripture, ***"But as for you, you thought evil against me; but God meant it unto good... (Genesis 50:20)."*** Every time the thought of this meeting would come to my mind, I read this scripture. Every time my heart began to beat rapidly at the thought of attending this meeting, I read this scripture. I remember one day I was leaving the gas station and I stopped at the traffic light and the thought of the meeting came to my mind. I pulled over and took out the devotional and read this scripture. I read this scripture numerous times up until the day of the meeting. I even read it before I entered the building where the meeting was being held and before anyone could step into the room, I pulled the devotional out from my purse and read this scripture.

When the meeting finally got underway, I thought for sure I was going to be interviewed by a panel, but it was only one person. She first read the report to me and then asked me to tell her what happened. I then proceeded to tell her my side of the story. As I was speaking, she looked at me with a very firm look on her face, I could not tell whether she believed me or not. As I kept talking, I seemed to have said something which resonated with her. She then looked over to me and nodded in agreement. She said, "Yea. I know what that feels like." She asked me more questions during the interview, and I answered them. She then got up from her chair with my paperwork in her hand, she walked over to the trash bin, ripped up the complaint against me and dropped it in the trash. She said, "Okay, we're done." I looked at her and asked, "Do I need to wait for a decision in the mail." She said, "No, it's over. You're fine." I could not see myself, but I could imagine the expression that was on my face. I was shocked! I could not stop thanking her. I walked out of the office thanking God because I knew it was only God who had given me the victory. God's Word went to work in that room. He put me with the person, who would give me the results, He wanted me to have. Everyone, and I mean everyone that had faced the same allegations as mine had lost. But God had given me the victory! I "renewed my mind" to His Word and just like the Woman with the issue of blood, His Word did for me what nobody else could. **Faith** in God's Word gave me the victory! This is what "renewing your mind" to the Word of the Lord does, it magnifies your **Faith** in God.

Romans 12:2

2And be not conformed to this world: but be ye transformed by the renewing of your mind, that you may prove what is that good and acceptable, and perfect, will of God.

God wants you in His good and acceptable and perfect will. He wants you whole and prosperous in every area of your life! "Renew your mind" to the Word of God, so you too, can be fully persuaded to go in and possess your promised land!

FAITH UNDER FIRE

T hat the trial of your Faith, being much more precious than of gold that perisheth, though it be tried with fire, might be found unto praise and honour and glory at the appearing of Jesus Christ (1 Peter 1:7).

One morning I got out of bed around three o'clock. I went to my office and began reading, praying and meditating—enjoying the time I was spending with the Lord. It was during this time I decided, I was going to pray and record my prayer. The reason I wanted to record my prayer is because I wanted to remember exactly what I prayed for and I wanted to be able to go back and check them off as God answered each one of my requests. As I picked up my cell phone and hit the voice recorder button to start, I started speaking about the events that transpired in me and my family's life from the year 2010. Let me tell you, my life changed dramatically over the course of this year. This is the year I like to say, I became "Saved for Real." I say this because throughout my life, I had responded to many altar calls. I would respond to them believing and receiving the message of salvation, but afterward I would find myself doing the same dumb things I did before going to the altar. During those years, I was a struggling teenage mother. I had my first daughter at the age of sixteen. I was tired of bad relationships and struggling financially. I wanted change badly, but I did not know how to bring forth this change.

In the year 2009, one day I was thinking about and assessing the years of my life. I was tired of the same existing circumstances that were greatly affecting me and my children's lives. I realized something had to change. It was in that moment, desperate for change, I decided to call out to God and give my life over to His will for my life. When I cried out, with all sincerity I uttered, "God, I just want to do your will. I do not want to live like this any longer."

This was a defining moment in my life. It was in that moment, I was declaring, enough is enough! I was establishing a boundary by making the decision, I will not continue to live like this any longer. When I did, things begin to change in my life. Little by little, they were changing. I began to lose interest in some of my old behavior patterns and trust me, I was quite pleased.

As previously mentioned, the year 2010 was a year of astronomical change for me. God really began to show me He was indeed answering my cry from 2009. This was the year I had a couple of amazing encounters with the Holy Ghost, I will never forget. The first encounter was at a meeting I attended. This meeting was totally life changing. I have never felt the power of God anywhere, as it was this day. The power of God was so strong that I could not contain myself. When I walked up for prayer the minister who was conducting the prayer, did not even touch me. She just motioned her hands as if she were tossing something over to me, and my body just fell back. I was balling and shaking so much. When I finally got up, I headed back toward my seat. Before I could sit down, I heard the voice of the Lord say, "Say goodbye to the old her and everything associated with her." From that day, my life began to change so fast. I felt like a new person. The things I used to do; I had no desire to do them anymore.

2 Corinthians 5:17

[17]Therefore if any man be in Christ, he is a new creature: old things have passed away; behold, all things are become new.

A couple of months later, I had another encounter with the Holy Spirit. This encounter was a powerful visitation from the Holy Spirit on December 16, 2010. Around 4 o'clock in the morning, I was awakened from my sleep, I arose and partially sat up in the bed. I began to hear these words audibly, *"I Hear the Sound of Abundance Rain."* I heard it over and over and over again. It was a soft gentle melodic voice, and there was an indescribable sound accompanying the voice. It was absolutely mystical! It was the voice of the Holy Ghost! Astonished, by what was happening I began looking around my room. I just sat there in awe. I could not believe what was happening, but it was happening. After the voice stopped speaking, I laid there gazing up to the ceiling. I said, "Lord, I don't know what just happened here, but it must be something good!"

This incredible experience made me think about the story in 1 Kings chapters 17 and 18. The story speaks about a time, there was no rain in the land for a period of three and a half years. As a result, there was an extreme drought in the land. The story shares how the prophet Elijah prayed for rain and the rain came. What I did not quite understand was how this would apply to my life. But I was excited! I felt like something good was about to happen!

During this time in my life, I was on welfare and low-income housing. God then began to deal with me to come off both forms of aid. At the time I was unemployed and in school because this is what God had me to do in this season of my life. A year prior to this, I lost my job as I explained in the chapter "Where is your Faith." But prior to working at this job, I had been on these two-government programs for some years. When I did obtain employment, and was able to come off welfare, I was so excited. When I lost my job, it was during the economy crash and I was discouraged because I had to revert to welfare after the unemployment checks ended. But during the time of my employment, God had been impressing upon me to go back to school. Going back to school was not something I was particularly happy about. I was already in my thirties and was not thinking about returning to school. Honestly, I felt that ship had long sailed. I was looking forward to seeing my children attend and graduate from college, not me.

When I lost my job, I began applying for other jobs. Let me just say, it was not happening. Eventually, around a year later I gave into the Word of the Lord and went to enroll in school. It appeared as soon as I made the decision to obey God, there were several program grants being cut and some were being done away with altogether. I became discouraged and wondered, "Lord, how am I going to be able to do this?"

When the Lord impressed upon me to come off government aid, I was still unemployed. But I felt an urgency to do what God said no matter what my conditions were. To be honest, I was tired of living like this. I wanted a better life and I did not want this life or mindset passing from generation to generation. I wanted my children to know this was not the life to live. I did not even know how I got there. But I knew God had a much better life in store for us. So, I complied with God and wrote letters to both agencies requesting to be removed from both programs. Coming off the housing program was the hardest. This program offered me and my family a roof over our heads. It did not matter how low my income was or how many times it changed. We would still have a roof over our heads. For example, because I was going to school and because my income was so low, I did not have to pay any rent. The housing subsidy paid the whole amount to my landlord. Not only did I not have to pay any rent, the housing authority sent me a check every month. To walk away from this was extremely difficult but I wanted to be obedient to the Lord and I wanted see change!

I was truly facing the unknown not knowing what was going to happen once I obeyed God. But I had to have **Faith** that God would be with me no matter what. One day, I wanted to eventually purchase a home. You see, I have always had a desire to live in a home that was my own. Staying in this program would not have allowed that. Not only would staying in the program prevented me from owning a home, it would have kept me trapped in the confines of poverty. This would have caused me to spend my life as an impoverished renter. Not ever knowing what it would be like to own my very own home and have the financial freedom I have always dreamed about. To be able to live the life God had originally created for me without settling for less. I figured if God was calling me out from these systems, He must have a plan in place. I just did not know what it was. But there is a promise located in the New Testament where we read Peter saying to Jesus personally, *"Lo, we have left all, and followed thee."* And Jesus answered and said, *"There is no man that has left house, or brethren, or sisters, or father, or mother, or wife, or children, or lands, for my sake, and the gospels, But he shall receive an hundredfold now in this time, houses, and brethren, and sisters, and mothers, and children, and* *lands, with persecutions; and in the world to come eternal life* (Mark 10:28-30)." And what about this promise, *"And God is able to make all grace (every favor and earthly blessing) come to you in abundance, so that you may always and under all circumstances and whatever the need be self-sufficient [possessing enough to require no aid or support and furnished in abundance for every good work and charitable donation]* (2 Corinthians 9:8)." These are incredible promises to have and to hold on to!

I did not go public with every family member or any friends with the decision I made. I believe I only shared this with two family members. I did not want to hear any negativity or the opinions of others, even though I knew they would only be voicing their concerns.

These were times of trials and testing – my **faith** was under fire! My family endured some serious hardships during these times. Eventually, we were evicted from our home. My grandmother and cousin passed away within six months of each other. They were the only two people I confided in regarding my decision. My son was getting into trouble and was eventually sentenced to time in jail. I was devastated. Because of the stress, sickness entered my body (I will speak more about this in the chapter "Testimony of **Faith-Style** Living"). I began doing horribly in school and my family thought I was absolutely nuts! They were probably thinking it was just another dumb life decision and I was deserving of the consequences.

This situation reminds me of when Moses left the comfort of Egypt to dwell in an unfamiliar land for forty long years. Hebrews 11:24-26 states, *"By Faith Moses, when he was come to years, refused to be called the son of Pharaoh's daughter; Choosing rather to suffer affliction with the people of God, then to enjoy the pleasures of sin for a season; Esteeming the reproach of Christ greater riches than the treasures in Egypt: for he had respect unto the recompense of the reward."*

Now, by all means I was not leaving royalty and riches behind like Moses, but I was leaving the comfort of having something I needed. Can you imagine what the people in Moses' circle was thinking about him for leaving the status and wealth of Egypt behind? Although Moses originally descended from Hebrew slaves, Moses was an Egyptian prince. When Pharaoh's daughter took him in and adopted him as her own child, Moses became royalty because he was adopted into the royal family. But when Moses became of age and witnessed the mistreatment of his people, the Hebrews, he became dissatisfied with the Egyptian lifestyle. Instead, Moses chose to suffer with the people of God rather than to enjoy the pleasures of sin for a season (Hebrews 11:25).

Surely, there were some people that did not agree with Moses' decision. Even while reading Moses' story in the Bible today, there may be some that say, "Wow, Moses turned his back on the status, riches, notoriety and comforts of Egypt to go live on the backside of a desert." But like Moses, instead of looking back to what I was losing, I needed to keep my eyes on the One who was calling me out of this lifestyle of bondage and limitation, no matter the consequences.

Hebrews 11:27

27By Faith he forsook Egypt not fearing the wrath of the king: for he endured, as seeing him who is invisible.

Moses resided on the backside of the desert until it was time for God to call him out. God had an amazing purpose and plan for Moses' life. Moses would assist God with His plan to deliver the Israelites from the hands of their Egyptian taskmasters. By this time, generations of Israelites had been enslaved for hundreds of years. The Israelites were so vexed by the mistreatment they suffered; they began to cry out to God for deliverance.

Exodus 2:23

23And it came to pass in process of time, that the king of Egypt died: and the children of Israel sighed by reason of the bondage, and they cried, and their cry came up unto God by reason of the bondage.

God heard the children of Israel's cry and decided it was time for them to be released from captivity. God appeared to Moses in the form of a burning bush, instructing Moses to return to Egypt. When God began to communicate His plan to Moses, naturally, Moses had reservations about what God was asking him to do. Moses had been living his new life for forty years. Moses was married and had a new family. Moses made many excuses, justifying in his own mind, why he could not adhere to God's request. Let us take a look at the many excuses Moses made to God.

Exodus 3:11

11And Moses said unto God, Who am I, that I should go unto Pharaoh, and that I should bring forth the children of Israel out of Egypt?

Exodus 4:1

¹And Moses answered and said, But, behold, they will not believe me, nor hearken unto my voice: for they will say, the Lord hath not appeared unto thee.

Exodus 4:10

¹⁰And Moses said unto the Lord, O my Lord, I am not eloquent, neither heretofore, nor since thou hast spoken unto thy servant: but I am slow of speech, and of a slow tongue.

Throughout their entire conversation, God addressed every concern Moses shared. God assured Moses; He would be with him every step of the way. After God persuaded Moses to take on his new life's assignment, it was time for Moses to return to Egypt. When Moses arrived in Egypt, Moses met with his brother Aaron to share God's plan for their deliverance. Afterwards, Moses and Aaron assembled with the other Israelites to share God's plan.

Exodus 4:29-31

²⁹And Moses and Aaron went and gathered together all the elders of the children of Israel:

³⁰And Aaron spake all the words which the Lord had spoken unto Moses, and did the signs in the sight of the people.

³¹And the people believed; and when they heard that the Lord had visited the children of Israel, and that He had looked upon their affliction, then they bowed their heads and worshipped.

Can you imagine how excited the Israelites were to hear, God sent them someone to relieve them from years of pain and suffering? Now, it was time for Moses and Aaron to confront Pharaoh and give him the Lord's command, *"Let my people go!"* Moses, Aaron and the children of Israel's **Faith** would be tried at this time. Let us take a look at what transpired next.

Exodus 5:1-3

¹And afterward Moses and Aaron went in, and told Pharaoh, Thus saith the Lord God of Israel, Let my people go, that they may hold a feast unto me in the wilderness.

²And Pharaoh said, Who is the Lord, that I should obey his voice to let Israel go? I know not the Lord, neither will I let Israel go.

³And they said, The God of the Hebrews hath met with us; let us go, we pray thee, three days' journey into the desert, and sacrifice unto the Lord our God; lest he fall upon us with pestilence, or with the sword.

As you can imagine, Pharaoh was not happy to hear the Lord's command. Pharaoh was most likely thinking within himself (paraphrasing), "How dare these Hebrews come to me speaking about a God I know nothing of and demanding I free my slaves. I'm the king of Egypt!"

After Moses released the Word of the Lord, Pharaoh became angry. He became so angry that he commanded the children of Israel's work to be made more rigorous. Pharaoh was subjecting them to even more cruel and severe bondage. Pharaoh used his brutal tactics to shift the blame for the children of Israel's punishment onto Moses and Aaron.

Pharaoh was most likely thinking the Israelites would not think to send Moses and Aaron to him again with this request. Let us take a look at what transpired next. These next verses illustrate extreme **Faith** under fire!

Exodus 5:4-19

⁴And the king of Egypt said unto to them, Wherefore do ye, Moses and Aaron, let the people from their works? Get you unto your burdens.

⁵And Pharaoh said, Behold, the people of the land now are many, and ye make them rest from their burdens.

⁶And Pharaoh commanded the same day the taskmasters of the people, and their officer saying,

⁷Ye shall no more give the people straw to make bricks, as heretofore; let them go and gather straws for themselves.

⁸And the tale of bricks, which they did make heretofore, ye shall lay upon them; ye shall not diminish aught thereof: for they be idle; therefore they cry, saying, Let us go and sacrifice to our God.

⁹Let there more work be laid upon the men, that they may labour therein; and let them not regard vain words.

¹⁰And the taskmasters of the people went out, and their officers, and they spake to the people, saying, Thus saith Pharaoh, I will not give you straw.

¹¹Go ye, get you straw where you can find it: yet not aught of your work shall be diminished.

¹²So the people were scattered abroad throughout all the land of Egypt to gather stuble instead of straw.

¹³And the taskmasters hasted them, saying, Fulfil your works, your daily task, as when there was straw.

¹⁴And the officers of the children of Israel, which Pharaoh's taskmasters had set over them, were beaten, and demanded, Wherefore have ye not fulfilled your task in making brick both yesterday and to day, as heretofore?

¹⁵Then the officers of the children of Israel came and cried unto Pharaoh, saying, Wherefore dealest thou thus with thy servants?

¹⁶There is no straw given unto thy servants, and they say to us, Make brick: and behold, thy servants are beaten; but the fault is in thine own people.

¹⁷But he said, Ye are idle, ye are idle: therefore ye say, Let us go and do sacrifice to the Lord.

¹⁸Go therefore now, and work; for there shall no straw be given you, yet shall you deliver the tale of bricks.

¹⁹And the officers of the children of Israel did see that they were in evil case, after it was said, Ye shall not minish aught from your bricks of your daily task.

All these verses were cited, so you could see exactly what transpired between Moses, Pharaoh and the children of Israel. The Israelites were being treated much worse than before God sent Moses to help them. Because of Moses and Aaron's demands, Pharaoh stopped supplying the Israelites with the materials they needed to do their work. They were now expected to locate the materials they needed to perform their work which took a lot of time. And they were still expected to fulfill their daily quotas. Because of this, the children of Israel became so furious with Moses and Aaron.

Exodus 5:20-21

²⁰And they met Moses and Aaron, who stood in the way, as they came forth from Pharaoh:

²¹And they said unto them, The Lord look upon you, and judge; because ye have made our savour to be abhorred in the eyes of Pharaoh, and in the eyes of his servants, to put a sword in their hand to slay us.

After hearing the Israelite's complaints, Moses was infuriated and went to God for answers.

Exodus 5:22-23

²²And Moses returned to the Lord, and said, Lord, wherefore hast thou so evil entreated this people? Why is it that thou hast sent me?

²³For since I came to Pharaoh to speak in thy name, he hath done evil to this people; neither hast thou delivered thy people at all.

In the next chapter, God assures Moses He will deliver the children of Israel, but their deliverance would come in the way God would choose to deliver them. God was going to show Pharaoh and every other pagan king, who the one true living God is. The Lord said to Moses, *"Now shalt thou see what I will do to Pharaoh: for with a strong hand shall he let them go, and with a strong hand shall he drive them out of his land. And God spake unto Moses and said unto him, I am the Lord (Exodus 6:1-2)."*

Before Moses returned to Egypt, God communicated to Moses the amazing promise He had for the Israelites. God was giving them a picture of their future as an assurance to their deliverance. God was going to allow the Israelites to receive compensation for the years they were enslaved, their freedom, and a new home in a new land. Let us take a look at the promise God gave to Moses for the children of Israel prior to Moses' arrival in Egypt.

Exodus 3:15-22

15And God said moreover unto Moses, thus shall thou say unto the children of Israel, The Lord God of your fathers, the God of Abraham, of Isaac, and the God of Jacob, hath sent me unto you; this is my name forever and this is my memorial unto all generations.

16Go, and gather the elders of Israel together, and say unto them, The Lord God of your fathers, the God of Abraham, Isaac, and Jacob, appeared unto me, saying, I have surely visited you, and seen that which is done to you in Egypt:

17And I have said, I will bring you up out of the affliction of Egypt unto the land of the Canaanites, and the Hittites, and the Amorites, and the Perrizites, and the Hivites, and the Jebusites, unto a land flowing with milk and honey.

18And they shall hearken to thy voice; and thou shall come, thou and the elders of Israel, unto the king of Egypt, and ye shall say unto him, the lord God of the Hebrews has met with us; and now let us go, we beseech thee, three days journey into the wilderness, that we may sacrifice to the Lord our God.

19And I am sure that the king of Egypt will not let you go, no, not by a mighty hand.

20And I will stretch out my hand, and smite Egypt with all my wonders which I will do in the midst thereof; and after that he will let you go.

21And I will give this people favor in the sight of the Egyptians; and it shall come to pass, that, when you go, ye shall not go empty;

22But every woman shall borrow of her neighbor, and of her that sojourneth in her house, jewels of silver, jewels of gold, and raiment; and ye shall put them upon your sons, and upon your daughter's and ye shall spoil the Egyptians.

God had an incredible life planned for the children of Israel. God had a promised land waiting for them. It was a land that flowed with milk and honey! It was a land that God designed to perpetually provide them with everything they would need and more. Let us read the description of the land located in Deuteronomy chapters 8 and 11.

Deuteronomy 8:7-9

7For the Lord thy God bringeth thee into a good land, a land of brooks of water, of fountains and depths that spring out of valleys and hills;

8A land of wheat, and barley, and vines, and fig trees, and pomegranates; a land of olive oil, and honey;

9A land wherein thou shalt eat bread without scarceness, thou shalt not lack anything in it; a land whose stones are iron, and out of whose hills thou mayest dig brass.

Deuteronomy 11:11-12

11But the land, whither ye go to possess it, is a land of hills and valleys, and drinketh water of the rain of heaven:

12A land which the Lord thy God careth for; the eyes of the Lord thy God are always upon it, from the beginning of the year even until the end of the year.

We can see God had a prepared, provision-filled place awaiting the Israelites' arrival. This place was a picture of heaven on earth! Although the Israelites' **Faith** was tried and tested during this time, not only would they walk out of Egypt as pure gold, they would leave Egypt with plenty of gold in their hands! God allowed the Israelites to walk out of Egypt with the wealth of Egypt, just as He promised.

Exodus 12:35-36

35And the children of Israel did according to the word of Moses; and they borrowed of the Egyptians jewels of silver, and jewels of gold, and raiment;

36And the Lord gave the people favor in the sight of the Egyptians, so that they lent unto them such things as they required. And they spoiled the Egyptians.

Wow, what a deliverance! The children of Israel were set for life! Although they encountered more cruelty from the Egyptians, God was setting them up to come out of Egypt with the wealth of the people that were enslaving them. Glory to God!

James 1:2-4

2My brethren, count it all joy when you fall into divers temptations;

3Knowing this, that the trying of your Faith, worketh patience.

⁴But let patience have her perfect work, that ye may be perfect and entire, wanting nothing.

Another story that demonstrates **Faith** under fire, is the story of Abraham. In *Genesis 12:1 it says, "Now the Lord had said unto Abram, get thee out of thy country, and from thy kindred, and from thy father's house, unto a land that I will shew thee."* Someone reading the story of Abraham's life for the first time might wonder why God would call Abraham away from his country and relatives at 75 years old. Why would God be asking Abraham to leave everything and everyone he loved behind? We can learn the answers to these questions in the book of Joshua, it provides us with a little history on Abraham's family.

Joshua 24:2

²And Joshua said unto all the people, Thus saith the Lord God of Israel, Your fathers dwelt on the other side of the flood in old time, even Terah, the father of Abraham, and the father of Nahor: and they served other gods.

According to the book of Joshua, Abraham and his family worshipped idols. They believed in and served several false gods and not the one true living God. This information about Abraham's family causes me to wonder if Abraham desired a different life beyond the life he was living. Did Abraham, somehow know deep down in his heart, the one true God loved him and had a different life planned for him. Whatever the case, God did in fact have an amazing plan for Abraham's life. A life Abraham could have never imagined for himself. In reading Genesis 12:1 in the Amplified translation, I noticed something I do not think I have ever noticed before. Please read the scripture below!

Genesis 12:1 AMPC

¹Now [in Haran] the Lord said to Abram, Go for yourself [for your own advantage] away from your country, from your relatives and your father's house, to the land that I will show you.

This scripture verse implies, what God was asking Abraham to do, was for Abraham's own advantage! Please proceed to read the next two verses!

Genesis 12:2-3 AMPC

²And I will make of you a great nation, and I will bless you [with abundant increase of favors] and make your name famous and distinguished, and you will be a blessing [dispensing good to others].

³And I will bless those who bless you [who confer prosperity or happiness upon you] and curse him who curses or uses insolent language toward you; in you will all the families of the earth be blessed [and by you they will bless themselves].

Do you see the amazing promises and blessings God was bestowing onto Abraham? It sounds like God was giving Abraham the deal of a lifetime! But wait. Abraham may have had some reservations about leaving his family and the region he lived in for most of his life. All these things were familiar to him for so many years. God was asking Abraham to leave his place of comfort and venture out into the unknown. But I do not believe Abraham had any reservations about what God was asking him to do. The book of Hebrews reveals how receptive Abraham was to God's request.

Hebrews 11:8 AMPC

[8][Urged on] by Faith Abraham, when he was called, obeyed and went forth to a place which he was destined to receive as an inheritance; and went, although he did not know or trouble his mind about where he was to go.

Abraham had great **Faith** in God! This verse implies, even though Abraham did not know where he was going, it did not trouble his mind to know where he was going. This causes me to wonder if Abraham had a desire for change. Was it on the mind and heart of Abraham that it had to be more to life than this?

Although Abraham was obedient to the Word of God and willingly took a step of **Faith**, Abraham did encounter some troubles along the way. When Abraham departed from Haran, Abraham did arrive at his destination, the country of Canaan. But later it says, Abraham continued to journey southward. I am not sure why Abraham left Canaan but afterward he encountered a grievous famine. It would be in this moment Abraham's **Faith** in God would be tested.

When Abraham was preparing to depart from Haran, the Bible clearly states he took all the substance he had gathered (Genesis 12:5). This tells me that Abraham was not without means on this journey. Plainly said. Abraham was not broke! Abraham made a living in his country and he had plenty to sustain him and his family before he left Haran. But to escape the famine, Abraham made the decision to depart from where he was and to travel to Egypt. He decided to live in Egypt temporarily until the famine subsided.

Before Abraham and Sarah entered Egypt, Abraham said to Sarah, *"Therefore it shall come to pass, when the Egyptians shall see thee, that they shall say, This is his wife: and they will kill me, but they will save thee alive. Say, I pray thee, thou art me sister: that it may be well with me for thy sake; and my soul shall live because of thee (Genesis 12:12-13)."*

The very thing Abraham feared would happen, did in fact happen. As soon as Abraham and Sarah entered Egypt, the Egyptians immediately noticed Sarah's beauty.

Genesis 12:14-15

14And it came to pass, that, when Abram was come into Egypt, the Egyptians beheld the woman that she was very fair.

15The princes also of Pharaoh saw her, and commended her before Pharaoh: and the woman was taken into Pharaoh's house.

Can you imagine how devastated Abraham must have been? His wife was in the home of another man. Although this was a very challenging time for Abraham, the Egyptians treated Abraham well because of Sarah (Genesis 12:16).

Genesis 12:16

16And he entreated Abram well for her sake: and he had sheep, and oxen, and he asses, and menservants, and maidservants, and she asses, and camels.

Abraham was given a great supply of material wealth, but his wife was still in another man's home. This could not have been a good feeling for Abraham despite the gifts he was given. But the most amazing aspect of Abraham's story is how God used this challenging time to bless Abraham's life immeasurably.

God used the famine and the apprehension of Abraham's wife to transfer the wealth of the wicked into Abraham's hands. God did not have this king take Abraham's wife, but He used the situation to permit Abraham to be recompensed for his pain and suffering. Now it was time for God to deliver Abraham's wife out of the hands of Pharaoh and return her to her husband. God was not going to allow Pharaoh to keep Abraham's wife in his home a moment longer. Let us take a look at what transpired between God and Pharaoh.

Genesis 12:17-20

¹⁷And the Lord plagued Pharaoh and his house with great plagues because of Sarai Abram's wife.

¹⁸And Pharaoh called Abram, and said, What is this that thou hast done unto me? why didst thou not tell me that she was thy wife?

¹⁹Why saidst thou, She is my sister? so I might have taken her to me to wife: now therefore behold thy wife, take her, and go thy way.

²⁰And Pharaoh commanded his men concerning him: and they sent him away, and his wife, and all that he had.

Genesis 13:1-2

¹And Abram went up out of Egypt, he, and his wife, and all that he had...

²And Abram was very rich in cattle, in silver, and in gold.

Look at everything that was added to Abraham's life! I guess we can see the purpose of Abraham leaving Canaan and traveling to Egypt. God had a plan to prosper him! But wait, there is more! God blessed Abraham with the wealth of a pagan king not once but twice in Abraham's life. You can read about the second transfer of wealth in Genesis chapter 20. The Bible later states, **God blessed Abraham in all things (Genesis 24:1)!** This was truly for Abraham's own advantage!

1 Peter 5:10-11

¹⁰But the God of all grace, who hath called us unto his eternal glory by Christ Jesus, after that ye have suffered a while, make you perfect, stablish, strengthen, settle you,

¹¹To him be glory and dominion for ever and ever. Amen.

I could not have completed this chapter without the mention of this story. In the book of Daniel lies a story that exhibits extreme **faith** under fire, literally! It is the story of three Hebrew boys who were forced to go and live in Babylon after their country was besieged by the Babylonian king, Nebuchadnezzar. The three Hebrew boys, Hananiah, Mishael and Azariah, entered Babylon as teenagers. As a part of their captivity protocol, their names were later changed to Meshach, Shadrach, and Abednego. They were assigned to serve in the Babylonian king's palace. Meshach, Shadrach, and Abednego were not just any children, they were privileged and knowledgeable children, they were descendants from the king of Judah's seed.

Daniel 1:4

⁴Children in whom was no blemish, but well favored, and skillful in all wisdom, and cunning in knowledge, and understanding science, and such as had ability in them to stand in the king's palace, and whom they might teach the learning and the tongue of the Chaldeans.

While Meshach, Shadrach, and Abednego were working in Nebuchadnezzar's palace, the king decided to build a golden statue (idol) for all the people of Babylon to worship. After the statue was built, there was a decree issued regarding the statue. Let us take a look at the king's decree.

Daniel 3:4-6

⁴Then an herald cried aloud, To you it is commanded, O people, nations, and languages,

⁵That at what time ye hear the sound of the cornet, flute, harp, sackbut, psaltery, dulcimer, and all kinds of musick ye fall down and worship the golden image that Nebuchadnezzar the king has set up;

⁶And whoso falleth not down and worship shall the same hour be cast into the midst of a burning fiery furnace.

As we read in the scripture verse above, the king's decree was; when the music played, everyone in Babylon had to bow down and worship the golden image no matter who you were, where you were from or what you believed. The decree further stated; whoever did not comply with the king's request, they would be thrown into a burning fiery furnace to die. So, when all the people of the land heard the instruments, they had to bow down and worship the golden image.

Daniel 3:7

⁷Therefore at that time, when all of the people heard the sound of the cornet, flute, harp, sackbut, psaltery, and all kinds of musick, all the people, the nations, and the languages, fell down and worshipped the golden image that Nebuchadnezzar the king has set up.

When the decree came, everyone except the three Hebrew boys bowed down to worship the golden image. It was then brought to the king's attention, Meshach, Shadrach, and Abednego did not bow down to worship his statue. When the king heard this, he became angry and confronted the Hebrew boys. Let us take a look at the Hebrew boys' response to the king.

Daniel 3:16-18

16Shadrach, Meshach, and Abednego, answered and said to the king, O Nebuchadnezzar, we are not careful to answer thee in this matter.

17If it be so, our God whom we serve is able to deliver us from the burning fiery furnace, and he will deliver us out of thine hand, O king.

18But if not, be it known unto thee, O king, that we will not serve thy gods, nor worship the golden image which thou hast set up.

Wow, these three Hebrew boys were bold! You can hear **Faith** in their words! These boys had some serious **Faith** in God! Shadrach, Meshach, and Abednego were threatened to be thrown into an actual burning fiery furnace, but they were not moved, they held onto their convictions. They chose to remain faithful to their one true living God.

Nebuchadnezzar was so angry, the Bible states, *"He was full of fury* (Daniel 3:19)!" In his anger, he instructed his mighty men to adjust the furnace seven times hotter than it was before. The king then commanded them to grab hold of Meshach, Shadrach and Abednego and tie them up. The mighty men tied them up and proceeded to throw them into the furnace. The flames were so hot that the very men who threw them into the furnace were killed by the flames themselves. Let us take a look at what transpired when the three Hebrew boys were in the burning fiery furnace.

Daniel 3:23-27

23And these three men, Shadrach, Meshach, and Abednego, fell down bound into the midst of the burning fiery furnace.

24Then Nebuchadnezzar the king was astonied, and rose up in haste, and spake, and said unto his counselors, did not we cast three men bound into the midst of the fire? They answered and said unto the king, true, O king

25He answered and said, Lo, I see four men loose, walking in the midst of the fire, and they have no hurt; and the form of the fourth is like the Son of God.

26Then Nebuchadnezzar came near to the mouth of the burning fiery furnace, and spake, and said, Shadrach, Meshach, and Abednego, ye servants, of the most high God, come forth, and come hither. Then Shadrach, Meshach, Abednego came forth of the midst of the fire.

27And the princes, governors, and the captains, and the king's counselors, being gathered together, saw these men, upon who's bodies the fire had no power, nor was an hair on their head singed, neither were their coats changed, nor the smell of fire have passed on them.

Glory to God! Everyone reading this story should be inspired in some way or another regarding their **Faith**. These three

Hebrew boys held onto their convictions! They told the king as politely as they could, they were not going to bow down and worship his idol. They knew God would deliver them!

There are so many remarkable aspects to this story, but I will only discuss three of them. First, Nebuchadnezzar witnessed the three men who were tied up and thrown into the fire, were no longer bound! Second, Nebuchadnezzar witnessed another man walking in the fire with them! The Bible states, Nebuchadnezzar looked into the furnace and said, *"Lo, I see four men loose, walking in the midst of the fire, and they have no hurt; and the form of the fourth is like the Son of God* (Daniel 3:25)." Glory to God! This story is amazing! Their extraordinary **Faith** brought Jesus to the scene personally! Third, the Son of God showed up and kept them untouched, and unharmed. The fire could not burn them or kill them! Jesus ensured their safety amid an impossible situation. Jesus came to show this wicked king who the one true living God is. Nebuchadnezzar knew that what he witnessed; no idol could ever do. During Shadrach, Meshach and Abednego's time of severe trial and testing, Nebuchadnezzar witnessed that God was with these boys!

Daniel 3:28-30

28Then Nebuchadnezzar spake, and said, Blessed be the God of Shadrach, Meshach and Abednego, who has sent his angel, and delivered his servants that trusteth in him, and have changed the king's word, and yielded their bodies, that they might not serve nor worship any god, except their own God.

29Therefore I make a decree, that every people, nation, and language, which speak anything amiss against the God of

Shadrach, Meshach, and Abednego, shall be cut in pieces, and their houses shall be made a dunghill; because there is no other God that can deliver after this sort.

30Then the king promoted Shadrach, Meshach, and Abednego, in the province of Babylon

Shadrach, Meshach, and Abednego held on to their convictions! They fought the good fight of **Faith** (1 Timothy 6:12). Shadrach, Meshach, and Abednego went from being almost killed, to being promoted by the same king who was trying to kill them. This is what I call **Faith-Style** living!

James 1:12

12Blessed is the man that endureth temptation: for when he is tried, he shall receive the crown of life, which the Lord hath promised to them that love him.

I am so thankful these stories in the Bible exist. God has made them available to us to serve as examples to us. They are **Faith** builders and **Faith** encouragers for us. These stories also exist to remind us, when we cry out to God for change or God calls us out of certain situations, He is not obligated to deliver us in the way we would choose to be delivered. And He rarely delivers us in the most comfortable ways we would choose for ourselves. God knows the best route of deliverance for His children.

Writing about these stories and sharing my own **Faith** testimonies have caused me to see the most important aspect of them all. God was giving all of us a lesson on **Faith-style** living. Again, what is this **Faith**? Hebrews 11:1 describes it as, *"Now Faith is the substance (ground, confidence) of things hoped for, the evidence of things not seen."*

As I was reading over the definition of **Faith** again, I felt impressed to look up the definition for ground. The legal dictionary defines ground as, a rational motive, basis for a belief or conviction for an action taken. When we transfer this definition over to **Faith** it means, we have a rational motive, the basis to believe and conviction for the action taken to obtain God's promise.

I heard these adages spoken by two powerful men of God regarding living by **Faith.**

1). "If you are willing to look like a fool for a while," Bishop T.D. Jakes.

2). "Your **Faith** will often put you in a place of ridicule," Dr. Bill Winston.

Child of God, when you live by **Faith,** not everyone in your circle will understand why you believe what you believe or why you do the things you do. When God gives you a promise, you must be like a track and field relay runner. Take hold of the promise, focus and run with all your might until you reach the finish line. The manifestation of your promise!

In every story provided throughout this book, you can see God was delivering all of us from some type of man-made system. *As "People of Faith" we should know, we are not confined by or limited to the practices of this world and its ways.* When we live God's way, we will be ushered into the supernatural realm of prospering God's way.

1 John 5:4 WNT

4For every child of God overcomes the world; and the victorious principle which has overcome the world is our Faith.

I am so glad I stepped out on the Word of God regarding leaving government aid. When I put my trust in God, He blessed my life in some amazing ways! It was during these times of trials and testing; God was relieving me from the pains of my past. He was using the fiery furnace to extinguish every impurity that would keep me from walking out my God-given destiny. This book is a product of being in that fiery furnace. May it be a blessing to every one of you.

Isaiah 48:10 NASB

10Behold, I have refined you, but not as silver; I have tested you in the furnace of affliction.

Job 23:10 HCSB

10Yet He knows the way I have taken; when He has tested me, I will emerge as pure gold.

Faith-Style living: The Just shall live by **Faith**! There's Just no other way to live!

TESTIMONY OF FAITH-STYLE LIVING

As we come to the close of this book, it is my prayer that you have come into the knowledge of how important **Faith** is to the believer. Living in a world where most are saturated with the ways of the world, we must really learn how to live God's way. We must aim ourselves at being God pleasers and not man pleasers. No matter how foolish or imprudent we may seem to others. We must always remember what the Bible teaches us about who we are. We are in this world but not of this world (John 17:16). As "People of **Faith**" when we are believing God to make the impossible, possible in our lives, the biggest test of our **Faith** will be to have the patience to endure no matter what we are seeing with our natural eyes. We must stand on our beliefs and call those things that be not as though they were until we see the manifestation of our promise (Romans 4:17).

I know how difficult it can be to hold on to your profession of **Faith**, especially when you are seeing people living in a way totally opposite from you and it seems like they are getting everything they want. But do not be dismayed or discouraged. And please do not give up. If **Faith** in God is all you have, what you have is irrevocably priceless!

You know why living by **Faith** is so important to God? When you look at the way the world system is set up, money is a huge factor in everything. It tells us how we can live, where we can live, what we can and cannot afford, and what we can and cannot buy. I believe the reason why God wants us to live by **Faith** is because He wants our priorities in the right place. You see, when you live by **Faith,** you are looking to God to meet your needs and not what you can achieve in your own strength. As I have said many times already, **Faith** is God's modus operandi. It is the way of life God established from the beginning of time. It was by the Word of God and **Faith,** the earth and everything in it was made.

Hebrews 11:3 NET

By Faith we understand that the worlds were set in order at God's command, so that the visible has its origin in the visible.

We can see by reading the verse above when God created the world, He did not use anything that was visible to the natural eye. God used His **Faith**-filled Words to bring forth the results He wanted. This brings us back to the definition of **Faith**, *"Now Faith is the substance of things hoped for, the evidence of things not seen (Hebrews 11: 1)."*

The Bible reveals to us the condition of the earth, prior to God's supernatural intervention. It describes the earth as without form, void, and dark. Although the earth was in this condition, we do not read anywhere where God said (paraphrasing), "This place is hopeless. It has no form. It is empty and it is dark. There is nothing I can possibly do to change this!" No, not at all. God is the Supreme Being and Creator. God did not allow the physical appearance of the earth to deter Him from turning the earth into the place He knew it could be. God decided to take this structureless, empty and dark place and form it into what He wanted it to be. As I mentioned in the chapter "Where **Faith** Began" God is not a fan of lack or darkness, so He immediately went to work shaping and filling the earth. God turned the earth into the beautiful, provision filled place He knew it could be. There are many beautiful places in the earth today, but I truly believe the Garden of Eden was so beautiful and extravagant that we have not yet seen anything like it! It was a picture of heaven on earth! We cannot even imagine the splendor it held. The point I am trying to make here is, God did not use anything that was visible to the natural eyes to create this highly esteemed work of art. God used His Word spoken in **Faith** to turn the earth into what He wanted it to be!

God's incredible example of **Faith** demonstrated in Genesis chapters 1 and 2, is the same **Faith** God desires for us to live by today. God does not want our primary focus to be on what we can see. No not all! That is not the life God had in mind for His children. God is unwavering in the way He want His children to live. The Just to live by **Faith**! God does not want His children seeing things, money, or people as our only source of supply. It is our **Faith** in God that meets and supplies our every need.

Philippians 4:19.

¹⁹But my God shall supply all your need according to His riches in glory by Christ Jesus.

God wants **Faith** to be the priority of the believer. **Faith** in God is infallible. Things, money and people are not. We must be completely honest with ourselves if we want to get on the right path of **Faith-Style** living. In Matthew chapter 6, Jesus implores us to get our priorities straight. Jesus tells us "twice" to take no thought for our lives. Jesus is telling us God knows we have need of these things. If God cares for the birds of the air, and clothes the grass in the fields. How much more will He do for the people of **Faith**? The people God created in His image and after His likeness.

While going over these things with the disciples, Jesus makes the comment, *"O ye of little **Faith** (Matthew 6:30)?"* Why does Jesus tell the disciples they have little **Faith**? *I believe it was because the disciples kept going back to natural thinking while Jesus was teaching them supernatural living. Jesus was delivering them from their old way of life!*

As God's elect, our **Faith** should always be in Him. When we put our **Faith** in God, He will bless us to live the abundant life His Son came to give us! Let us read over these verses again!

Matthew 6:30-33 MSG

If God gives such attention to the appearance of wildflowers - most of which are never seen - don't you think he'll attend to you, take pride in you, do his best for you? What I'm trying to do here is to get you to relax, to not be so preoccupied with getting, so you can respond to God's giving. People who don't know God and the way He works fuss over these things, but you know both God and how He works. Steep your life in God-reality, God-initiative, God-provisions. Don't worry about missing out. You will find all your everyday human concerns will be met.

These are powerful verses of scripture! Again, Jesus is teaching us all about priority. He is showing us where our **Faith** and confidence should be. Our **Faith** should be in God, who will provide us with what we need, to live in the place He has placed us to live. This is what God did for Adam and Eve with the Garden of Eden. If God provided all these things for them, we must believe He will provide for us as well.

In reading over these verses again, I know what Jesus is asking us to do, will definitely take some **Faith** for us to do. Why? Because Jesus' teachings are so contrary to the ways of the world. The world's system teaches us to get a good education and a career as if these things will guarantee us the life we desire to live. As I have mentioned many times, there is absolutely nothing wrong with having a good education and a good career. God can and will use these things to bless us. But God wants us to put first things first and this is, to seek first the Kingdom of God and His righteousness, with the promise of everything we need being added to us!

Matthew 6:33

³³**But seek ye first the kingdom of God, and His righteousness; and all these things shall be added unto you.**

Abraham's story is the perfect example of seeing this scripture in operation. Abraham's magnificent **Faith** in God afforded him everything he could possibly need and want. Abraham's **Faith** in God along with obedience to God's Word added undeniable riches to Abraham's life. Abraham had such a spectacular testimony; Abraham's servant is shown telling Abraham's relatives back home, all the wonderful things God has done in Abraham's life. Let us take a look at Abraham's servant, sharing Abraham's incredible testimony!

Genesis 24:35-36

³⁵**And the Lord hath blessed my master greatly; and he is become great: and he hath given him flocks, and herds and**

silver, and gold, and menservants, and maidservants, and camels, and asses.

[36]And Sarah my master's wife bare a son to my master when she was old: and to him hath he given all that he hath.

Not only did Abraham's servant share with Abraham's relatives, how wealthy God made him, the servant also shared news about the miraculous birth of Abraham and Sarah's son! This had to be an incredible surprise to Abraham and Sarah's family. I am sure they knew Sarah was barren. And now, to hear, they have a son together, what a testimony! Many years after Abraham's departure from his country, we can see Abraham's servant having the privilege of telling Abraham's family, all the great things God has done in Abraham and Sarah's life.

God blessed Abraham with even more miracles in his old age. After Abraham's wife Sarah died, Abraham married Keturah, and went on to have many more children in his old age.

Genesis 25:1-4

[1]Then again Abraham took a wife, and her name was Keturah.

[2]And she bare him Zimran, and Jokshan, and Medan, and Midian, and Ishbak, and Shuah.

[3]And Jokshan begat Sheba, and Dedan. And the sons of Dedan were Asshurim, and Letushim, and Leummim.

[4]And the sons of Midian; Ephah, Epher, and Hanoch, Abida, and Eldaah. All these were the children of Keturah.

Wow, what a powerful testimony! Abraham stepped out in **Faith** and was greatly rewarded! Everything Abraham wanted, and so much more was added to his life. Every miracle Abraham experienced was attributed to having **Faith** in God. Abraham went from having no children at the age of 75, to having many children by the time of his death, a hundred years later. Abraham lived a full and amazing life!

Abraham's journey with God greatly demonstrates, God's hand of faithfulness on Abraham's life. We can clearly see how the miracle working power of **Faith** blessed Abraham's life in some extraordinary ways. You see, Abraham did not limit God. Abraham welcomed the hand of God in every area of his life. This decision alone ushered Abraham into an incredible life of **Faith-Style** living. Let us read what Abraham's descendant, king David, had to say about living by **Faith**.

Romans 4:6 MSG

⁶David confirms this way of looking at it, saying that the one who trusts God to do the putting-everything-right without insisting on having a say in it is one fortunate man.

David's words come down to one thing and this is having **Faith** in the Word of God to do exactly what it says it will do. If we do not make God's way our priority, we will think it is by our own strength our needs are met. God warns the children of Israel of this very thing. Let us take a look at what God said to the Israelites.

Deuteronomy 8:13-18

¹³And when thy herd and flocks multiply, and thy silver and thy gold is multiplied, and all that thou hast is multiplied;

¹⁴Then thine heart be lifted up, and thou forget the Lord thy God, which brought thee forth out of the land of Egypt, from the house of bondage;

¹⁵Who led thee through that great and terrible wilderness, wherein were fiery serpents, and scorpions, and drought, where there was no water; who brought thee forth water out of the rock of flint;

¹⁶Who fed thee in the wilderness with manna, which thy fathers knew not, that he might humble thee, and that he might prove thee, to do thee good at thy latter end;

¹⁷And thou say in thine heart, my power and the might of mine hand hath gotten me this wealth.

¹⁸But thou shalt remember the Lord thy God: for it is he that giveth thee power to get wealth, that he may establish his covenant which he sware unto thy fathers, as it is this day.

In these verses we can see God reminding the children of Israel of four important truths. First, it was God who protected them from all hurt, harm and danger in the wilderness. Second, it was God who fed them and kept them. Third, it was God who gave them power to acquire all the wealth they had and not by their own hands. Fourth, it was their **Faith** in God that sustained them those forty years in the wilderness and not anything they could do for themselves. For this reason, God wants us to make Him our priority and not our careers and money because sometimes, unfortunately, we allow our careers and money to take us away from God. Then our lives will be about our agenda and not God's agenda. And we will see ourselves as our own source of supply. But when we do it God's way, we will know it is God who has blessed us with everything we have, including our money. It is God we serve and not our money!

Matthew 6:24

²⁴No man can serve two masters: for either he will hate one and love the other; or else he will hold on to the one, and despise the other. You cannot serve God and mammon.

Even though God knows we need money to live in this earth, God still wants our primary focus to be on Him. For this reason, the Bible implores us to, "Walk by **Faith** and not by Sight." This verse is important to **Faith** living because when your focus is on money alone, you will perceive money as your source of supply. For the believer, **Faith** in God is our source of supply because money cannot buy everything.

God is a God of no limits. He is both limitless and boundless. There is nothing He cannot do! Even though many may believe money can meet every need you have, it truly cannot. As previously mentioned, the children of Israel had a whole lot of money, but their money could not bring them out of their wilderness experience nor could it get them into the promised land. God reminded the children of Israel; it was Him that sustained them and provided for them and not the silver and gold they were carrying. God made it very clear it was only through His power; they were able to obtain the wealth they had. God wanted the children of Israel to see, He was their total source of supply. If they would have just considered all the great miracles God performed on their behalves, they would have known they had absolutely nothing to worry about. God was teaching the Israelites, although they could not physically see Him, He was there for them and He would take care of them no matter what. God wanted their total trust and confidence (**Faith**) in Him.

Every need the children of Israel had in the wilderness was not supplied by the money they had. Their needs were met and supplied by the God who was watching over them. Money did not free them from bondage and money did not part the Red Sea. When they entered the wilderness, wilderness meaning a void place, there was absolutely nothing physically there to sustain them or provide for them. But you see child of God, this is exactly the way God wanted it. These were the perfect conditions for the children of Israel to learn exactly who God was and all He could do for them. If they would only believe! It was God and not the silver and gold they were carrying that caused manna and quail to fall from the sky when they were hungry. It was God who caused water to come out of a rock when they were thirsty. It was God who kept their bodies in perfect health and their clothes in perfect condition as they traveled in the wilderness for forty long years.

Nehemiah 9:21

21Yea, forty years didst thou sustain them in the wilderness, so that they lacked nothing; their clothes waxed not old, and their feet swelled not.

I know this may be shocking for many and contrary to what many may think, money does have its limitations. But **Faith** in God is unlimited, and we can clearly see an example of this in the lives of the children of Israel. **Faith** can do and bring us things no amount of money in the world can such as love, joy, peace, healing and contentment. This reminds me of a story in the New Testament about a man who was lame from his birth, meaning he could not walk. And because this man could not walk, every day he would have the people carry him to the gate of the temple. He would lie down at the gate every day asking the temple goers for money.

What is interesting about this story is this man thought the money he collected daily was the answer to his problems, but he would soon learn what he really needed was something he thought was totally impossible! This story is both powerful and amazing! Let us take a look at what transpired when this man had an encounter with Apostles Peter and John.

Acts 3:1-7

[1]Now Peter and John went up together into the temple at the hour of prayer, being the ninth hour.

[2]And a certain man lame from his mother's womb was carried, whom they laid daily at the gate of the temple which is called Beautiful, to ask alms of them that entered into the temple;

[3]Who seeing Peter and John about to go into the temple asked an alms.

[4]And Peter, fastening his eyes upon him with John, said, Look on us.

[5]And he gave heed unto them, expecting to receive something of them.

[6]Then Peter said, Silver and gold have I none; but such as I have give I thee: In the name of Jesus Christ of Nazareth rise up and walk.

⁷And he took him by the right hand, and lifted him up: and immediately his feet and ankle bones received strength.

You see, this man did not receive the money he expected to receive. Instead, he received exactly what he needed and so much more! This man received his healing and his newfound **Faith** in God. He no longer had to lay out at the temple gate anymore seeking handouts. He was healed and made whole! He could get up and go praise God inside the temple like everyone else.

Acts 3:8-10

⁸And he leaping up stood, and walked, and entered with them into the temple, walking, and leaping, and praising God.

⁹And all the people saw him walking and praising God:

¹⁰And they knew that it was he which sat for alms at the Beautiful gate of the temple: and they were filled with wonder and amazement at that which had happened unto him.

This man received a powerful testimony! And his testimony was made viable through his **Faith** in the name of Jesus Christ. You see, the money he was begging for everyday at the temple gate did not and could not heal this man, but **Faith** in God did! Now did this man need money. I am sure he did because his condition may have prevented him from working. But the healing he received was the true answer to his problem and I know it changed his life forever. It was through **Faith** his limitation was removed. He could now go and make his own money!

Acts 3:16

[16]And his name through faith in his name hath made this man strong, whom ye see and know: yea, the faith which is by him hath given him this perfect soundness in the presence of you all.

This incident reminds me of a time when my husband asked a visiting pastor to pray for me. My husband never did say in what regards I needed prayer and the visiting pastor never asked. He just walked over to me, placed his hand over the top of my head and he began to pray. His entire prayer for me was for God to give me peace. As he was praying, I sat there thinking, "Peace, what is he talking about peace. I need some money. I need a place to live. I need my body healed. What is he talking about peace? When I get the money and I can take care of my needs, then I will have peace!"

Although I was thankful for the prayer, at that time I did not believe this man prayed for what I was really in need of. Do you know it was not until maybe a year or so later, it dawned on me, this visiting pastor prayed over me exactly what I needed at this specific time in my life? I needed peace in my situation. I needed peace in knowing that no matter what was going on in my life, I needed to have **Faith** in God. I needed to have **Faith** He would bring me through and to really understand this truth would have brought total peace to my situation. Now did I also need money? The answer is a resounding yes! But all the anxiety I was experiencing had driven me to a place of unrest which then greatly affected my body. I believe it was in this situation God was trying to grow me up and show me no matter what was going on in my life, I needed to have total trust and confidence (**Faith**) in Him. I thought the answer was money, but the real answer was **Faith** in God. Just like the children of Israel and the man at the gate called Beautiful, God gave me exactly what I needed when I needed it! Glory to God!

God is our Heavenly Father, and we are His children. When we think we know what is best for us, believe me He knows better than we do. You see, sometimes we are just looking to meet a need we may have at this moment in our lives, but we must remember, God knows our end from our beginning. He knows what is down the road, and around the corner and He is the Author and Finisher of our **Faith**. He knows what is best for us in the long run. For this reason, God is adamant about His children living by **Faith**. He wants our lives to reflect His way of doing things and being right which will cause us to live the life He created for us to live. This is a life without limits! He also wants us to use our **Faith** to tap into the things He has already provided for us before the foundation of the world. We must remember our God is limitless. He is not constrained by money, people or things and He does not want His children constrained by them either. For this reason, it is so important for us to walk by **Faith** and not by sight. Let me give you an example. If you are constantly looking at your own abilities and the money you have, and God is trying to send you into places you do not have the money for, you are going to miss out! **Faith** in God can give you access into places your money cannot. **Faith** can get you money, but money cannot get you **Faith**!

Now as I said before, there is absolutely nothing wrong with having money, but we must make **Faith** living our priority. We must remember money, people and things are temporal, but **Faith** in God is eternal. It is the seen verses the unseen, in which the unseen wins every time! Now let us take a look at the definition of **Faith** once again.

Hebrews 11:1

¹Now Faith is the substance of things hoped for, the evidence of things not seen.

Do you see the emphasis that is placed on the unseen? The verse says, **Faith** is the substance of things hoped for, it is the evidence of things not seen. **Faith** is the substance meaning, it is a real physical matter of which a person or thing consists and has a tangible solid presence. So, although we cannot see our **Faith,** our **Faith** is a real physical matter. It is tangible! It is more real than anything we can see!

2 Corinthians 4:18

¹⁸While we look not at the things which are seen, but at the things which are not seen: for the things which are seen are temporal; but the things which are not seen are eternal.

This brings me back to the testimonies I gave in the earlier chapters. I often ask God, why did He show me so much in such a short period of time. As I was pondering this question, it dawned on me, it could have been the evidence I needed to write this book. But most importantly God was teaching me how to live by **Faith.** He was teaching me, how to seek first His kingdom and His righteousness, with the promise of everything I needed being added to me.

The testimonies I used for this book derived from the principles Jesus taught in Matthew 6:24-33. I have discussed these scripture verses many times already, but they are truly the foundation for living by **Faith**. So, you can see it all comes back to the unseen!

God was teaching me, how to walk by **Faith** and not by sight. When I followed the leading and the prompting of the Holy Ghost, I was blessed in ways I could not have imagined. For example, when I worked at the telemarketing company and I made a vow to God I will not leave the position until He opened another door of opportunity for me, I did not realize it at the time, but this was me exercising my **Faith** in God. I did not know when or if God would open another door for me, but I had to believe He would. And He did!

What I am about to discuss next is very important. Please consider my words in these two testimonies. Earlier, I mentioned a time when I needed a car so badly and I desperately did not want to pay a car note. When I was going through this ordeal, I did not have the money to purchase a car or to make a down payment on the car. So, this meant I would have to borrow the down payment, pay the car note every month, pay insurance every month and pay back the loan for the down payment. I knew this would be a struggle for me to do. I did not even have the car yet and I could already feel the weight of the burden on me. When God spoke to me to sow a seed into a specific ministry, I had no idea what God was up to. I just wanted to obey what the Holy Spirit was instructing me to do. If God said it, I wanted to do it and that was the bottom line.

After I received the car and the money to purchase my kids school clothes, I looked back over the situation and thought, this is what the sowing of that seed was all about. God was presenting me with an opportunity to trust Him to provide for me in my time of need. When I exercised my **Faith** in God, God blessed me and my children tremendously! He took away the burden and the stress. Just thinking about it makes me happy all over again!

This testimony I am about to share really blesses my heart and makes me think of the bigness of our God. I shared this testimony in the chapter "**Faith** and Honor in God." I spoke about the first time I tithed. I remember this miraculous event like it was yesterday. When God was speaking to me about tithing, I had no idea what He was up to. All I know is I wanted to obey God. These are some of the things that were going on at the time. First, I was thinking about looking for a second job because the pay was not enough to raise three kids and pay bills. Second, the hours I was working were not working out because I had to work overnight a couple days a week and I did not feel comfortable leaving my kids alone at night. As you can see, I had a couple of dilemmas going on at the time. If I did obtain a second job, this really would not have been a solution to my problem because it would have created another problem, which was more time away from my kids. The other dilemma was my employer preferred employees who did not work a second job because they needed us to be available for emergency situations. This was a huge dilemma for me because I enjoyed my job and I did not want to leave my position. Most importantly, I knew the Lord had placed there.

As I was thinking about what to do about my situation, I received information that one of the daycare workers was resigning. This opened the door for me to be offered her position. This was great because now I would be working Monday through Friday, from 8am to 4pm. So, my transition into the daycare position would have resolved all my problems. My kids would only be home alone for about an hour until I came home. This was a huge relief. I was excited about the change of positions! As well as the new hours and the small increase in salary I would be receiving. This change in positions would also afford me the opportunity to get a part-time job if necessary. The daycare workers were not required to be on call, so this was a huge benefit for me. Although this new position would have worked out wonderfully, God had another plan in mind. When God began speaking to me about tithing, I had no idea He was presenting me with another opportunity to exercise my **Faith**. I took that opportunity and not long after, God had blessed me with a totally unexpected surprise! God blessed me to be promoted to a supervisor position! Not only was I blessed with great working hours, the promotion took me from an hourly position to a salary position. It also came with a nice increase in salary. I went from almost receiving a small hourly pay raise to receiving hundreds of dollars more a month, which meant thousands of dollars more annually. Glory to God! You see what happened when I listened to and obeyed God? In all these instances, God was showing me how to operate by **Faith**.

When God was presenting me with these opportunities to sow into His Kingdom, as I mentioned I needed more money myself. I had many financial obligations, so naturally I did not have the money to give on either occasion. But when I put my **Faith** in God and trusted Him, God blessed me in ways I could not have made possible on my own. While doing the study for this chapter, the Lord opened my eyes to something interesting in the verse below.

Matthew 6:24

24No man can serve two masters: for either he will hate one and love the other; or else he will hold on to the one,

and despise the other. You cannot serve God and mammon.

If you look back over the last two testimonies I discussed, you can clearly see the instructions God gave me involved money. In the natural, I could not afford to give the money, I needed someone to give me some money. Take another look at the scripture verse above. Again, Jesus is teaching us all about priority. Jesus is showing us in this passage of scripture, who our one and only source is. When you look back over the testimonies I gave, and look at the scripture verse above, can you see God demonstrating His Word in them? Can you see God was teaching me in every scenario I provided, including the first one that did not involve money, who my one and only source is? God gave me a choice in both situations. The choice being who was I going to trust and believe? And most importantly, who was I going to serve? Was I going to trust God and serve Him or was I going to trust in the money by holding on to it? This is a very valuable lesson. In the testimonies you can see, when I put my **Faith** in God, everything I needed was added to me. It happened just like Jesus said it would in Matthew 6:33. My **Faith** in God produced the results it said it would. When I put my **Faith** in the unseen, it brought miraculous results I could see every time!

By the way, you remember I spoke about the trouble I was having in school. Well, God blessed me with the determination and perseverance I needed to finish my education! And I was blessed to participate in two graduation ceremonies within one year of each other! I completed three degrees! I graduated from the local community college in 2016, with an A.A. in Liberal Arts and Humanities and an A.S. in Business Real Estate. And I was blessed to graduate from the greatest university in the world. Oral Roberts University in 2017, with a B.S. in Communication!

When I think about the goodness of God, I get excited all over again! I have thoroughly enjoyed rehearsing and sharing my personal testimonies. These are resounding evidence of **Faith-Style** living! I feel like our elders in Hebrews 11:2, by **Faith** I have received a good testimony!

What is even more astounding about this life of **Faith** we have been blessed to live, is every born-again believer has been given the greatest testimony ever, *"And they overcame him by the blood of the Lamb, and by the word of their Testimony (Revelation 12:11)."*

In Jesus Christ we are more than conquerors. We are destined overcomers!

It is my prayer; you have come into the knowledge of how truly important **Faith** is to the life of the believer. **Faith** is so relevant to the life of the believer, that even Jesus asked the question, *"Nevertheless when the Son of man cometh, shall He find Faith on the earth (Luke 18:8)?"*

God wants you in **Faith**! It is impossible to please Him without it!

Faith-Style living is the True way of living for the believer!

Faith-Style: The Christian's Mantra for Victorious Living!

Made in the USA
Middletown, DE
15 February 2022

61226071R00176